"Conard provides **a much-needed reappraisal of the role of in-equality** in a free-market economy. The most crucial insight of economics is that incentives matter, and those incentives will inevitably show up as an unequal distribution of economic resources. Conard argues forcefully that the well-intentioned policies of reducing inequality in the short term are not necessarily beneficial in the long term, as inequality and economic growth are closely linked."

> —*George J. Borjas*, Robert W. Scrivner professor of economics and social policy, Harvard Kennedy School, and author of *Labor Economics* and *Immigration Economics*

"Ed Conard **reminds us that inequality sends a signal of what society lacks most; in America's case, entrepreneurship and risk-taking**. That is why it is highly rewarded. Intellectual and political attacks on those who use these attributes will prove to be counterproductive."

> —*Lawrence Lindsey*, CEO of the Lindsey Group LLC and former director of the National Economic Council

"In this **significant contribution to economic thought**, Ed Conard extends our theory that equity and risk-underwriting constrain growth and uses it to identify important consequences for economic policy."

> —*Bruce Greenwald*, coauthor (with Joseph Stiglitz) of *A New Paradigm in Monetary Theory*, and Robert Heilbrunn professor of finance, Columbia Business School

"Economists tend to be enslaved by their models, and too often their work is obscure, unimaginative, and irrelevant. Conard's visionary take on the constraints to growth and their effect on inequality is **nothing short of revolutionary**."

> —*Kevin Hassett*, resident scholar and director of research for domestic policy, American Enterprise Institute

# The Upside of Inequality

# THE UPSIDE

## —— *of* ——

# INEQUALITY

## How Good Intentions
## Undermine the Middle Class

# EDWARD CONARD

PORTFOLIO / PENGUIN

*For my wife and daughter,*
*my mother, who died this year,*
*and my sister, who kept her alive.*

---

An imprint of Penguin Random House LLC
375 Hudson Street
New York, NY 10014

ISBN 9781595231239 (hardcover)
ISBN 9780698409910 (e-book)

Printed in the United States of America
1   3   5   7   9   10   8   6   4   2

Set in ITC New Baskerville and Promemoria

# CONTENTS

# INTRODUCTION

I wrote *Unintended Consequences* in 2012 because I was concerned that in the aftermath of the financial crisis misguided economic policy would lead to slower-than-necessary growth. The financial crisis had called the value of free enterprise into question in the mind of the public, and I wanted to set the record straight.

The U.S. economy had grown robustly for nearly two decades leading up to the financial crisis. But the U.S. economy ran enormous trade deficits with China, Germany, and Japan—economies with large surpluses of risk-averse savings. These economies used risk-averse savings to fund large trade surpluses that indirectly necessitated large increases in U.S. borrowing and lending—chiefly subprime mortgages—to maintain full employment. This expansion of credit destabilized U.S. banks. When real estate prices fell 30 percent, it sparked a panicked run on an inherently unstable banking system.

Rather than diagnosing the problems properly, demagogues on the left and right claimed that ill-advised monetary policy, misguided regulation, and debt-fueled growth—fraudulently devised by reckless bankers—had created unsustainable prosperity. The public bought those views despite two decades of historic U.S. productivity growth that could only have been achieved with hard-earned investment, risk-taking, and innovation.

In *Unintended Consequences*, I explained why the U.S. economy was gradually growing more productive than Europe and Japan—namely, because higher payoffs for successful risk-taking were gradually building

U.S. institutional capabilities. More valuable on-the-job training, large synergistic communities of experts, highly motivated and trained talent, and equity in the hands of eager risk-takers had compounding effects on the value of successful risk-taking. I recommended lower marginal tax rates to maintain higher payoffs in the face of slower growth in the aftermath of the financial crisis. The Obama administration did the opposite.

I cautioned that holding the banks responsible for bank runs, instead of just loan losses, at a time when they were already reluctant to lend, would slow growth. I recommended strengthening government guarantees of banks and the Fed's ability to function as the lender of last resort but charging banks and borrowers for these guarantees. The Obama administration did the opposite.

Most Keynesian economists insisted that the government need only borrow and spend idle savings to create growing demand. They also claimed that a credible threat of inflation would accelerate growth by discouraging unused savings that slow growth. I predicted that constraints to growth would prevent these policies from having positive long-term effects and that the private sector would dial back risk-taking in response to these policies, slowing growth further. I argued that America should not distort the economy by inflating the money supply to discourage saving nor increase unproductive government borrowing and spending in an effort to put unused risk-averse offshore savings to work. Instead, I recommended that the country should deal with the problem of idle savings directly—by demanding balanced trade with trade partners like China, Germany, and Japan. While trade is critical for growth, trade deficits are not. The Obama administration did the opposite.

To foster growth, the U.S. government borrowed and spent $6 trillion and inflated the money supply four-fold in order to buy another $3 trillion of privately held financial securities. Perhaps the recession would have been worse without these efforts, but eight years after the financial crisis, growth remains anemic and productivity growth has fallen to historic lows. Financial crises likely slow recoveries, but eventually the economy rebounds. No rebound ever materialized, nor is one in sight. Instead, slow productivity growth portends continued difficulties. While it's true that institutional capabilities allowed the U.S. economy to recover faster than other high-wage economies, they were already producing faster growth in the two decades prior to the recession.

Because my business partner, Mitt Romney, was running for president when *Unintended Consequences* was published, the media held up my book as a defense of the 1 percent. At the time, a leading proponent of income redistribution wrote, "the biggest surprise, on opening *Unintended Consequences,* lies in discovering that this book isn't about income inequality at all."[1] The critics' demand for a comprehensive defense of income inequality planted the seeds for this book.

Since 2012, accusations that crony capitalism and the success of the 1 percent slow middle- and working-class income growth have only grown louder. While the incomes of the 0.1 percent have soared, the growth of middle-class and working-class incomes has continued to remain slow. Many insist that this gap has grown because the wealthy are rigging a zero-sum game to take what rightly belongs to others. *The Upside of Inequality* addresses these accusations head-on and explains why income redistribution hurts the middle and working class.

Advocates of income redistribution cavalierly insist that we can redistribute the income of successful entrepreneurs, financiers, and leaders without slowing growth. Austan Goolsbee, President Obama's former chairman of the Council of Economic Advisers, for example, insists that the growth in the 1990s provides evidence that taxes and payoffs for risk-taking have little, if any, effect on risk-taking and growth, since the boom came after President Clinton raised marginal taxes, which cut payoffs for success.[2] Though increased tax rates would ordinarily dampen investment, during the '90s the rising payoffs for success, even after taxes, were great enough to spur increased high-tech entrepreneurialism and investment. This is hardly evidence that payoffs for risk-taking don't matter. Quite the contrary, it shows that incentives matter even if they are affected by more than just taxes.

Played out over time, the differences in growth and middle-class prosperity between countries that have decreased incentives (through increased income redistribution) and those that have not are startling. Look at the differences between Europe and the U.S.; East and West Germany; and Communist China versus Hong Kong, Taiwan, and China today. There are enormous and compounding costs to dulling incentives for entrepreneurial risk-taking with few, if any, exceptions. As payoffs for success have risen, entrepreneurial risk-taking has accelerated U.S. growth relative to other high-wage economies with more equally distributed incomes. Because of this growth, today, median U.S. household incomes are 15 to 30 percent higher than Germany, France, and Japan.[3]

If redistribution isn't the solution to slow income growth, what is? Some claim low-skilled immigration and trade with low-wage economies slow middle- and working-class wage growth. Many economists, however, insist that these are not the culprits. They claim that the low-cost imports make everyone better off, that opportunists will employ displaced and immigrant workers, and that competition will force employers to invest in order to increase productivity, which is essential for maintaining high wages.

If there were no constraints on growth, these economists might be right. But if resources essential to increased productivity, like capital, constrain growth, then trade and immigration may reduce wages by diluting these resources over a greater number of workers. With interest rates near zero, capital is clearly not constrained. Instead, properly trained talent and the economy's capacity and willingness to bear risk constrain growth in today's innovation-driven economy.

Today displaced workers wait for entrepreneurs, companies, investors, and other properly trained risk-takers to create jobs that employ them at high wages. But these resources are in short supply. And when high-wage jobs do appear, displaced workers find they are competing with the 40 million foreign-born adults and their 20 million native-born adult children who are also looking for work.[4] Because of these constraints, both trade with low-wage economies and low-skilled immigration slow middle- and working-class wage growth. Unfortunately, few economists take these noncapital constraints into consideration.

Instead, Keynesian economists continue to insist that investment waits for demand and that government spending and the threat of inflation will accelerate growth. But thirty years in business have taught me that, contrary to what Keynesians say, investment rarely waits for demand. Investors wait for good ideas, like the iPhone, that create their own demand and for properly trained talent needed to commercialize ideas successfully.

Business runs hard just to stay in place. Companies are continually innovating, investing, and taking risks to avoid losses caused by improvements made by competitors. Competition drives most of the value created by business into the pockets of customers, not investors. And payoffs for success drive the ferocity of competition. Competition between innovators creates middle-class prosperity, not well-intended but misguided government policies.

Business has also taught me that competitors succeed because they provide customers with more value than alternatives. The powerful reasons for their success make improvements hard to find. Most ideas for improvement look good in theory because the theory is wrong. In the real world, it takes a lot of failure to find a glimmer of true insight. Advocates of change rarely take the unlikelihood of finding real improvements into consideration.

This book lays out an explanation of the economy that recognizes the complexity and robustness of the economy, the power of incentives, and the rights of all mankind to enjoy the value produced by the talents of its lucky recipients. Along the way, it punctures today's most popular myths about income inequality and the economy. Ultimately, it lays out a plan for growth that takes today's constraints to growth into consideration.

If you take nothing else away from this book, I want you to remember this: Higher payoffs for success increase the supply of properly trained talent, and these higher payoffs motivate innovators, entrepreneurs, and investors to take risks. These two effects loosen the current constraints on growth, which frees the economy to grow faster. Faster growth increases middle- and working-class wages when the supply of lesser-skilled labor is constrained. Otherwise, it increases employment rather than wages. With smaller payoffs, growth would be even slower than it is.

Naturally, higher payoffs increase income inequality by increasing the wealth of successful innovators, entrepreneurs, and one-in-a-thousand CEOs who are essential to the competiveness of our most important institutions. But when success bubbles up from a large sea of failure, should we begrudge them their payoffs when their success improves life for all of us? Of course not. We should celebrate our good fortune. It's time to stop blaming the success of the 1 percent and embrace the upside of inequality: faster growth and greater prosperity for everyone.

## Part I

# THE WORLD
# AS WE FIND IT

## Chapter 1

# THE CAUSES OF
# GROWING INEQUALITY

I t seems as though you can't pick up a newspaper today without reading an article blaming the 1 percent for the stagnant wages of the
middle class.[1] If people aren't accusing the 1 percent of using crony
capitalism to steal what they haven't earned, then they are accusing
them of inventing technology that hollows out the middle class or stifles
the advancement of the underprivileged by underfunding education.[2]

In 2003 renowned economists Thomas Piketty and Emmanuel Saez
burst into the public's consciousness with convincing evidence that
income inequality had increased dramatically, especially in the United
States, and that middle- and working-class incomes had stagnated.
Their work showed that income inequality had increased not so much
because of an increase in the earnings of the top 10 percent of Americans or the top 5 percent or even the top 1 percent, but chiefly among
the top 1 hundredth (0.01) of 1 percent.

Demagogues and politicians favoring income redistribution were
quick to link the success of the 0.1 percent to the alleged stagnant
wages of the middle class. They insisted that the rich were succeeding
at the expense of the rest of America. They seized on this linkage to
demand higher taxes on the rich for greater income redistribution.

In his 2013 book *Capital in the Twenty-First Century*, for example,
Piketty insisted the rich "by and large have the power to set their own

Figure 1-1:  Growth in Incomes by Level of Income

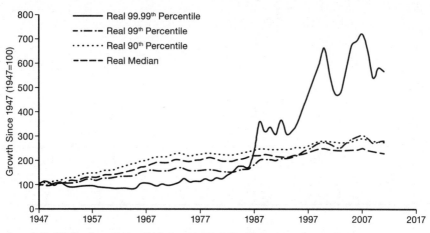

Source: The World Wealth and Income Database, Picketty, Saez et al., 2012, via "Visualizing Income Inequality in the U.S." Hirschman, 2013

remuneration, in some cases without limit and in many cases without any clear relation to their individual productivity," using nepotism, corruption, and corporate politics, or by conspiring with "hierarchical superiors."[3] According to Piketty, the 1 percent were merely the beneficiaries of gradually eroding social norms that previously held their pay in check. Success, he claimed, was earned at the expense of the middle class. The alleged growth of CEO pay from thirty times the median wage in 1980 to over three hundred times by 2007 for the largest companies is held out as prima facie evidence.[4]

The financial crisis of 2008 only fueled the flames of anger toward the wealthy. Banks were accused of predatory lending, the sale of fraudulent securities, and ultimately for recklessly causing the "Great Recession." The 1 percent were held responsible.

The list of allegations and complaints against the most successful Americans continued unabated. The technology they create supposedly hollows out middle- and working-class jobs. They own and manage companies that lay off employees and hire offshore workers. They are accused of failing to provide appropriate funding for education and other benefits that may alleviate poverty and increase income mobility or allow for infrastructure investments that may spark faster economic growth.

At first glance, these accusations seem reasonable. The growth of middle-class and working-class incomes has slowed. Crony capitalism does exist. Automation and offshoring seem to have reduced the number of high-paying factory jobs. Companies like Apple, Google, and Facebook scarcely seem to employ any Americans, especially not middle- and working-class Americans. Academic test scores are not improving. And it seems impossible to break the generational cycle of poverty.

Yet despite these facts, the growth of the U.S. economy has accelerated relative to other high-wage economies with more equally distributed incomes—the opposite of what one would expect if crony capitalism or other unfair means of income distribution had increased in the United States on a scale necessary to account for rising income inequality. U.S. employment grew twice as fast as employment in Germany and France since 1980.[5] This growth has created a home for 40 million foreign-born adults, their 20 million native-born adult children, and the 20 million children of these 60 million adults.[6]*

And America has achieved this employment growth at median household incomes that are 15 to 30 percent higher than other high-wage economies, such as Germany, France, and Japan.[7]

Careful scrutiny of the evidence reveals U.S. median household incomes have grown as fast as, or faster than, other high-wage economies.[8] Piketty and Saez's use of tax returns instead of household income ignores the fact that an increasing number of workers live alone instead of in families with more than one worker and that an increasing portion of workers' pay is now provided as untaxed health and retirement benefits, which are difficult to measure. Middle-class tax rates have also fallen as government services have grown.

At the same time, workforce participation has fallen as Americans have grown more prosperous. Social Security and Medicare, for example, now allow older workers to retire instead of working. It's misleading to count them as households without earned income. And the demographics of the workforce have shifted toward lesser-skilled Hispanic immigrants who logically earn less than more highly skilled

---

*I have rounded numbers throughout this book. Time periods were taken from sources available at the time of writing (2015). The years 1979 or 1980 are often used as an initial period because of the comparability of the U.S. Census data.

Americans on average. When these factors are properly considered, real wages have grown more robustly than they appear to have. And there has been no hollowing out of the middle class whatsoever. Belief that wages have stagnated nevertheless persists.

The notion that the growing success of America's 0.1 percent is the cause of slower middle- and working-class wage growth is mistaken. Entirely independent forces drive the two phenomena.

As the economy grows, it values innovation more. As such, successful innovators who achieve economy-wide success, like Steve Jobs or Bill Gates, grow richer than innovators have in the past. It's simple multiplication. And they grow richer relative to doctors, schoolteachers, bus drivers, and other median-income employees whose pay is limited by the number of people, or customers, they can serve.

At the same time, information technology has opened a window of new investment opportunities and increased the productivity of the most productive workers.

Moreover, in today's knowledge-based economy, companies can scale to economy-wide success with little need for capital. Successful innovators need not share their success with investors. Successful individuals like Google's Larry Page and Facebook's Mark Zuckerberg look like corporations of a bygone capital-intensive era.

Without much need for capital, start-ups become all-or-nothing lotteries. The chance for enormous payoffs attracts a larger number of more talented gamblers. More gamblers produce more outsized winners, and more innovation, too—whether the risk-adjusted returns are good, on average, or not.

Their success has compounding benefits. It provides American workers with more valuable on-the-job training, at companies like Google and Facebook, than they can get in other high-wage, slower-growing manufacturing-based economies. It creates synergistic communities of experts, like Silicon Valley. And it puts equity into the hands of successful risk-takers who use their equity and expertise to underwrite further risk-taking that produces more innovation, faster growth, and compounding benefits. Higher and more certain payoffs coupled with the growing success of others motives increased risk-taking.

No surprise, the U.S. economy has produced a disproportionate share of innovation. As a result, the nation has more income inequality but also faster employment growth at higher median incomes than other high-wage economies. Rising income inequality is the by-product of an economy that has deployed its talent and wealth more effectively than that of other economies—and not from the rich stealing from the middle and working classes.

In truth, the outsized success of America's 1 percent has been *the* chief source of growth exerting upward pressure on domestic employment and wages. The success of America's 1 percent is an asset, not a liability.

In the face of the evidence, it's no surprise that even Paul Krugman, a leading liberal economist, admits, "I'm actually a skeptic on the inequality-is-bad-for-performance proposition. . . . The evidence . . . is weaker than I'd like."[9]

At the same time, a near-unlimited supply of low-skilled, low-wage workers—both offshore and immigrant—has put downward pressure on lesser-skilled wages relative to higher-skilled wages. The U.S. economy's ongoing shift from capital-intensive manufacturing to knowledge-intensive services increased the demand for properly trained talent and reduced the need for capital. Normally, the increased availability of capital would make it easier to raise the productivity and wages of lower-skilled workers. But competition from an abundance of low-wage offshore workers combined with the productivity gains it demands from domestic producers with higher-wage workers leaves a smaller and smaller share of less-skilled workers employed in highly productive capital-intensive manufacturing jobs.

Today U.S. growth demands properly trained talent and a capacity and willingness to take the risks needed to produce innovation. A shortage of properly trained talent and of the economy's capacity and willingness to take risk limit the entrepreneurial risk-taking, investment, and supervision needed to expand higher-wage, lower-skilled American employment opportunities. As a result, an influx of low-skilled immigrant workers has increased lower-wage work. In turn, the availability of low-wage immigrant workers puts downward pressure on low-skilled wages.

It's true that trade with low-wage economies lowers the cost of goods more than the wages of domestic lower-skilled labor. Were that not the case, it would be cheaper to produce goods domestically, rather than import them. But middle- and working-class workers bear

100 percent of the burden of lower wages for only a portion of the benefits of lower-priced goods. The rich, retirees, and the non-working poor also enjoy the benefits of lower-priced goods but without suffering the cost of lower wages. So while international trade benefits everyone on average, because the costs are shared disproportionately, it slows middle- and working-class wage growth relative to the growth of everyone else's income.

Growing income inequality is a real phenomenon, but a misdiagnosis of its causes and consequences leads to policies that slow growth and damage an already slow-growing economy. If the public mistakenly blames the success of the 1 percent for the stagnant wages of the middle class, while leaving the true sources of slow-growing wages— trade, trade deficits, and immigration—unaddressed, a dangerous feedback loop is likely to ensue. Raising taxes on success will reduce risk-taking and innovation. This will slow growth and reduce middle-class wages, and, in turn, increase the demand for redistribution.

Politicians who rely on middle- and working-class votes may relish this dynamic. Some may even advance the misunderstandings necessary for the problem to endure. Unfortunately, they either don't realize or don't care if they're cooking the goose that lays the golden egg.

Lower marginal tax rates would increase the payoff for successful risk-taking needed to produce innovation. Higher payoffs would motivate increased risk-taking. And increased risk-taking would have gradually compounding effects on America's ability to produce innovation— more people motivated to acquire and use the proper training, more valuable on-the-job training, growing communities of experts, and equity in the pockets of knowledgeable investors. These capabilities would magnify the value and likelihood of success. In turn, this would motivate prudent risk-taking and accelerate growth just as it has in America relative to other high-wage economies.

But unless we cut government spending, which seems highly unlikely, lower taxes would blow a huge hole in the deficit in the interim. And lower marginal tax rates would increase income inequality.

A more practical solution increases the pool of properly trained talent. America is full of high-scoring talent unwilling to endure the training and take the risks necessary to grow the economy. Their reluctance sets the price for success.

America could take a number of steps to increase its pool of properly trained talent. It could reduce subsidies to students and colleges studying curricula that do little to increase employment—psychology, history, and English, for example. There is an enormous mismatch between what high-scoring students study and what employers value. As the rest of the world trains its talent and grows increasingly competitive, America can no longer afford to waste a large share of its talent.

America needs to replace the current ethos, which discourages students from learning practical skills, with one that insists that talented people have a moral obligation to put their talents to full use serving their fellow man—whether serving them as customers or philanthropically. America could also nurture high-scoring students from low-socioeconomic families, as large numbers of these students are failing to graduate from college.

But training the next generation of students more effectively will have little effect on growth for decades, and then only with a slow compounding effect that won't fully saturate the workforce for decades after that. And like all good intentions, it is unlikely to be implemented.

In the interim, America should recruit properly trained talent from the rest of the world through more logical immigration policies. It could also recruit employers with a lower marginal corporate tax rate, perhaps by offsetting lost tax revenues with a higher tax rate on capital gains or other taxes. These steps would not only have more immediate effects but may also reduce income inequality.

In the absence of substantial changes, retiring baby boomers threaten to eat our economy alive with their unquenchable demand for retirement benefits. And China looms as a growing existential threat to national security. Neither threat appears to be solvable on its own. Embracing ultra-high-skilled immigration is America's best shot at avoiding permanent damage from these otherwise unsolvable problems.

Unless we fully understand the economics underlying growing income inequality—both the accelerating growth in the payoffs for success and the slowing growth of middle- and working-class pay—we will not understand the corresponding consequences of alternative policy changes. Without these understandings, we are likely to damage the economy rather than accelerate employment and wage growth.

So let's begin by examining the economics underlying the growing success of the 0.1 percent before turning to slowing middle-class wage growth. Then we can scrutinize alternative explanations for the facts as we find them in the second part of the book, before considering alternative proposals for change and making recommendations in the last part.

## A Larger Economy Values Innovation More

While a number of economic factors drive the growing success of the 0.1 percent, this group grows richer for no other reason than the economy is growing larger. As the economy grows larger, the pool of customers grows larger. Today successful innovators, business leaders, and entertainers can serve more customers than they could have fifty years ago. As a result, the payback for economy-wide success is bigger than it used to be. An entertainer like Taylor Swift, for example, can reach a much larger market for her music than the Beatles could have in the 1960s.

Few people recognize the extent of the growth of the world economy. In 1964 the entire world economy was only as large as China's economy is today![10] That growth has had a big impact on the success of the most successful workers.

Over the same period, the incomes of doctors, schoolteachers, plumbers, and other tradesmen remain limited by the number of customers they can serve. The size of the economy doesn't change that. All other things being equal, economy-wide success, like Taylor Swift's success, will grow larger relative to the income of typical workers. This increases income inequality.

The pay of entertainers and other successful entrepreneurs grows larger relative to the pay of the typical workers, not because these innovators charge customers more. If anything, they are charging customers less and less. They earn more because they have more customers.

Taylor Swift's growing success doesn't come at the expense of her fans. They aren't paying more for her music; they are paying less. And they wouldn't buy her music if they didn't believe it was worth more than it cost, so buying her music creates value both for Swift and for her customers. Music is more valuable today because it makes more people happy.

For the same reason, the size of the largest companies has grown relative to the median pay of workers. The pay of CEOs has grown as companies have grown larger and more valuable. It's illogical for a CEO managing five employees to earn the same pay as one managing fifty thousand employees. As companies grow larger and more valuable, CEO pay has logically risen relative to the pay of the average employee. The ratio of CEO-to-employee pay may be clever rhetoric, but it's illogical economics.

It is no surprise, then, to find that as the world's population has grown, income inequality has grown around the world.[11] A more prosperous world values and rewards innovations—a new song or movie, a new technology, or a new insight—more highly than a less prosperous world. That's a good thing. The growing income of the 1 percent is the result of simple multiplication, not a deduction from the pockets of the less successful.

Were it the case that the world was becoming a less competitive "winner take all" economy, as economist Robert Frank postulates, or an increasingly concentrated "superstar economy" with relatively fewer "box office" successes, as economist Sherwin Rosen contends, we would expect the success of the 1 percent to be growing even faster than the success of the most successful corporations.[12] That hasn't been the case. Instead we find that the growth in pay of the highest-paid workers, as large as it is, lags behind the growth of the S&P 500 index. From 1979 to 2007, the S&P 500 index grew 500 percent after tax while the incomes of the top 1 percent have grown only 275 percent.[13] The economy has not grown less competitive, as Frank and Rosen claim. The world is simply growing larger, and that makes success more valuable.

# Information Technology Disproportionally Benefits the Most Productive Workers

The rise of information technology has increased income inequality in other ways as well. Information technology—computers, software, smartphones, and the Internet—not only has increased the productivity of trained talent, making their labor worth more, but it also has opened a window of new investment opportunities. A surge in the demand for properly trained workers has driven up their wages relative to lesser-skilled workers.

As technology augments the abilities of already productive workers, it increases the demand for workers who are trained in the use of technology. Assisted by computers, managers and entrepreneurs are now more effective than they have ever been before. They now have more accurate and comprehensive information to make decisions and more computing power to run "what if" planning scenarios. These tools increase their ability to serve customers more effectively and to find and commercialize new innovations that are beneficial to everyone. As a result, workers trained to use these tools have grown more productive.

Had computers merely increased the productivity of properly trained talent without also opening an even larger window of investment opportunities, higher productivity would have increased the supply of high-skilled workers relative to demand. High-skilled wages would have declined.

Fortunately, that did not happen. Information technology opened up more opportunities for employment than productivity gains expanded the capacity of high-skilled workers. Because demand for properly trained workers has exceeded supply, their wages have risen, albeit far more slowly than the payoff for successful innovation.

Information technology has given properly trained talent greater ability to add value. It has also opened a window of new investment opportunities. And at the same time, the world has grown more prosperous. A more prosperous world logically values innovation more. Given the circumstances, we should expect income inequality to rise.

# Information Technology Reduces the Need for Capital

A shift from a manufacturing economy to an information economy has also increased income inequality. Success in the modern information-intensive economy often requires substantially less capital than the manufacturing-based economy. Information technology scales to economy-wide success without much need for capital. Successful innovators often have less need to share the value they have created with investors. With less need to share their success with investors, success-ful innovators, such as Bill Gates, Steve Jobs, and Sergey Brin, have grown richer than they would have had they needed to rely on inves-tors. As a result, successful founders often look like large corporations of old. Their outsized success contributes to rising income inequality.

Successful IT start-ups no longer need large networks of buildings filled with expensive, long-lasting equipment and inventory to serve customers. Today's start-ups can often find, communicate with, and distribute information-intensive products and services to customers globally with minimal additional costs. In fact, today's successful start-ups often generate more cash than they consume.

With little need for capital investment, successful innovations like Google and Facebook can scale fully without much need for investors. Successful start-ups are often cash flow positive from the get-go. Today when entrepreneurs are successful, they often sell stock to the public only to establish its price so that founders can sell a small portion of their holdings.

Bigger payoffs from lottery-like success combined with less need for capital also motivates a greater number of talented individuals to take entrepreneurial risks. On average, if more people gamble, there will be more outsized winners even if the expected returns to gambling are poor. More lottery winners increase income inequality.

## Compounding Success Benefits the Most Productive Workers

As the success of American innovators increases, that success itself has compounding effects that increase the pay and productivity of the highest-paid Americans. We see these effects when we compare Amer-ica's growth with that of other countries.

In America, cutting-edge companies like Microsoft, Google, and Facebook give their employees valuable on-the-job training that in-creases their productivity. Together these well-trained employees cre-ate communities of experts, such as in Silicon Valley. Access to communities of experts further enhances productivity of properly trained workers. This expertise permeates into the larger economy as well-trained employees take jobs elsewhere, supervise others, and teach them what they have learned—what economists call "spillover effects."

Successful innovation also puts money into the hands of experts with better understandings of related investment opportunities than that of investors more broadly. Investment expertise reduces investment risk. Successful investments that find and commercialize more innovation enhance productivity further.

A better-trained workforce, larger communities of experts, and more knowledgeable investors increase the expected payoff for risk-taking—both the value and likelihood of achieving success. Like any game of chance, the higher the value and certainty for risk-taking, the more people will take risk. More risk-taking accelerates innovation and growth.

As well, the growing success of successful risk-takers raises the bar for success by diminishing the success of others. In large part, success is relative. Loss of status motivates talented workers to get trained properly, work harder, and take more risks.

Together these effects combine into a self-reinforcing feedback loop that gradually builds upon itself to create differentiated capabilities that accelerate growth. These capabilities include not only better-trained experts and investors but also more motivated entrepreneurs and investors who are more willing to take the risks necessary to produce innovation.

The failure of the rest of the world to spark the feedback loop that builds these institutional capabilities limits the productivity of other countries' most productive workers and prevents them from contributing their fair share of innovation in a world driven by information technology. A shortage of properly trained and productivity-enhanced talent in the rest of the world leaves low-hanging fruit for American innovators to pick. This further increases the value and pay of high-skilled American workers.

The compounding effects of these dynamics show in the pay of the highest-paid Americans relative to their counterparts elsewhere (see Figure 1-2, "Effect of Productivity on Wages"). Americans earn more because customers value their work more. Higher pay for properly trained talent and more success producing innovation increase income inequality.

Figure 1-2: **Effect of Productivity on Wages**

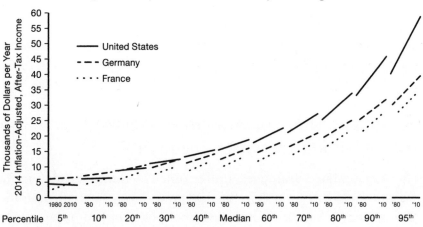

Source: "Luxembourg Income Study," via *New York Times*, 2014

Figure 1-3: **99 Percent's Share of GDP over Time**

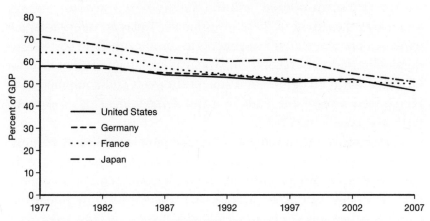

Source: "Income Distribution, Aggregate Demand and Current Account: A Sectoral Perspective," Behringer & van Treeck, 2013

The increased pay of the highest-paid workers is coming not at the expense of the rest of the workforce but from returns captured by investors. In both the United States and Germany, the bottom 99 percent of citizens earned 49 percent of GDP in 2007, despite America's top 1 percent earning 18 percent of all income earned by labor, versus the German top 1 percent earning only 12 percent of labor's income (see Figure 1-3, "99 Percent's Share of GDP over Time"). Relative to Germany, the additional share of GDP earned by America's 1 percent comes entirely from the investors' share of GDP, and not the share earned by the 99 percent.[14] The same is true, albeit to slightly lesser degrees, in comparisons with France and Japan.[15] Again, this split increases the pay of the highest-paid Americans without diminishing the pay of the other 99 percent.

# A Greater Share of Resources Devoted to Innovation Increases Inequality

Given its unique advantages, unlike other high-wage economies in which capital costs as a share of GDP are growing faster than in the United States, America is investing brainpower in lieu of capital. As America devotes a greater share of its resources to producing innovation, it will produce a greater number of outsized successes. In turn, this increases inequality.

America's antiquated manufacturing-based accounting system masks the extent of these investments. Today accounting largely expenses people-related investments as an intermediate cost of production, rather than recognizing them as capital goods that increase GDP, the way it recognizes investments in plant and equipment. Unrecognized investment leads to an understatement of investment, GDP, and productivity.*

Conservative measurements that take people-related investments into account, such as those employed in a 2006 study published by the Federal Reserve Board entitled "Intangible Capital and Economic Growth,"[16] show significant increases in people-related investments. According to the study's estimates, intangible investments rose from about 7 percent of non-farm-business output in the late 1970s to 10 percent in the early 1990s to about 14 percent today. Intangible investments rose dramatically in the 1990s when productivity accelerated (see Figure 1-4, "U.S. Investment in Intangibles as a Percentage of GDP").

Given America's heavy investment in knowledge-intensive intangible assets, it hardly seems coincidental that total factor productivity—productivity growth from innovation and know-how rather than from

---

* This mismeasurement grew so untenable that in 2013 the U.S. Bureau of Economic Analysis took its first steps to account properly for intangible investment.

Figure 1-4: U.S. Investment in Intangibles as a Percentage of GDP

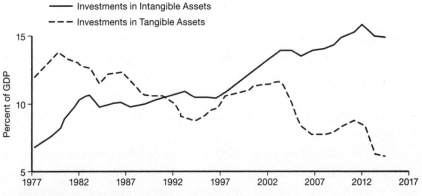

Source: "Intangible Capital and Growth," Corrado et al., 2012, via *BusinessWeek*

greater capital investment or education per worker—surged from a growth rate of 0.5 percent per year from 1974 to 1995 to 1.75 percent a year from 1995 to the economic peak preceding the financial crisis.

America's increased productivity growth relative to other high-wage economies stems from increased investment in intangibles—*not* magic. Nor should it come as a surprise that intangible investment rates in Germany and France, where productivity growth has been slower, were only 60 to 70 percent of those in the United States when measured as a percent of GDP in 2006. The less advanced economies of Italy and Spain invested at half that rate. Only the United Kingdom, which has grown as fast as the United States over the last two decades, albeit from a lower base of productivity and prosperity, has invested in intangibles at a rate comparable to that of the United States.[17]

It's true that productivity growth has recently waned and that investment declined significantly in the aftermath of the financial crisis.[18] But since the recession, Internet-related investment has come roaring back. One only need go to Silicon Valley to witness the phenomenon. The place is on fire. Google, Facebook, Amazon, and Apple have increased investment to $60 billion per year in 2014 from less than $10 billion in 2000.[19] Together with venture capital's $50 billion per year of funding, tech-related investment has eclipsed the 2000s' extraordinarily high $100-billion-per-year inflation-adjusted investment levels.[20]

Skeptics of America's dynamism often point to the declining number of start-ups.[21] But the reality is more complex than a superficial count of start-ups indicates. The consolidation of the retail and restaurant sectors by national chains like Walmart and Darden (the owner of Olive Garden) distorts the data of the U.S. economy, decreasing the number of mom-and-pop entrepreneurial start-ups. Mom-and-pop retail start-ups largely take market share from one another, rather than growing the economy. Taken as a whole, they do little to increase employment.

Start-ups that grow large increase employment, and those companies are predominantly high-tech start-ups.[22] Successful high-tech start-ups require a subset of entrepreneurial risk-takers—ones that are both very smart and uniquely trained.

While it's true that high-tech start-ups spiked briefly in 2000, there has been a gradual upward trend in the rate of high-quality start-ups since the early 1990s. In fact, 2014 represents the second-highest level of activity since the short-lived spike of 2000 (see Figure 1-5, "High-Potential U.S. Start-Ups").[23] And in the San Francisco Bay Area—the hub of high-tech start-ups—high-quality start-up activity is substantially higher than it was at the peak in 2000.[24] This hardly represents evidence that high-quality start-ups are waning—quite the opposite.

Others point to the recent slowdown in productivity as evidence of waning investment in innovation.[25] But a slowdown in productivity growth can occur for a variety of reasons, independent of the amount of effort devoted to innovation. Add-on innovation in the wake of breakthroughs like the Internet, e-mail, personal computers, and smartphones initially accelerates productivity and then eventually slows as opportunities to pick low-hanging fruit are exhausted— "fished out" in economic parlance. Meanwhile, breakthroughs come intermittently and unexpectedly. Increased regulation can sap management's attention and subsequently slow productivity growth. Dodd-Frank and the Affordable Care Act swamped the economy with regulation. A reduction in the rate of further gains from education and capital investment slows productivity growth independent of innovation. And investment and risk-taking clearly retreated in the aftermath of the financial crisis, as evidenced by a 40 percent to

Figure 1-5: High-Potential U.S. Start-Ups

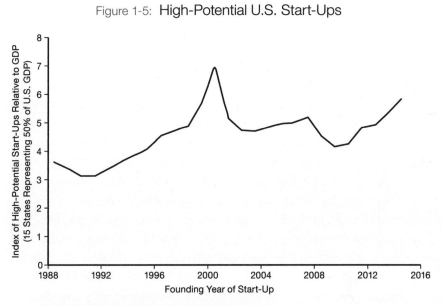

Source: "The State of American Entrepreneurship," Guzman and Stern, 2016

50 percent reduction in accumulated business investment from 2007 to 2013 relative to historical norms.[26]

Because productivity growth ebbs and flows independent of the resources expended, productivity growth relative to other high-wage economies is a truer measure of America's ability to produce innovation. By all measures, effort (the amount of resources devoted to innovation) and outputs (productivity growth relative to other high-wage economies) of U.S. investment to produce innovation appear to be both substantially higher and more successful.

There are also reasons to believe productivity growth is higher than it appears to be. The Boskin Commission and decades of follow-up work by Northwestern University's Robert Gordon, for example, also find understatement of productivity growth. This understatement largely stems from the U.S. Consumer Price Index's failure to fully account for the value of replacing old goods with more valuable innovations—for example, by replacing landline-based telephones with smartphones. Properly accounting for these productivity gains boosts GDP growth upwards of 1 percent per year, which is substantial since GDP grows only 2 to 3 percent a year.[27]

Goldman Sachs economists Jan Hatzius and Kris Dawsey reach the following conclusion about slowing versus unmeasured productivity growth:

> Measured productivity growth has slowed sharply in recent years. . . . But is the weakness for real? We have our doubts. Profit margins have risen to record levels, inflation has mostly surprised on the downside, overall equity prices have surged, and technology stocks have performed even better than the broader market. None of this feels like a major IT-led productivity slowdown. One potential explanation that reconciles these observations is that structural changes in the U.S. economy may have resulted in a statistical understatement of real GDP growth. There are several possible areas of concern, but the rapid growth of software and digital content—where quality-adjusted prices and real output are much harder to measure than in most other sectors—seems particularly important.[28]

Despite the recent slowdown in productivity growth, it's not hard to imagine vast improvements in Internet-search capabilities, computing capabilities converging on consciousness, and genetic engineering that transform the human race in the long run. Historically we have seen nothing but surprisingly large improvements in our standards of living. So it's hard to see us nearing a "fished out" pool of opportunities.

If the economy *does* reach a point of significantly diminishing returns to information-intensive innovation, and investment slows, income inequality will likely narrow considerably. But is that a good thing?

The short-term ebb and flow of productivity growth should not blind us to the long-term historic trend. The economy has devoted a greater share of resources to innovation. Today the U.S. economy invests by hiring smart people to improve the future—to invent applications for iPhones and to capitalize on the information collected by Google. It no longer builds plants and equipment. Because of this shift, income inequality has grown.

Consistent with this shift in investment from traditional investment in capital goods, like plant and equipment, to innovation with widely dispersed lottery-like returns, a 2015 study by the McKinsey Global Institute shows that "since 2000, the average variance in returns on capital for North American firms has been more than 60 percent higher than the levels that prevailed from 1965 to 1980."[29] The study finds that "this trend toward greater variability in corporate performance is playing out at the sector level. . . . The margin gap between the top quintile firms (by profit margin) and median firms in idea-intensive industries has widened by 20 percent in the past decade, more than in any other group of industries. In return on invested capital, the gap between top performers and the median has grown by 25 percent."[30]

In contrast, to information-intensive investments, the study reports:

> While idea-intensive firms run away with the profits, companies in capital-intensive industries are feeling a growing squeeze. The average after-tax profit margin in industries producing capital goods is roughly half the average of IT firms. . . . In addition, the margin spread between capital-intensive firms at the fifth and 95th percentile of profitability is much smaller than the spread in idea-intensive industries. . . . In these [capital-intensive] industries, it is much harder for winning firms to pull away from the pack.[31]

While competition between traditional companies is narrowing the gap between winners and the rest of the pack, innovation in information technology is widening the distribution of returns and subsequently increasing income inequality.

Whether innovation becomes harder to find—and there is evidence that it is becoming harder to produce—it doesn't mean that the payoffs for success or the amount of U.S. resources devoted to innovative activities will correspondingly dwindle, at least not in the short run.[32] Growing global markets, relatively diminished competition from the rest of the world, less required upfront investment, and less opportunity in other endeavors can all offset a reduction in the probability of success from innovation. As the U.S. economy devotes more resources to these lottery-like investments, income inequality will grow at the highest end of the wage scale.

# Increased Risk-Taking Increases Inequality Even If the Returns Are Subpar

Even though a handful of fortunate innovators are making outsized returns, it does not mean that on average innovation's profitability has increased and that entrepreneurial risk-takers, investors, and properly trained talent are merely benefiting from outsized risk-adjusted returns. Nor is it necessary for average returns to increase for inequality to rise. As more resources are devoted to finding and commercializing innovation, overall return on investment is likely to decline.[33] Even if returns are declining in general, the shift toward innovation's more widely distributed lottery-like returns—and away from traditional investments—can increase outsized success. Scrutinizing only the successful 1 percent (or 0.1 percent, or 0.01 percent) ignores the true cost of success, namely the cost of failure. Ignoring the cost of failure creates a distorted view of the value of success.

A more accurate measure of return on investment incorporates both the value of success and the cost of failure. This measure is the "expected value" of success—the value of success multiplied by the likelihood of success.

A ninetieth-percentile earner used to be a doctor, lawyer, or corporate executive with a lifetime of near-certain employment.[34] In the twenty-first century, a top graduate is likely to be working in a high-tech start-up with a remote prospect of success and facing a lifetime of disruptive career changes that will likely end badly late in his career—as an obsolete fifty-year-old without great prospects for high-wage employment. It's true that one in one hundred may get very lucky, but given the uncertainties those one hundred face, are they really better off than their parents were?

It's disingenuous to measure growth in the pay for the one lucky success while ignoring the fate of the other ninety-nine who didn't succeed. A more accurate measure of pay includes not only the small number of successes but also the larger pool of workers from which they are drawn. It's disingenuous to consider the 0.1 percent in isolation. Instead we also need to include the large pool of very talented failures—failures critical for finding that one lucky success. The group of failures will likely earn less than their similarly skilled peers—the ones who became doctors and lawyers instead of failed Internet entrepreneurs.

There are numerous reasons to believe the overall returns to investment that produce innovation may be subpar. Proprietary ideas have been notoriously hard to guard. Economists have typically described ideas as non-excludible goods. Unlike physical goods, which only their owners can use, ideas are available for anyone to use but for know-how and legal restrictions, such as patents. Non-exclusivity makes it harder to use ideas to create sustainable competitive advantages critical to generating above-average returns. While it's true that networks of users give companies like Google and Facebook competitive advantages from economies of scale, most ideas afford no such opportunity. Non-exclusivity makes competition more capable than it otherwise may be.

As well, we don't see cash-rich technology companies like Google, Facebook, Apple, and Microsoft stretching to invest their cash in product development despite these companies possessing deep and far-ranging expertise and superior capability to commercialize viable innovation. Quite the opposite: we see these companies hoarding cash and buying back their shares. That's odd behavior if the returns are superior.

It's a misnomer to suggest high-tech companies are accumulating offshore cash simply to avoid taxes. They can and do use intermediaries—namely, banks—to borrow offshore cash and buy back their shares domestically to distribute cash to shareholders. They hold cash regardless.

In part, the investment opportunities may be so broad that tech companies with valuable franchises can't afford to pursue every possible opportunity and threat to their business. Instead they may hoard cash to maximize their market value so they can outbid competitors to buy unexpected emerging technologies that threaten their existing business if necessary. The threat of technological disruption may be too high for companies with valuable franchises, like Google, to close off their options by using all their cash, whether for investment or distributions to shareholders. If companies are hoarding cash to protect themselves from emerging technologies, it indicates that the risk of loss from unexpected disruptive innovation is high.

It's also possible that entrepreneurialism has grown so prevalent that companies like Google and Facebook—with limited upside to their market value—can no longer attract the most productive innovators. That would be consistent with the opening of a broad window of investment opportunities, albeit opportunities that disrupt existing businesses.

In those circumstances, large companies may not be able compete successfully by relying exclusively on internal resources for product development. Surely, a multifaceted approach is better than relying on a one-dimensional strategy.

It's also possible that clever employees may be learning to scour their work environments more thoroughly for good ideas and abscond with them. Frankly, it may be unprofitable to produce innovation systematically without first randomly stumbling upon a good idea.

Entrepreneurial employees may be able to circumvent laws that protect corporate assets by passing good ideas to friends. If employees steal a significant number of good ideas, internal development will be less profitable.

The gradually accelerating turnover in the Fortune 500 is consistent with a growing risk of technological disruption. "In the 1920s and 1930s the turnover rate in the S&P 90 averaged about 1.5% per year. A new member of the S&P 90 at that time could expect to remain on the list, on average, for more than sixty-five years. . . . In 1998, the turnover rate in the S&P 500 was closer to 10%, implying an average lifetime on the list of ten years, not sixty-five!"[35] Surprisingly, "of the five hundred companies originally making up the S&P 500 in 1957, only seventy-four remained on the list through 1997. And of these seventy-four, only twelve outperformed the S&P 500 index itself over the 1957–1998 period."[36]

The changing fortunes in technology are even more tumultuous. The fifteen largest technology companies in 2000, at the peak of the Internet bubble, have lost 60 percent of their market value—$1.35 trillion as of December 2015. Nortel, a $200 billion company in 2000, is bankrupt today. On the same date, EMC's market value was a quarter the size. Cisco's was a third the size. Intel's market value was 40 percent smaller as of December 2015. Only one, Microsoft, had a higher market capitalization.[37]

While these apparent juggernauts were declining in value, fifteen companies with combined market capitalization less than $10 billion in 2000 are now worth over $2 trillion today. Apple's market value, a has-been in 2000, has grown from $6 billion to over $650 billion today.[38] With turnover like that, the values of established franchises are surely less than they would be otherwise, no matter the valuations financial markets currently place on them.

As hard as it may be for established companies to produce innovation profitably, it is surely even harder for independent start-ups and investors who lack the full breadth of expertise and capabilities necessary to commercialize viable innovations. Given the plethora of start-up-related risks, assets that reduce risk, such as teams of properly trained talent, proven supervision, an infrastructure for commercializing innovations, and synergies with existing businesses, are more valuable than they otherwise would be. Without them, stand-alone start-ups funded by independent investors are likely to be riskier and less profitable.

And unlike bets on exogenously driven growth—population growth, education-driven productivity growth, rural migration to more productive cities, two decades of pent-up demand first from the Great Depression and then the Second World War, and the growth of mass production and related capital investment—where every investor more or less has the same access to insights whether they truly have any insight or not, investing in technology increasingly requires technology-specific expertise and insight. Every fundraiser designs his or her start-up's investment sales pitch to sound like a miraculous cure for cancer. Outside investors must acquire the necessary knowledge to avoid systematically investing in unworthy opportunities. Over and over again, one should expect investors to spend money evaluating new opportunities only to discover the investments are not worth making. Costly due diligence reduces investment returns and makes investing more expensive than it appears to be.

As such, Joe Stiglitz questions whether rich households invest directly in young start-ups that are critical to innovation and growth.[39] He fails to see that rich households need not invest directly in start-ups to motivate high-tech entrepreneurialism.

Silicon Valley is full of entrepreneurs looking to create companies that will be highly valued by public market investors—chiefly wealthy households that either buy equity in successful start-ups directly through initial public offerings or through their ownership in other highly valued, public high-tech companies like Google and Facebook—*if* they are successful start-ups.

That's not to say returns to innovation are poor. No one knows. But without the benefits of exogenous growth, given the near certainty of widespread failure, and with competition from the growing amount of investments in intangibles like research and development, it would not be surprising to find below-average returns even though outsized success is rising. Income inequality may nevertheless rise as the dispersion of returns widens even though the increased risk necessary to produce a handful of outsized successes and the high failure rates needed to produce those returns may not represent the walk in the park they appear to be.

## Loss of Status Drives Irrational Risk-Taking

As poor as the risk-adjusted returns on start-ups may be for investors who can diversify their risk by investing in many start-ups, they are surely much worse for individual entrepreneurs. Unlike investors who enjoy average returns by investing in many projects, founders and their teams risk everything on a single start-up. As such, they bear undiversified project-specific risks that investors avoid through diversification. Most will end up with little to show for their work. At the very least, they are putting the latter half of their careers and their retirement at risk.

In part, individuals may be joining start-ups because of a lack of good opportunities elsewhere. Waning investment opportunities from other exogenous sources of growth may have accelerated the shift to innovation-driven growth. In large part, necessity is the mother of invention. An increasing lack of both alternative investment and employment opportunities increases the willingness of talented workers to take entrepreneurial risks.

People also seem attracted to playing lotteries. In the lead-up to 2000, for example, when Internet payoffs exploded, young business students forsook high-paying, high-status careers to pursue far-fetched

Internet start-ups. In the lead-up to 2007, talented workers similarly flocked to risky hedge funds despite the near impossibility of beating average market returns in an effort to win big. The same thing is happening today in Silicon Valley—an explosion of unlikely-to-succeed start-ups fueled by talent seeking outsized payoffs.

Rising payoffs for state lotteries also lure an increasing number of people into taking irrational risks. Gambling increases, despite the fact that the expected payoff—the size of the payoff multiplied by the chances of success—remains poor. State lotteries collect far more money than they pay out. As a result, participants lose money on average.

Gamblers seem to systematically overestimate their capacities, underestimate the risks, and value a two-dollar payoff *more* than twice as much as a one-dollar payoff contrary to the economic theory of diminishing marginal utility. That theory posits a second car is less valuable to its owner than the first, the third is less valuable than the second, and so forth.

So it ought to follow that an additional dollar is similarly less valuable as one's wealth grows. But money confers status, notoriety, and other things people desire beyond just the goods they consume. Or, at least, if people without money believe it confers these things, then the opportunity to own money may offset, at least partially, the increasingly declining value of wealth as payoffs grow larger.

Perhaps more important, status seekers lose status when others succeed. As a result, the most talented students no longer want to be doctors and lawyers. They go to business school and join start-ups despite the long odds of success. Loss of status drives them to take ill-advised risks in an effort to regain their lost status as potential lottery winners.

No surprise, microeconomic experiments that randomly distributed relatively large rewards to poor Kenyan villagers found that "the bigger the handouts to others in their village, the greater the dissatisfaction of the non-recipients."[40] According to *The Economist,* a study published in the *Journal of Public Economics* in 2005 found that "we tend to look exclusively at those better off than us. . . . When the lot of others improves, we react negatively, but when our own lot improves, we shift our reference group to those who are still better off."[41]

Fortunately for the rest of us—the chief beneficiaries of entrepreneurial risk-taking that produces innovation—the outsized success of a handful of entrepreneurs made talented workers feel a loss of status. Those workers ramped up high-tech entrepreneurial risk-taking despite the risks.

## Conclusion

A frenzy of highly skilled entrepreneurial risk-taking is benefiting the U.S. economy. The U.S. economy continues to produce billion-dollar unicorns—venture-backed privately owned start-ups with billion-dollar valuations—at a substantially faster pace than Europe and with valuations that are substantially larger.[42] From January 2014 to March 2016 alone,* the number of U.S. unicorns has grown from 32 to 88, despite 18 companies exiting the list after going public, with a combined value growing from $75 billion to over $300 billion.[43] Over the same period, European unicorns have grown from 2 to 16 (less two public offerings), with $9 billion of combined value increasing to $35 billion.[44] During a time when large European start-ups created $26 billion of addition value, the United States created $225 billion of additional value—almost ten times as much!

While it's true that American consumers will benefit from a cure for cancer even if it's discovered by a Chinese company, American workers benefit *more* when the successful innovators are also American. At the very least, company's founders, investors, and workforce disproportionately spend their gains in the United States, which pumps up the demand for goods and services made by lesser-skilled Americans.[45]

Since 1980, the U.S. economy has increased employment nearly 50 percent—more than twice the growth of that of Germany and France, and more than three times the growth of Japan, while providing median after-tax incomes for American families that are 15 to 30 percent higher than those of Europe and Japan. This is an unheard-of difference in performance.

And that difference in growth would have been greater still were it not for the disproportionate benefit of U.S. innovation, which accelerated the rest of the world's growth.

---

* As of the time of this writing.

Successful American innovators also increase tax revenues as rich Americans pay a disproportionate share of taxes.[46] Increased tax revenues provide more government services and benefits to lesser-skilled Americans. And a larger U.S. economy is also better able to defend itself militarily. It would be shortsighted to leave these opportunities to other economies to discover and commercialize when they are available to America even though they increase income inequality.

As other sources of growth have waned, information technology fortunately opened a large window of new investment opportunities. More so than the rest of the world, the U.S. economy capitalized on these opportunities.

IT increased the productivity of the most productive workers. With investment opportunities growing faster than productivity gains, the pay of the most productive workers grew.

A positive feedback loop ensued that further increased the productivity of the most productive worker. Better-trained workers and investors increased the likelihood and payoff for successful innovation. Like any game of chance, better odds increase the risk-taking needed to produce innovation.

A larger economy also increased the value of innovation. And unlike capital-intensive manufacturing, IT reduced the need for capital investment to scale to economy-wide success. These factors magnified the value of success and the pool of eager and talented risk-takers.

More risk-taking increases the number of fortunate successes even if the returns to risk-taking don't improve significantly. Success diminishes the status of others. Loss of status drives many status seekers to regain their lost status by taking ill-advised risks. More risk-taking produces innovation that is beneficial to all of us.

Despite the success of America's economy, demagogues have demonized the success of America's 1 percent as a liability that hollows out the middle class, lowers wages, and damages the fabric of American society.[47] But were it not for the successes of America's most successful workers, U.S. employment growth would have slowed further, as employment growth did in Europe and Japan.

The outsized success of America's 0.1 percent is the true source of its growing income inequality. Growing income inequality is a byproduct of the success of the U.S. economy. This success has been shared broadly by the rest of the economy. If anything, America should try to entrench and expand its position as a hub of innovation by encouraging its best and brightest students to get the kind of training demanded by customers, and to take the risks necessary to produce more innovation.

## Chapter 2

# THE REASONS FOR SLOWING WAGE GROWTH

T he soaring wages of the highest-paid workers is a by-product of America's differential success in the age of information. Given this success, we might have expected middle- and working-class wages to have grown more. Instead their growth slowed.

Advocates of income redistribution have been quick to blame the success of the 1 percent for this slowing wage growth. Their arguments, however—that success is unearned, technology hollows out the middle class, and poor-quality education unnecessarily holds back students—are suspect. More likely, trade, immigration, and manufacturing productivity gains, which have hollowed out manufacturing employment, have flooded the economy with a near-unlimited supply of lesser-skilled workers. This increased supply in combination with resources that constrain growth—namely, properly trained talent and the economy's capacity and willingness to take risk—hold back wage growth.

In an economy constrained only by labor, trade and immigration grow the economy without reducing wages—no different than population growth. Additional workers increase demand. Increased demand spurs investors to invest more capital. With the same amount of capital invested per worker—namely, plant and equipment—workforce productivity and wages remain constant.

If capital were constrained, however, more workers would reduce the amount of capital invested per worker. Less capital invested per worker would reduce productivity and wages.

In a knowledge-intensive economy, capital doesn't constrain growth. Properly trained talent and the economy's capacity and willingness to take risks constrain growth.

The increased availability of capital in a knowledge-intensive economy spurs investment in the industries of low-wage economies, where, unlike services, manufactured products can be shipped around the world to compete with products made with high-wage labor. The high saving rate of the Chinese and German economies adds to the availability of capital.

The increased availability of capital also spurs domestic high-wage manufacturers to increase productivity where it is economical to compete with low-wage offshore manufacturers. The combination of the two—offshore sourcing and domestic productivity growth—reduces the demand for high-wage, lesser-skilled manufacturing workers.

It's true that when consumers and investors spend their savings from buying lower-cost offshore goods on domestic goods and services, it increases the demand for domestic labor. But displaced high-wage, blue-collar workers depend both on entrepreneurs and other investors to take the risks necessary to create new jobs for them and on properly trained talent to engineer and supervise work as productive as their previous capital-intensive manufacturing jobs—no easy tasks. Properly trained talent and the economy's capacity and willingness to take risk, however, are constrained resources in the knowledge-intensive economy. If resources are constrained, trade with low-wage economies will put downward pressure on low-skilled wages.

If trade with low-wage economies didn't lower the cost of goods more than the wages of domestic lower-skilled labor, it would be cheaper to produce the goods with domestic labor. So trade makes everyone better off on average. Lesser-skilled workers, however, suffer the entire burden of lower wages but capture only a portion of the benefits from lower-priced offshore goods. Much of the benefit is captured by the rich, retirees, and the non-working poor, who enjoy lower-priced goods but without the cost of lower wages. As a result, trade lowers the relative incomes of the middle and working classes.

An influx of low-skilled immigrants only adds to the strain on constrained resources. If risk-takers and properly trained talent fail to create jobs for low-skilled immigrants that are as productive as the jobs of the lesser-skilled, native-born workers on average, lower-wage immigrants working in less productive jobs will bid down wages, further lowering the relative incomes of the middle and working classes.

It's true that if low-skilled immigrants contributed proportionally to constrained resources, an influx would not reduce wages. But surely they do not contribute proportionally to these resources.

At the same time, information technology opens a window of attractive investment opportunities that competes with displaced workers for the attention of properly trained talent and the economy's willingness and capacity to take risk. Successful IT start-ups like Google and Facebook tend not to employ low-skilled workers directly. Instead, attractive investment opportunities raise the pay of properly trained talent and successful risk-takers, and their increased demand employs lesser-skilled workers in other lines of works—waiters and landscapers, for example. But an influx of low-skilled immigration spreads a given increase in the demand of properly trained talent and successful risk-takers over a greater number of lesser-skilled workers who compete with one another to satisfy that demand. Again, this lowers the relative incomes of the middle and working classes.

As more and more lower-skilled workers compete to satisfy a given increase in the demand of properly trained talent and successful risk-takers, wages are driven down to waiters-waiting-on-waiters wages—that is, to the value of low-skilled workers serving each other without the added benefit of constrained resources. In a theoretical economy without constrained resources, lower-skilled workers are, in effect, already earning waiters-waiting-on-waiters wages that can fall no further. Trade and immigration have no effect in that world. Unfortunately, we don't live in that world.

Trade deficits only exacerbate the problem. With balanced trade, Americans buy goods that employ offshore workers, and offshore economies buy goods that employ American workers. With trade deficits, offshore economies loan America proceeds from the sale of goods to Americans rather than buying American goods. To reach full employment at the highest possible wages, consumers, risk-takers, and properly trained talent must borrow that money and put it to work creating jobs lost to trade deficits. Trade deficits just strain constrained resources further.

Ultimately, in a world with constrained resources, growth can manifest itself in two ways: Where the supply of labor is restricted—as it was in the 1950s and 1960s—growing demand drives up wages. Where the supply of labor is unrestricted, as it is today, growth drives up employment.

Since 1980, the U.S. economy has increased employment by nearly 50 percent—more than twice the growth of that of Germany and France, and more than three times the growth of that of Japan.[1] And that difference would have been greater still were it not for the disproportionate benefit of U.S. innovation, which accelerated the rest of the world's growth.

Because of this growth, today America is home to nearly 40 million foreign-born adult immigrants and their 20 million native-born adult children—a very large proportion relative to the rest of America's 140 million eighteen- to sixty-five-year-old population.[2] In truth, *no other high-wage economy has done more to grow the world's middle class and working class than America's.*

It's disingenuous to close one eye, ignore America's extraordinary employment growth relative to its peers, and claim that the outsized success of America's 1 percent has slowed the growth of middle- and working-class incomes. The outsized success of America's 1 percent has been *the* chief source of growth exerting upward pressure on domestic employment and wages.

# Trade with Low-Wage Economies and Other Changing Circumstances Slow Middle-Class Wage Growth

The U.S. economy has changed significantly since the end of World War II, when increased capital investment in the face of a shortage of lesser-skilled workers raised wages. Today a slowdown in exogenously driven growth; trade with low-wage economies; domestic manufacturing productivity gains; a population fully saturated with education; a growing supply of lesser-skilled domestic labor; and constraints on the assets that create highly productive, lower-skilled employment—namely, entrepreneurial risk-taking, investment, and properly trained talent—slow middle- and working-class wage growth.

A dearth of births in the Great Depression restricted the supply of labor in the 1950s and 1960s when the economy rebounded after two decades of damage—first from the Great Depression and then from World War II. At the same time, interstate highways and television created enormous American mass markets. Capital-intensive companies like General Motors and Procter & Gamble raced to exploit unrealized economies of scale and hire lesser-skilled workers to operate their machinery. This window of opportunity opened at a time when World War II killed a large number of working-age men in Europe and Japan, both of which were rebuilding economies destroyed by the war and, as a result, were temporarily less able to compete. With minimal international competition, the window for American businesses temporarily opened even wider.

Meanwhile, America was the first nation to send a significant portion of its students to college.[3] It discovered a large pool of talented workers that grew more productive with education. The success of America's college graduates not only increased the productivity of both skilled and unskilled workers, but also further reduced the supply of lesser-skilled labor.

With a much larger share of students not yet graduating from high school, Europe and Japan needed several decades before they were able to duplicate America's educational success. Again, the temporary lack of international competition opened a window of opportunity that accelerated American growth.

With a shortage of labor in the face of growing manufacturing demand, agricultural technology freed rural workers to capitalize on these opportunities. World War II pulled young farm boys off the farm. Higher wages made factory work more attractive when they returned. Rural farmhands consequently migrated to inherently more productive cities, which further increased their capacity to add value.

These favorable exogenous trends (two decades of pent-up growth, the value of mass markets and related capital investment, education, and rural migration) combined with waves of population growth (first from the baby boom, then from the increased workforce participation of women, and finally from immigration) accelerated growth. With manufacturers racing to hire workers in order to satisfy growing demand, wages rose.

To satisfy growing demand, manufacturers invested more capital—both plant and equipment—and employed more workers. At the same time, they substituted capital for workers. They automated tasks by investing more capital per worker to make workers more productive. This dynamic employed an increasing number of workers in increasingly more capital-intensive jobs. This raised the productivity of the marginal worker.

Fast exogenous growth also reduced investment uncertainty. Eventually, growth absorbs excess capacity. Less risk lowers the cost of capital, which accelerates investment. Rapid growth over the last twenty-five years similarly reduces investment risk in China today.

Ultimately, competition forces investors to share the value they create with customers and workers. When employers compete for workers, the least productive employer sets the wages for a given skill level. That employer's workers would gladly take work at higher wages if it was available. When employers that are more productive need more workers, they bid up wages and drive the least productive employers out of business. As marginal producers raise their productivity—what economists call their marginal product of labor—to survive, wages rise. Under these conditions, competition for workers seems to lead to a never-ending spiral of productivity improvements and wage increases.

These circumstances led economists to believe that income inequality narrows as countries grow richer—what economists call a Kuznets curve, after Simon Kuznets, the economist who theorized it. In agrarian economies, where a small cabal of landowners initially controls the means of production, industrialization of those economies often broadens ownership of the means of production and raises wages, which narrows income inequality. Similarly, where a broad base of uneducated talent becomes educated, income inequality again may narrow.

But this provides a cautionary tale. Economists often make their bones by discovering generalizable truths. Economic circumstances, however, affect the application of these generalizable truths. Consider a chess game: in general, a queen may be more valuable than a knight, but in particular circumstances, the knight is superior. Chess players must continually study the changing circumstances of each new position to apply generalizable truths correctly. You simply can't get very far in chess with generalizable truths alone, nor can you with economics.

Most economic models assume labor and capital constrain growth, but circumstances have changed. Now properly trained talent and the economy's capacity and willingness to bear risk constrain growth. This has far-reaching consequences.

The economy, like biology, is a nested hierarchy of positive feedback loops, where each issue bears on many other issues. Biologists expected that decoding the human genome would lead to a host of drug discoveries, but they quickly discovered unexpected complexities. Genes have multiple purposes. They work in conjunction with one another and through redundancies. Proteins alter how genes express themselves. Glycomes, namely sugars, affect proteins, and environmental circumstances affect both. Because of these complexities, decoding the genome has not resulted in the straightforward discoveries for which scientists had hoped.

The same is true of economics. Failure to see all the linkages is the chief source of flawed macroeconomic reasoning. In fact, demagogues often ignore or oversimplify complex linkages to make their proposed solutions look better on paper than they actually are in reality. A proper diagnosis of the economy requires careful delineation of randomly changing and logically evolving circumstances.

In a post-industrial economy, a Kuznets curve hasn't described reality. In an economy saturated with education, for example, information technology, and not education, augments the value of cognitive skill. Unlike the saturation of education, this has increased income inequality. As computerization converges on cognition, the value of human creativity may later decline. There may be no generalizable governing principle whatsoever. The ebb and flow of outcomes may be entirely circumstantial.

Unfortunately, circumstances favorable to lesser-skilled workers in the 1950s and 1960s ran their course. Exogenous sources of growth slowed. America saturated its talent with education. Further gains have proved difficult to achieve. The migration of rural America to the cities is over.

Competition drives manufacturers, who can ship their products around the world, to relocate their factories offshore to low-wage economies. Domestic manufacturers must increase their productivity (e.g., auto assemblers), specialize (e.g., GE), move production offshore (e.g., toys and appliances), or never start producing in the first place (e.g., electronics) to compete successfully against lower-wage offshore producers. These outcomes all displace workers, who must find employment elsewhere.

The increased availability of capital, from both the shift from a capital-intensive economy to a knowledge-intensive economy in high-wage economies and the high saving rates in many low-wage economies, like China's, accelerates investment offshore that reduces manufacturing employment in high-wage economies.

Productivity gains from capital investment now hollow out manufacturing employment and drive unskilled workers to the harder-to-manage service sector, where productivity growth has been slower. Meanwhile, the baby boom, the increased participation of women in the workforce, immigration, and international trade greatly increased the supply of labor, especially lower-skilled labor.

Displaced workers must depend on entrepreneurial risk-takers, properly trained talent, and investors to find and commercialize new sources of employment with productivity and wages comparable to their prior capital-intensive manufacturing jobs. The ease of finding such work should not be taken for granted. To the extent these resources are in short supply, an increase in the number of job seekers—whether from displaced workers, newly arriving immigrants, or population growth—strains resources critical to job creation.

Balanced trade should return an equivalent amount of income and employment to the United States from offshore economies as offshore economies buy U.S. goods with the dollars they earn by selling Americans products. And U.S. consumers should spend their savings from lower-cost products—whether produced offshore or domestically—on other products and services that employ Americans, generally on domestic services that low-wage offshore labor cannot perform. Were that not the case, trade would not balance.

If the supply of U.S. labor were constrained, this increased domestic spending would increase wages independent of productivity gains. This dynamic buoys the demand for domestic labor. To the extent displaced workers can find work at wages higher than the lower wages of offshore workers, the economy as a whole is better off. The savings of lower-cost goods outweigh the reduction of wages. After all, offshore production is cheaper *because* displaced domestic workers can find work at higher wages. Were that not the case, it would be cheaper to produce imported goods with domestic workers.

Similarly, innovation and capital investment have historically lowered the cost of goods more than they have lowered the wages of lesser-skilled labor. The introduction of tractors, for example, did not result in the starvation of the displaced farmers. Quite the contrary—the lower cost of food allowed displaced workers to find work as teachers and carpenters, jobs that were uneconomical when the cost of food was astronomically high. The lower cost of food makes these jobs economical.

Agriculture converted to tractors en masse because the value of the newfound work was greater than the now-lower cost of food. Were that not the case, tractors would have been uneconomical investments— growing food with labor instead of capital would have been cheaper. Technology and capital investment are economical because they are cheaper than the value of the displaced labor.

As is the case with most all investment, competition forced all surviving farmers to buy tractors to avoid losses when competition lowered the cost of producing food. Competition between farmers lowered the price of food. In turn, this reduced the return on investment in a tractor to the cost of capital. So consumers, not investors, captured most of the value of tractors through the lower cost of food. Since even as recently as 1960, the cost of food in the United States has fallen from 18 percent of GDP to 10 percent.[4]

Luddites have always feared that displaced workers would be unable to find work at wages greater than the now-lower cost of goods, even though the history of technology tells a contradictory tale. When they smashed the looms, the Luddites could never have imagined that we would pay people to drive us to perform physical exercise, brew our coffee one cup at a time, and even swirl the foamy milk to make it pretty. These jobs became economical *because* of the lower cost of goods.

So far, the U.S. economy has employed an enormous influx of low-wage workers, both immigrants and offshore workers, with little, if any, decrease in median wages. If, on average, displaced lesser-skilled U.S. workers can find work at high enough wages—that is, with a high enough marginal product of labor—the lower cost of imported goods may increase the value of their wages because their wages can purchase more.

But while it's true that trade with low-wage economies may lower prices more than wages, an economy like America's buys products made with low-wage, lesser-skilled labor and sells products made with high-skilled labor—such as operating systems produced by Microsoft, Apple, and Google. Middle- and working-class workers bear the burden of lower wages while retirees, the non-working poor, and higher-skilled workers and their families—where 20 percent of the families earn 50 percent of the after-tax pay—share the benefits of lower-priced goods. The cost and benefits are not distributed proportionally. As such, trade will slow middle- and working-class wage growth relative to the rest of the economy.

Christian Broda and John Romalis of the University of Chicago and David Weinstein of Columbia University, however, present evidence that the resulting lower prices of imported goods disproportionately benefit low-income households. Lower-income families spend a disproportionate share of their income on low-cost imported goods sold at stores like Walmart, relative to richer households. The Consumer Price Index doesn't reflect this fact. Instead, it produces a price index for the average person—what economists call a representative agent.

Broda, Romalis, and Weinstein estimate that the cost of living for the poor is 25 percent less expensive than the Consumer Price Index (CPI) suggests, and that subsequently "current poverty rates [2005] are less than half of the official numbers."[5] Using a different methodology, the University of Chicago's Bruce Meyer and the University of Notre Dame's James Sullivan find a difference between actual and official poverty rates of a similar magnitude over the same period. These mismeasurements of income may also exaggerate the extent of rising income inequality and slowing middle-class wage growth.

There is, however, an important difference between low-income households, especially households with the lowest quintile of income, and low-wage workers. Many low-income families are not working full time or even part time. Their adult members are retired, disabled, sick, unemployed, or headed by single mothers with young children. Only about 3 percent of full-time workers live in poverty.[6]

Because government aid enables low-income (non-working) families to consume substantially more than they earn, trade likely lowers the cost of their consumption more than it lowers the price of their labor, because they don't work much. So while both the poor and the rich share in the benefits of lower prices from trade with low-wage economies, lower-skilled workers bear 100 percent of its burden. It would hardly be surprising, then, to find that the benefits of trade and immigration increase inequality by holding back middle- and working-class wage growth more than others—even if they make everyone richer.

Evolving circumstances have changed the relative growth rates of the pay of highly skilled and less-skilled high-wage workers. Conditions favorable to less-skilled workers in the 1950s have given way to less favorable conditions today. Investments in capital and education no longer accelerate lesser-skilled wage growth. Constraints on the resources that accelerate growth—risk-taking and properly trained talent—slow middle- and working-class wage growth further. While trade with low-wage economies makes everyone better off on average, it also slows middle- and working-class wage growth relative to the rest of the economy.

# Low-Skilled Immigration Strains Constrained Resources, Which Slows Wage Growth Further

The effect of immigration on wages is more concerning than trade. Unskilled immigrants largely compete with domestic workers at prevailing wage rates when resources are constrained. To the extent an increase in the supply of labor pushes down wages, it only reduces the cost of goods proportionally. In that case, middle- and working-class workers suffer 100 percent of wage reduction for only a portion of the similarly sized benefits.

An influx of workers should push down the marginal product of labor and reduce wages. If prospective employers had found more profitable work for workers than their existing jobs, these jobs would already exist. Newly created jobs are presumably the next best alternative to existing jobs—that is, less profitable than existing jobs—and should, therefore, have lower pay.

Workers who take these jobs would gladly take a higher-paying comparably skilled job for a nickel more than they are currently earning. Their lower wage sets the pay for all similarly skilled work.

To address these concerns, advocates of trade and immigration insist that immigrants and offshore workers complement rather than compete with American workers, and that competition will force domestic employers to invest the capital necessary to raise the productivity of immigrants and displaced workers back to the productivity of the rest of the workforce—what economists call capital deepening.[7]

Some even claim restrictions on immigration have left trillions of dollars of unharvested value "lying on the sidewalk."[8] They believe trade and immigration only raise the rest of the world's wages to America's with little, if any, adverse effect on the level and growth rate of American wages. But you have to digest a lot of hard-to-swallow assumptions to get all the way there.

In effect, they see the economy as waiters waiting on waiters—that is, on average, the economy serves itself. In that economy, the addition of another waiter is of no consequence. Without constraints, supply creates its own demand at prevailing wages.

If waiters previously saved enough capital to seat themselves as customers, then another waiter will save and invest enough money to add another seat of restaurant capacity. From this perspective, economic growth has no constraints other than the know-how to achieve its current level of productivity.

The economy, after all, has always grown to employ the children of its workers. What difference does it make if new workers are grown children, immigrants, or offshore workers?

And in an economy of waiters and dishwashers, if unassimilated immigrants are compelled to wash dishes, it frees dishwashers to work as higher-paid waiters. Everyone supposedly benefits. Dishwashers complement rather than compete with waiters.

Proponents of trade and immigration are confident, perhaps even cavalier, that businesses will capitalize on the availability of lesser-skilled labor, that competition between employers will force companies to invest to raise the productivity of new workers to the rest of the workforce, and that the economy will grow proportionally. Were this not the case, an increase in the supply of lesser-skilled, lower-wage labor would reduce lesser-skilled wages as lower-wage workers bid down wages.

Historically, savings have limited investment. But since the recession, trillions of dollars of bank deposits have sat unused neither lent nor borrowed.[9] And prior to the recession, lending largely increased household consumption through subprime mortgage lending. Borrowers did not use these funds for business investment. The availability of savings for investment does not seem to limit growth.

Nevertheless, liberal economists Larry Summers and Paul Krugman are reluctant to agree with the underlying logic of trade and immigration advocates who state that supply creates its own demand. Summers's theory of secular stagnation (discussed at length in chapter 5) asserts that a shortage of investment opportunities currently limits growth despite a surplus of unused savings.[10] That hardly represents a world without constraints to growth where supply—in this case, savings— creates its own demand, quite the contrary.

Krugman adamantly denies the notion that supply creates its own demand. He insists:

> One of the intellectually horrifying things about the response to economic crisis was the way many economists . . . seemed utterly unaware that Say's Law—the proposition that supply creates its own demand . . .—had been refuted three generations ago.[11]

Again, Krugman is implicitly admitting there are constraints to growth even during times when savings sit unused.

University of California, Berkeley, economist David Card, one of the chief architects of these theories, admits that if immigrant labor competes rather than complements the existing workforce, or if capital investment is fixed, or at least doesn't rise proportionately to maintain worker productivity fully, wages will fall.[12]

Card's qualification applies to any economic constraint that restricts investment, especially constraints that restrict investment at a time when savings sit unused.

There are three constraints that can restrict investment even when savings sit unused—the limits of our know-how, properly trained talent, and the economy's capacity and willingness to bear risk.

It's hard to believe that we have fully exploited the limits of our know-how when median U.S. family incomes peaked at $57,800 in 1999 and have since fallen back to $53,700 in 2014; unskilled dishwashers earn less than unskilled factory workers; and full-time Hispanic workers earn less on average than their non-Hispanic counterparts.[13] Each indicates opportunities for growth without additional insights.

It is similarly hard to believe know-how is the binding constraint to growth when savings sit unused in a world full of capital deepening opportunities and where investors have overcome political risks associated with investing abroad, as evidenced by capital pouring into low-wage economies like Mexico's and China's.

With one of the highest levels of capital investment per worker in the world, and correspondingly with one of the highest levels of GDP per worker, America's productivity has demonstrated the value of additional capital investment to the rest of the world.[14] Savings sit unused despite opportunities to duplicate America's investment success without the need for new insights.

It's true that lack of infrastructure as well as political and legal uncertainties increase the riskiness of investments outside the United States and that the value of low-wage labor offsets the higher offshore risks when competing to supply high-wage rather than low-wage economies. Nevertheless, companies and their investors have raced to build offshore manufacturing to produce goods for both high-wage economies and the local economy. Given the magnitude of these investments, it is hard to believe that international risks alone account for the much lower capital investment per worker throughout the world.

More likely, properly trained talent and the economy's capacity and willingness to bear risk limit growth. The U.S. economy has unused savings that it is reluctant to invest—whether domestically or aboard—without better engineering and supervision to manage the risks and more equity to bear potential losses. Chapter 5 discusses these unconventional constraints further. Suffice it to say here that if constraints limit growth, then trade and immigration spread a limited amount of income over a greater number of workers.

If the income of the highest-skilled workers is limited in the short run, for example, and their spending raises the pay of lesser-skilled workers when the supply of lesser-skilled workers is limited, then another lesser-skilled worker—a waiter, for example—drives their wages back down toward waiters-waiting-on-waiters pay unless waiters contribute proportionally to the resources that constrain growth. Surely they do not.

Similarly, if lesser-skilled immigrants and displaced workers depend on higher-skilled entrepreneurs and investors to find and commercialize new employment opportunities, then wage growth will slow at the margin if constrained resources don't grow proportionally to the workers seeking work.

If project-management skills or companies' capacity and willingness to bear risk slow automotive manufacturers—who are racing one another to invest in Mexico to take advantage of cheap labor—from investing at an even faster rate, then devoting constrained resources to Mexican investment slows domestic investment in the United States. This slows domestic productivity growth, reduces the marginal product of labor, reduces wages, and increases income inequality.

If innovation and entrepreneurial risk-taking limit the growth of high-wage economies at this time, then additional workers, who fail to produce that growth, slow wage growth. To the extent finding and harvesting information-related innovations consumes a limited amount of entrepreneurial risk-taking and properly trained talent, and these efforts produce a minimal amount of lesser-skilled domestic employment—for example, Apple, Google, Facebook, and Microsoft—then the addition of lesser-skilled workers reduces their wages further still.

If innovation employs an increasing share of properly trained talent that would otherwise supervise less-talented workers and make them more productive, then low-skilled immigration reduces wages by diluting the available supervision.

We can see this measured in the military. While the quality of enlisted marines has increased since the draft ended in 1972, the test scores of commissioned officers have dropped significantly—approximately ten IQ points.[15] The same thing is likely occurring throughout the entire economy. The quality of blue-collar supervision is probably declining, and the productivity growth of lesser-skilled workers is slowing as a result.

Similarly, the most talented women are no longer schoolteachers who educate our children. They are doctors, lawyers, and business executives. Lesser talent may reduce the effectiveness of teachers and the outcomes of students.

Opportunities in engineering and computer programming have stripped factories of critically needed, higher-skilled mechanics and foremen. American manufacturers, who employ armies of blue-collar workers, have a hard time competing with German and Chinese factories that still have higher-skilled workers in those skilled positions. Lack of manufacturing talent limits U.S. investment in manufacturing.

And if a limited number of successful innovators and properly trained talent pay a disproportionate share of the taxes, to the extent lower-skilled immigrants consume more government benefits than they contribute in tax revenues, it reduces the government benefits available to others (see Figure 10-1, "Federal Government Expenditures and Taxes by Household Type").

Implicit in most economic arguments, and especially arguments that low-wage immigrants and offshore workers do not diminish U.S. wages, is the notion of *all other things being equal.* For example, immigration may not lower wages if the ratio of higher-skilled to lower-skilled workers or the availability of savings per lower- and higher-skilled worker remains constant. But "other things" rarely ever remain constant relative to one another.

Overly simplified economic theories that assume capital alone increases the productivity of labor are mistaken. Risk-taking and properly trained talent constrain growth. Unless low-skilled immigration contributes proportionally to constrained resources, which it does not, it slows lesser-skilled wage growth relative to what would have been the case if the supply of lesser-skilled labor had been restricted.

# Trade Deficits Strain the Economy's Capacity and Willingness to Take Risk and Reduce Wages Further

Unlike immigration, trade deficits add to the available workforce without also adding to demand. Trade deficits simply export jobs to offshore workers. Prior to the financial crisis, trade deficits reached a whopping 6 percent of GDP.[16] That represents an enormous increase in the supply of labor—principally low-skilled labor.

To run trade surpluses, exporters must lend importers like the United States the proceeds from the sale of goods to Americans, rather than using the proceeds to buy goods that employ Americans. Surplus exporters do this by buying U.S. government–guaranteed debt. With a limited amount of safe government-guaranteed debt, risk-averse savers who would have bought safe government debt lend their money elsewhere—namely, to banks, as deposits available to be lent.

To reemploy U.S. workers idled by trade deficits, the U.S. economy must borrow and spend these newly created deposits. If these deposits sit idle, U.S. growth, employment, and wages will be lower than they would be if the economy used all its available resources—chiefly, labor idled by trade deficits.

Of course, the economy can always reach full employment by cutting wages, in effect, by spreading a given amount of labor income over a greater number of workers. To reach full employment at the highest possible wages, the economy must fully utilize all its resources.

To put risk-averse savings to work, someone must bear the risk of using those savings. With a limited capacity and willingness to bear risk, a portion of this capacity must be used to regain employment lost to trade deficits rather than using it to grow employment and wages further.

As U.S. business has grown increasingly profitable, it has had less need for debt to finance investment. Instead, business has increasingly self-funded its growth. It is true that companies have used debt to buy back shares, pay dividends, finance mergers, and fund leveraged buyouts. But unlike investment, these transactions do not consume savings. They merely exchange savings and ownership rights to future cash flows between one owner and another, which leaves savings unused.

With fewer productive uses for savings, at least at the margin, America indirectly loaned risk-averse foreign savings lent to the United States by surplus exporters, like China and Germany, and once upon a time Japan, to poor subprime homeowners. Unlike richer homeowners, these homeowners borrowed against the rising value of their homes and behaved as if they won the lottery. They used the proceeds to increase their consumption.[17]

Rising home prices and innovative Wall Street financing—structured finance and loan syndication—found investors, chiefly foreign investors, to bear the risk of loaning money to subprime consumers with limited income to repay such loans. In the wake of the financial crisis, those investors are gone.

At the same time, surplus exporters like China used their savings to build empty apartment buildings while Germany loaned their savings to Greece. None of these unwise uses represent productive investments that permanently increase productivity or growth.

Now that government regulations have stifled lending to subprime homeowners, and lenders and borrowers haven't yet found viable alternative uses for risk-averse savings, these savings sit idle in the aftermath of the financial crisis.[18] No surprise, growth has slowed, employment has recovered slowly, and wage growth has been lackluster.

Trade deficits export jobs. To regain lost jobs, America must take the risk of borrowing and spending risk-averse savings. This strains the economy's limited capacity and willingness to bear risk. Without trade deficits, this capacity could be used to grow employment and increase wages. Unless domestic saving rates decline or trade deficits narrow, employment and wage growth are likely to remain slower than they otherwise would be. Until then, the economy must find new uses for risk-averse savings and investors willing to bear the risk of putting these savings to work to grow the economy faster.

# Empirical Studies Claiming Trade and Immigration Have Minimal Effects Are Unconvincing

To address the thorny issues of trade and immigration, economists have turned to empirical studies to determine the degree to which trade and immigration affect middle- and working-class wage growth. The economic circumstances are so complex, however, that the conclusions remain unresolved.

In a seminal study, David Card insisted that after the Mariel boatlift of 1980, when Fidel Castro released 125,000 Cuban immigrants to

Florida—60 percent of whom were high school dropouts—wages barely fell in Miami.

London School of Economics economist Gianmarco Ottaviano and University of California, Davis, economist Giovanni Peri claim, "US-born workers (with at least a high school degree) who accounted for 90% of the US-born labor force in 2004, gained from immigration [from 1990 to 2004]. Their real wage gains in the long run range between 0.7% and 3.4% while even in the short run they either gain (high school graduates) or have essentially no wage change (college graduates). . . . The wage losses . . . are concentrated among previous immigrants who experience most of the competition from new immigrants." They argue, "This result stems from the imperfect substitutability between US- and foreign-born workers so that immigration increases the wages of US-born at the expenses of a decrease in wages of foreign-born workers."[19]

University of Cape Town economist Lawrence Edwards and Harvard economist Robert Lawrence, using data from the 1990s and early 2000s, find, "Trade is not a major source of increasing U.S. wage inequality. . . . The goods exported by developing countries are highly imperfect substitutes for those produced by developed countries. This means that for the most part, unskilled U.S. workers are not competing head to head with their counterparts in developing countries." Despite their unflinching conclusions, Edwards and Lawrence caution, "There is always the possibility that 'but for trade' U.S. wage inequality might have fallen."[20]

Unfortunately, studies claiming trade and immigration have minimal effects often depend on evidence from the 1990s when median wages accelerated after the commercialization of the Internet, e-mail, and cell phones. An influx of lesser-skilled workers may have freed greater-skilled workers to capitalize on employment opportunities afforded by the faster growing economy at that time.

Given the complexity of the economy and the constant flux of circumstances, it is near impossible to isolate the effect of one factor independent of all the others. Studies should overwhelmingly fail to find effects even when there are effects. That's why studies that find evidence of statistically significant effects are so highly prized. As such, we should exercise great caution when we use studies that find minimal effects to conclude there are, in fact, minimal effects.

Even if trade slows middle- and working-class income growth, empirical studies that attempt to measure trade's effect on income inequality ought to find little effect from trade. That would be the case, for example, if soaring payoffs for innovation produced by the 0.1 percent are the predominant reason for growing inequality, as is likely the case. They simply can't know what would have happened to wages if America's 0.1 percent had been less successful. It is not enough to say that wages did not decline, especially when advocates of income redistribution complain that wages haven't grown fast enough and blame the success of the 1 percent.

As the economy and wage growth have slowed, economists have grown increasingly skeptical that offshore and foreign-born workers complement rather than compete with domestic workers.[21]

Harvard economist George Borjas's recent reassessment of David Card's highly influential study of the Mariel boatlift, for example, found substantial downward pressure on the wages of similarly skilled workers—"perhaps as much as 30 percent."[22] While Peri criticizes Borjas's workforce sample as too small, Borjas notes his results are, nevertheless, statistically significant and that the "only way to make sure your lying eyes see the 'right' wage trend is to enlarge the sample in ways that are, at best, questionable and, most likely, just plain wrong."

More broadly, Borjas's research finds that where immigration increases the number of workers in a skill group by 10 percent, it reduces wages by 4 percent.[23]

While it is true that some immigrants may perform work that native-born Americans may be eager to leave behind (migrant workers picking crops, for example), with 60 million foreign-born immigrants and their native-born adult children, it stretches credibility that all these workers are largely complementary—that they merely free up the rest of the workforce to do more productive work. The distribution of Hispanic wages, for example, albeit lower on average than native-born workers, overlaps significantly with the rest of America's middle- and working-class workforce. And there are plenty of native-born workers who, when freed from performing some tasks, are nevertheless incapable of doing more skillful work.

With automotive and other manufacturers pouring capital into

Mexico, and with Mexico supplying an increasing share of North American production, it grows harder and harder to believe these Mexican autoworkers complement rather than compete head-to-head with American workers for jobs and investment capital.[24]

If offshore labor truly complemented American workers rather than merely displacing them, and if the supply of immigrant workers truly increased capital investment until their productivity matched domestic workers, we should see a frenzy of capital investment boosting the productivity of unskilled workers. We see the opposite.

Low-skilled employment is not growing in highly productive capital-intensive sectors like manufacturing, for example. Instead, we see capital investment producing productivity gains that exceed the growth in the demand for manufactured products, which, in turn, hollows out manufacturing employment. Lower-skilled employment has subsequently grown in less productive service sectors like retail, restaurants, household employment, and healthcare.[25] In turn, low-skilled immigrant labor has skewed toward employment in these sectors.[26]

Pro-trade and immigration theories assume that businesses will capitalize on the availability of lesser-skilled labor, and competition will force employers to invest capital to raise the productivity of new and displaced workers up to the rest of the workforce. Otherwise, an increase in the supply of labor will put downward pressure on wages. If employers face difficulties in finding employment for displaced workers, it's a strong indication of significant constraints to growth.

The evidence is worrisome. After comparing geographically distinct U.S. labor markets affected differently by trade, MIT labor economist David Autor concludes:

Alongside the heralded consumer benefits of expanded trade are substantial adjustment costs and distributional consequences. These impacts are most visible in the local labor markets in which the industries exposed to foreign competition are concentrated. Adjustment in local labor markets is remarkably slow, with wages and labor-force participation rates remaining depressed and unemployment rates remaining elevated for at least a full decade after the China trade shock commences. Exposed workers experience greater job churning and reduced lifetime income. At the national level, employment has fallen in U.S. industries more exposed to import competition, as expected, but offsetting employment gains in other industries have yet to materialize.[27]

It is an ominous finding, especially when the trade deficit simultaneously flooded the U.S. economy with offshore savings that businesses could have used to fund new investment. Entrepreneurs, companies, and investors did not rush in to capitalize on the newly available supply of labor or capital. And in the absence of these constrained resources, incomes fell. That's a clear indication that constrained resources—namely, properly trained talent, which likely moved away in tough times, and the economy's capacity and willingness to take risk—had previously raised middle- and working-class pay above waiters-waiting-on-waiters pay.

It is not enough to say that some dislocated workers face hardship that they could have avoided by moving to faster-growing regions of the United States, like the San Francisco Bay Area. If risk-taking and talent don't constrain growth, where were the entrepreneurs and investors who should have rushed in to take advantage of underutilized labor in these regions and competed fiercely enough to restore high wages?

Clearly capital in combination with constrained resources previously raised pay higher than would have been the case otherwise. Without an abundance of constrained resources, capital sat unused and wages fell back to waiters-waiting-on-waiters wages—the opposite of the economics underlying trade and immigration theories that claim they have no effect on wages because resources are unconstrained.

With savings used to fund risky subprime mortgages, capital clearly did not constrain employment growth prior to the financial crisis. It largely increased household consumption. Nor have savings constrained growth since the financial crisis, as $2.4 trillion of bank deposits have sat unused.[28] This is a strong indication that something other than savings—most likely, properly trained talent and the economy's capacity and willingness to take risk—has constrained investment. If anything other than labor constrains growth, then immigration and trade deficits reduce wages.

The trend of America's middle- and working-class wages relative to the rest of the world's provides further evidence that global trade with low-wage economies is slowing middle- and working-class wage growth. According to the World Bank, real wages in the developing world have grown rapidly—40 to 80 percent cumulative from 1988 to 2008—while high-wage middle- and working-class incomes have scarcely grown.[29] The juxtaposition hardly seems coincidental.

## Conclusion

Conditions favorable to lesser-skilled workers in the 1950s and 1960s—two decades of pent-up growth, the value of mass production and related capital investment, more education, rural migration, and population growth—gave the false impression that productivity growth on its own increases median wages and that the wages of advanced economies naturally grow more equally distributed over time. Neither assumption has proved to be universally true.

When growth is constrained, supply and demand determine prices. Like all commodities, the value of an additional lesser-skilled worker sets the wages for these workers, not their average productivity. When more lesser-skilled workers are available, unless they increase constrained resources proportionally, lesser-skilled wages will be lower.

In our information-intensive economy, capital is neither a constraint to growth nor the sole determinant of productivity, as many oversimplified models of trade and immigration often assume. Today properly trained talent and risk-taking constrain growth.

In order to compete with low-wage manufacturers, capital investment now reduces employment and pushes workers into less productive jobs. The productivity of displaced workers sets the pay for similarly skilled workers.

When similarly skilled workers are producing less value in less productive and, by necessity, lower-paid jobs, workers in more productive, capital-intensive manufacturing jobs can no longer capture the additional value produced by their capital-enhanced productivity.

Wages are bid down to the wages affordable to an employer with jobs that are less productive.

Capital intensity no longer determines the productivity and pay of newly created jobs—for example, swirling milk in a cup of coffee brewed one cup at a time. The prosperity of the economy—where 20 percent of the workers earn 50 percent of the pay—and the scarcity of lesser-skilled labor, or lack thereof, set pay.

Low-skilled immigration just adds to the supply of lesser-skilled workers and holds down pay. Hispanic immigrants work in landscaping, for example—jobs supported by a minimal amount of capital and technology—because more productive work isn't available for them to perform. Rather than performing work that Americans are unwilling to do, low-wage immigrants likely perform work at wages Americans are unwilling to accept.

Low-wage immigrant labor may benefit the rest of the American workforce by performing work more cheaply. Some Americans may choose to own yards that require more yardwork if the cost of yardwork is cheaper, for example. And low wages may increase demand, which expands employment. But it likely does so by lowering the marginal product of labor and putting downward pressure on wages.

It is true that competition between companies with low-wage labor drives down the prices of their product and service offerings, and that lower prices increase the value of wages. But it is also true that working- and middle-class workers likely bear the greatest burden of lower wages while enjoying only a portion of the benefits of lower prices.

While advocates of redistribution are loath to admit it, a near-unlimited supply of lesser-skilled labor—from international trade that buys low-skilled labor and sells high-skilled labor, trade deficits that export employment without extensive borrowing and lending, and low-skilled immigration—has slowed U.S. middle- and working-class wage growth. Instead of wage gains, growth has produced large employment gains. This has chiefly benefited immigrants.

At the same time, lower-cost goods and services have disproportionately benefited higher-skilled workers and people who don't work.

To advocate both for more immigration *and* for faster wage growth for the working and middle class is to work at cross-purposes. It is a stretch to assume low-skilled immigration adds proportionally to constrained resources and disingenuous to suggest that it is politically verboten to believe otherwise.

It is an even greater stretch to pretend that the rising income of the 1 percent is responsible for the stagnating wages of others. Quite the opposite: the growing success of the most successful Americans has put upward pressure on employment and wage growth.

## Part II

---

# DEBUNKING
# MYTHS:
## Why Mitigating Inequality
## Is Not the Solution

# Chapter 3

# THE MYTH THAT INCENTIVES DON'T MATTER

R ather than acknowledging that trade and immigration have disproportionately slowed middle- and working-class wage growth, and that the outsized success of America's 0.1 percent is pushing up wages and employment, proponents of income redistribution have turned to a variety of arguments to blame the success of the 0.1 percent for the slow income growth of the middle and working classes. While the case against income redistribution is strong, its proponents are tireless in propagating myths that undermine arguments for a free economy.

No myth is more foundational to the crusade for income redistribution than the argument that payoffs for successful risk-taking don't matter.[1] Proponents of this myth deny that rewards for risk-taking incentivize innovation that drives increased prosperity. If proponents of this myth are correct, no other arguments are needed. We can simply redistribute the payoffs for success without discouraging the engineers of that success. We can have our cake and eat it too!

Finding arguments against the importance of incentives wanting, some proponents of redistribution insist that success is unearned.[2] If success is achieved through theft or unfair negotiation, then it can be redistributed without economic consequences. The evidence, however, runs contrary to these arguments.

Failing these arguments, others claim there is a shortage of investment opportunities, so we can tax and redistribute income that would otherwise be invested.[3] While risk-averse savings chiefly supplied by offshore savers no longer constrain growth, equity that underwrites risk now binds growth. Taxing success slows the creation and accumulation of equity. In turn, this slows growth.

Still others argue that success, while earned, nevertheless hollows out the middle class.[4] Like trade and immigration, the middle and working classes allegedly share disproportionately in the cost of success. Again, the evidence is unconvincing.

Last, some argue that while no one argument for redistribution accounts for the slow growth of the middle and working classes, they are nevertheless suffering death by a thousand cuts.[5] Were that the case, income mobility would be slowing. So far, we find no evidence of that.

The next five chapters address each of these myths at length, beginning with the first—the argument that incentives are unimportant.

Typically, arguments that deny the motivational effects of money fail to differentiate between the small, micro, short-term effects and the potentially large, gradually compounding macro effects over the long run.[6] They often point to the motivation of entrepreneurs long before they can logically expect large payoffs as evidence that large payoffs do not drive entrepreneurial risk-taking. Similarly, they point to the success of Bill Gates and others like him when marginal tax rates were higher.[7] Perhaps only curiosity or glory motivated them.

These arguments ignore the fact that high-tech entrepreneurialism was nascent prior to Bill Gates's windfall, and that it has accelerated greatly since. Surely, the successes of Bill Gates, Steve Jobs, Larry Ellison, Jeff Bezos, Sergey Brin, Larry Page, and the other technology billionaires have sparked an enormous army of wishful risk-takers in their wake.

In the short run, slightly higher tax rates may make imperceptible differences in the motivation of determined entrepreneurs. But these small differences have proved to have large compounding effects in the long run. The mechanics of these compounding effects are well understood.

Look at the enormous differences in growth and prosperity among similar countries that have dulled incentives by redistributing income: East Germany and West Germany; North Korea and South Korea; Hong Kong, Taiwan, and China today versus Communist China; and the United States relative to Europe. Played out over time, the differences are startling. And there are few, if any, exceptions.

Innovation is far more valuable to the rest of the economy than it is to successful innovators. As such, maximizing tax revenues and income redistribution in the near term has proved far more costly than maximizing innovation and growth over the long run. Incentivizing the risk-taking that produces innovation has been and always will be the key to growing middle- and working-class prosperity.

And yet advocates of redistribution are cavalier about the detrimental effects of diminished incentives, insisting that incentives have insignificant effects that can be ignored. Arguments for income redistribution persist in part because of dogmatic insistence that redistribution *must* work, despite the evidence. Wishful thinking, it turns out, is powerfully persuasive.

# Lone Geniuses Are Not the Predominant Source of Innovation

One of the first faulty assumptions underlying the idea that incentives don't matter is the notion that innovation largely stems from lone innovators, like Bill Gates, motivated by nonmonetary gains, like curiosity. The Bill-Gates-wasn't-motivated-by-money argument assumes a genius in a vacuum with a good idea creates innovation—as if we need only another genius to come along and stumble upon a new idea in order to accelerate growth. If it were just that simple!

Research shows that innovation evolves from a community of ideas, that these communities build on themselves and gradually magnify the payoffs for success that motivate the risk-taking needed to produce innovation.[8] As such, we need to build large communities of successful entrepreneurs.

The larger the community of thinkers, the faster ideas evolve. That's why large geographical centers of trade—Athens and Rome, for example—have produced so much innovation. Today communities of experts, like Silicon Valley and the Internet, are critical to the evolution of technology.

Success bubbles up from a community of hardworking innovators all pursuing the next advancement, learning from the insights of others, and competing with one another. Isaac Newton and Gottfried Leibniz invented calculus at the same time. Samuel Morse patented the telegraph hours before someone else applied for the same patent. And Hendrik Lorentz published the equation $E=mc^2$ before Albert Einstein. Each shared a common base of knowledge. The evolution of that knowledge and their familiarity with it was critical to their success.

At the same time, innovation is just a game of chance. Like mining for gold, the more the world searches, the more gold it will find. Because the chances of finding valuable innovation are small, we need to motivate a large community of wannabe innovators to produce a small number of successes.

Like any game of chance, the higher the payoffs, the more gamblers gamble. The more they gamble, the more innovation they find.

To accelerate growth in our information-intensive economy, we don't need just any gamblers. We need an army of brilliant, properly trained gamblers—talent that could otherwise earn high incomes with near certainty—willing to suffer near-certain failure for the remote chance of even greater success.

Proponents of the incentives-don't-matter line of attack argue that America's not-for-profit universities and government research provide the community of expertise in which entrepreneurs succeed. To a certain extent, surely that's true. But research by the Organisation for Economic Co-operation and Development (OECD) shows these communities fall short of the achievements of businesses. The report finds: "Research and development activities undertaken by the business sector seem to have high social returns, while no clear cut relationship could be established between R&D activities not undertaken by businesses [e.g., by governments and universities] and growth."[9]

Similarly, a paper published by the U.S. Bureau of Labor Statistics found: "The overall rate of return to R&D is very large, perhaps 25 percent as a private return and a total of 65 percent for social returns. However, these returns apply only to privately financed R&D in industry. Returns to many forms of publicly financed R&D are near zero."[10]

These findings certainly do not indicate that not-for-profit research predominantly drives innovation and productivity growth—quite the contrary.

Ultimately, valuable learning comes from serving demanding customers—who pay for performance—and from racing to serve those customers more effectively than competitors. It's the value of differentiated performance that allows customers to pay for innovation that has been successfully commercialized.

Evolution doesn't occur in a vacuum. Survival of the fittest drives evolution. The same is true of innovation. Without demanding customers, and competitors eager to satisfy them, theorizing wanders unproductively. Ideas aimed at satisfying customers' demands more effectively than competitors and the riches it brings predominantly drive innovation and economic growth.

Nor do ideas alone satisfy the demands of customers. Implementation is as important as ideas, even more important when competitors often have access to the same ideas. And implementation happens in the business world, not in the academic world.

Facebook wasn't a unique idea. There was Friendster, Myspace, and others. Facebook succeeded because an army of skillful accomplices fiercely implemented it. It takes a mix of talents to produce good ideas *and* implement them.

While some people love ideas, many people love money—especially the ones without ideas. Those people often turn to implementation as a means to success. Their expertise is critical to an economy's success.

Professors may be willing to forgo higher pay for the sake of intellectual status, but most people can't achieve status through intellectual achievement and so are motivated by status derived from other reasons, often money, especially implementers. Monetary payoffs fuel implementation and the army of talented entrepreneurs in Silicon Valley and other sectors of the economy. Those communities of experts accelerate U.S. innovation and growth.

Accelerating growth requires motivating top PhD students with valuable ideas, like Larry Page and Sergey Brin, to leave their tenured careers as college professors and get the training and take the risks necessary to commercialize innovations that truly increase productivity. Given the large army of tenured college professors who could be redeployed as entrepreneurs if ideas alone increased productivity, apparently, motivational pay is a lot longer than the current one-in-a-million chance at a Google-like payoff.

Let's not kid ourselves. Money paid by demanding customers who value improvements motivates the community of thinkers and doers who produce innovation that drives growth. Running experiments to satisfy the demands of customers in competition with competitors trying to do the same focuses and accelerates the learning that grows the economy, not theorizing in a vacuum.

Customers who value improvement, especially differentiated improvements, must, by necessity, concentrate payoffs in the hands of successful innovators—both the prudent and the imprudent. Socializing the risk, by paying everyone who tries rather than only those who succeed, destroys the very thing that motivates risk-takers—the opportunity for differentiation via outsized payoffs. It leads to what we see in academics—lots of ideas of questionable value without much tedious implementation that turns those ideas into value for others.

## The Benefits of Risk-Taking Compound Gradually

Those who argue against the importance of incentives make another big mistake. By focusing only on the short-term effects of incentives— the small changes in behavior a person makes tomorrow—they overlook the gradually compounding effects successful risk-taking has on the institutional capabilities that accelerate growth. These gradually compounding effects are the very thing that differentiate America from other high-wage economies—a better-trained community of experts that raises the productivity of innovators, increases the likelihood of success, subsequently motivates increased risk-taking, and ultimately accelerates growth.

Successful risk-taking produces companies like Google, Facebook, and the many businesses within their orbits. In turn, these companies give America's workforce more valuable on-the-job training than workers gain elsewhere. The expertise workers gain from this experience increases their chances for entrepreneurial success. Imagine the enormous differences in the odds of discovering the next Internet breakthrough in a cafe in Greece rather than in the workspaces of Google or a start-up in Silicon Valley. Like any game of chance, higher payoffs and better odds motivate increased risk-taking.

A growing critical mass of success creates communities of expertise, like Silicon Valley, where experts exchange ideas more frequently and are consequently more likely to find valuable innovations. Again, better odds of success afforded by large communities of experts motivate increased risk-taking.

The failure of the rest of the world to energize these positive feedback loops leaves more opportunities for American entrepreneurs to find and commercialize. This, too, increases their chances of success.

The growing success of successful innovators raises the bar for social status. The success of some diminishes the success of others. Loss of status motives talented workers to work harder and to take more risks. It drives them to risky start-ups with the possibility of higher payoffs. In America, the highest-paid workers are working longer hours than their counterparts elsewhere.[11] The most talented students no longer want to be doctors and lawyers. They go to business school and join start-ups. The larger the pool of properly trained talent seeking to be successful innovators, the more likely they are to find innovation that benefits everyone.

Furthermore, the payoffs for success put wealth—namely, equity willing to underwrite risk—into the hands of successful risk-takers who have more knowledge of investment opportunities than investors at large. More wealth and knowledge in the hands of expert investors lead to more, or at least more effective, risk underwriting, which is critical to innovation.

Thanks to the power of incentives, this self-reinforcing feedback loop has taken hold in America. It has increased the payoff for successful risk-takers relative to the rest of the world. In turn, higher expected payoffs—the size of the payoff times the probability of success—have gradually driven America's talented workers to get the training and to take the risks necessary to be more productive. If we reduce incentives, this feedback loop won't diminish in a day; rather, progress will slow over time.

Advocates of income redistribution ignore or deny the motivational effects of higher payoffs for risk-taking and their gradual compounding effects on the economy's institutional capabilities over the long run. Ignoring these effects makes their case much easier; without the need to compare the value of public expenditures with the cost of diminished incentives, advocates of redistribution are free to debate the merits of public expenditures in a vacuum. To make the case for redistribution, they measure the benefits of public expenditures over and above their cash cost without considering the costs of taxing success in order to raise the money.[12] Ignoring the motivational value of money lowers the cost of taxation and public investment significantly, making the case for redistribution look better.

To be fair, on the other side of the debate, advocates of lower taxes sell tax cuts by overpromising short-term economic benefits from the increased motivation of higher payoffs for success, when, in fact, these benefits evolve gradually and accumulate slowly over a long period. Europe can't cut taxes and expect to form quickly the institutional capabilities necessary for faster growth—a community of experts, like Silicon Valley, for example.

Given the slowly compounding effects of successful risk-taking on the economy's institutional capabilities, tax cuts are likely to reduce tax revenues long before they increase them. Unfortunately, these errors not only damage the credibility of these economists, but they also give advocates of redistribution an opening for counterarguments by shifting the debate to short-term tradeoffs instead of long-term tradeoffs.

You would expect serious economists, even if they did favor redistribution, to address the long-term consequences of diminished incentives, but no. Nobel Prize winner Peter Diamond and John Bates Clark Medal winner Emmanuel Saez provide a good example of how many economists who advocate for redistribution deal with the long-term compounding value of incentives—they simply ignore them!

In their argument for higher marginal tax rates, Diamond and Saez admit that "although we know much about behavioral responses to taxation in the short- and medium-term we have only a limited understanding of long-run behavioral responses that would also include educational and career choices. Such long-term responses are needed to calibrate optimal tax formulas."[13] Nevertheless, they propose tax policies based on the assumption that taxes have *no* long-term effect. Moreover, they explicitly assume the additional income earned by the rich has *no* value to the rest of society; that is, that it provides neither increased motivation for innovative risk-taking nor opportunity for the rich to use their wealth to make investments and underwrite increased risk-taking that chiefly benefits others. Instead, Diamond and Saez argue that "the social marginal value of consumption for top-bracket tax filers is small relative to that of the average person in the economy, and so . . . as a first approximation can be ignored."[14] Assumptions as extreme as these are disingenuous.

Why would they make such extreme assumptions? Because admitting to small negative long-term effects on growth has devastatingly large consequences in the long run. Look at the large and growing difference between the U.S. economy and that of Europe or Japan. Growth has been faster in the United States, and median U.S. family incomes are 15 to 30 percent higher.[15]

Denying the power of incentives and subsequently overlooking their gradual compounding effect on institutional capabilities leads some economists to make xenophobic claims that Americans and American culture are inherently more entrepreneurial than other high-wage economies, such as France's and Japan's—as if Americans are genetically superior.[16] If anything, research shows the inherent talent of the American workforce is lower, on average, than other high-wage economies.[17]

More likely, culture is largely a by-product of incentives, where higher payoffs lead to increased risk-taking. Americans take more entrepreneurial risks because their chances for success are significantly better than their counterparts in other high-wage economies.

Rather than comparing the growth rate of America today with other high-wage economies facing similar contemporary circumstances but with more equally distributed incomes (and substantially slower growth), advocates of income redistribution point to numerous counterexamples with glaring apples-to-oranges inconsistencies, which they conveniently overlook. For example, they compare today's growth rate with America's growth rate in the 1950s, when government was much smaller and circumstances were substantially different, and where corporate success—where tax rates were lower—drove growth rather than the entrepreneurial success of individuals—where tax rates were higher.[18]

Imagine if someone claimed modern training methods didn't produce more competitive athletes because athletes without this training were nevertheless winning championships in the 1950s. No one would take them seriously. Yet supposedly serious economists make exactly this argument all the time.

Or they compare America today with the 1990s, when the Internet, e-mail, and cell phones were first commercialized.[19] Those inventions had a substantial impact on boosting productivity akin to the invention of the telephone. The enormous payoff for deploying these technologies overwhelmed small changes in the tax rate. These economists also ignore the fact that growth pushed all government spending (i.e., federal, state, and local) to a low of 32 percent of GDP in the 1990s.[20]

Similarly, they point to the success of innovation in California despite the difference of a couple of points in the state tax rate, which is small compared with the enormous benefit of working alongside the experts in Silicon Valley.[21]

When making comparisons to contemporary Europe, advocates of income redistribution avoid comparisons to Southern Europe and focus exclusively on Scandinavia, where academic test scores are higher than those in America.[22] In knowledge-based economies, academic capabilities accelerate growth. America grows faster than Scandinavia despite lower American test scores more akin to Southern Europe.[23] To the extent Southern Europe grows faster than other parts of Europe, it is largely the result of lower wages, which America doesn't share.

Advocates of income redistribution avoid comparisons with the UK, Germany, and the rest of Europe because the UK and Germany have less equally distributed incomes and faster growth rates than their European counterparts.[24] They ask only whether small changes to the tax rates will have large effects in the short run, as if European nations could cut their tax rates and grow faster without first developing all the institutional capabilities America has gradually built over the last three decades.

If the case against incentives were stronger, advocates of higher taxes and greater redistribution wouldn't make such obviously flawed and biased comparisons. While it's true that some portion of America's success relative to its peers is attributable to its greater labor flexibility and economies of scale, the lion's share of the credit should go to high payoffs for successful risk-taking stemming from both lower taxes on success and the large gradually compound effect successful risk-taking has had on the payoff and likelihood of successful innovation. In turn, higher payoffs have motivated increased risk-taking and success. But rather than acknowledging the evidence, the most learned advocates of redistribution ignore any long-term consequences to decreasing incentives, despite enormous and growing differences between America and other high-wage economies.

## Customers Capture Most All of the Value Created by Innovation

A slowdown in growth, and the risk-taking that propels it, has far-reaching consequences that diminish the well-being of the middle and working classes. While innovators chase after the profits of success, almost all the value they create is captured by their customers. The late Steve Jobs may have made huge profits from his innovations, but his wealth was small in comparison with the value of the iPhone and its imitators to their users. In the long run, consumers benefited far more than he did. Motivating increased risk-taking that produces innovation is the key to growing middle- and working-class prosperity.

Producers, like Apple and Microsoft, are always in danger of falling behind their competitors and earning less profit as a result. They must continually innovate and invest largely to stay even with competitors and earn the same profits rather than investing to earn additional profits. When an innovator like Apple invents the iPhone, for example, competitors must respond or lose market share. The competitors may suffer losses as a result of new and risky innovations, and even if they succeed, the odds are good that they will do little more than maintain their earlier level of success.

When competition forces competitors to cut costs, lower prices, and improve quality to maintain their profits, customers, not investors, capture the benefits. And even when investors do create something new and different, they *still* rarely capture all the value they create. Economists often describe the belief that a successful innovator necessarily becomes rich as the "alchemist fallacy." Were someone to discover a way to turn lead into gold, rather than getting rich, that person would find the price of gold would fall precipitously.

Innovators who find better ways to do things rarely find their profits last. Historically, innovators have found it difficult to prevent competitors from copying their ideas, even with patent protection. Instead, knowledge has spread rapidly and competitors have quickly found ways to catch up. The window for what economists call "Schumpeterian profits" (named for economist Joseph Schumpeter)—for innovators to earn above-average returns before competitors find a way to copy their ideas—has been brief.

Just look at how quickly the leading mobile phone producers, once on the cutting edge of innovation, have lost their leadership. Motorola, Palm, Nokia, and BlackBerry are all shadows of their former selves. The iPhone already faces stiff competition from Google's Android operating system. Facebook faces a host of threats from alternatives like LinkedIn, Instagram, and Snapchat.* Even Google faces threats from an increasingly balkanized Internet that limits Google's use in countries like China. The payoff that innovators earn from their success is frequently short-lived.

The wealth that consumers capture, on the other hand, is long-lasting. Once productive ideas are discovered, their value lasts forever and even compounds as new ideas build on the ideas that come before them. The radio led to the phone, which, together with the computer, led to the Internet. Each innovation has lasting effects.

In truth, investors profit relatively little from their creations. A study by Yale economist William Nordhaus concludes, "Only a miniscule fraction of the social returns from technological advances over the 1948–2001 period was captured by producers indicating that most of the benefits of technological change are passed on to consumers rather than captured by producers." Nordhaus estimates that innovative producers capture less than 5 percent of the value their inventions create for society.[25] And those are the innovators who succeed!

Nordhaus cautions: "The low appropriability of innovation should caution investors about committing the alchemist fallacy. . . . Some

---

* Facebook acquired Instagram.

believed that such a virtual substance had been found in the electronic world [or in the information world as the case may be]. But the laws of economics teach us that were anyone to find such a miraculous substance, its value would quickly fall. . . . In retrospect, the laws of economics look like a safer bet than the lure of alchemy."[26]

Because the benefits of innovation garnered by the public are far greater than the payoff captured by successful innovators, it's surprising how eager the advocates of redistribution are to maximize taxes collected from innovators rather than to maximize the pace of innovation. They focus on the tail instead of the dog. Tax policy that seeks to maximize tax revenues in the short run is horribly shortsighted. A more logical policy seeks to maximize the pace of innovation and the benefits captured by the middle and working classes in the long run.

In my previous book, I argued that redistribution hurts the middle and working classes because they forgo more value from lost investment than they reclaim from redistributed income. While I argued that investment likely produces 20 times more value for consumers and workers than is captured by investors—in line with Nordhaus's estimates—my analysis was based on consumers and workers capturing only 3.8 to 5.7 times more value than investors.[27] I reasoned that no one would dispute estimates that conservative.

The New York Times erroneously reported (although perhaps intentionally so) that a 20-times multiplier was "crucial" to my argument.[28] The reporter admitted that "the idea that society benefits when investors compete successfully is pretty widely accepted."[29] The article used Dean Baker, "a prominent progressive economist with the Center for Economic and Policy Research,"[30] as expert testimony to dispute the 20:1 multiplier. The article reported: "Baker estimates the ratio is 5 to 1, meaning that for every dollar an investor earns, the public receives the equivalent of $5 of value."[31] Ironically, that's essentially the value I assumed in my calculations to avoid disputes with liberal economists like Dean Baker!

Very briefly, my reasoning was as follows: The top 5 percent of wage earners save 40 percent of their income on average, according to research from economist Karen Dynan, the chief economist of the United States Department of the Treasury under President Obama.[32]

A dollar of redistributed income therefore forgoes at least 40 cents of investment. Surely, the top 1 percent or 0.1 percent save and invest even more than 40 percent of their income. Bill Gates, for example, consumes only a miniscule share of his income. But to be conservative, I assumed a 40 percent saving rate at the margin.

If $1 of investment produces (only) $1 of value for investors and $4 of value for noninvestors,* for example, then 40 cents of forgone investment forgoes $1.60 of value for noninvestors. According to the U.S. Census, the middle 20 percent of income earners earned about 15 percent of aggregate income in 2013,[33] or 24 cents of the $1.60 captured by noninvestors. Were they to capture their proportionate share of the redistributed dollar of income, they would capture only 20 cents from redistribution—less value than the forgone value from investment.

In truth, according to the Congressional Budget Office (CBO), the middle 20 percent of non-elderly middle-class households captures far less than 20 percent of government spending—closer to 10 percent—because the elderly and the poor capture a disproportionate share of government spending (see Figure 10-1, "Federal Government Expenditures and Taxes by Household Type").[34] The non-elderly middle class captures an even smaller share of government spending if one allocates a disproportionate share of the value of military spending and interest expense from avoided taxes to the rich, as most liberal economists argue. None of this bodes well for the value of income redistribution from the rich to the middle class.

The working class—the twentieth to fortieth income quintile—captures about 8 percent of the $1.60 of value from 40 cents of investment captured by noninvestors, or 13 cents, and about 13 percent of government spending or 13 cents of a dollar of redistributed income (if military and interest expenses are allocated proportionally to people rather than income). But, again, this assumes that the rich save only 40 percent of their marginal income, that the value of investment captured by noninvestors is low, that the value of military and interest expense is proportional to incomes rather than people, and that successful investors don't pay a disproportionate share of taxes on their incomes. To appease skeptics, it stacks conservative assumptions upon conservative assumptions.

---

* I'm simplifying here. Read the more carefully reasoned calculation in my book *Unintended Consequences*, chapter 9, "Redistributing Income."

At Nordhaus's 20:1 ratio, the value of investment to noninvestors obviously overwhelms the value of redistribution for all but the poorest households—households that only participate indirectly in the economy through redistribution.

In a society that taxes successful risk-takers heavily but taxes most everyone else lightly—less than the cost of the government services they receive—and where workers and consumers capture most of the benefits from innovation, it is unwise to base tax policy on maximizing tax revenues in the short run. Yet this is exactly what Diamond and Saez do. Increases in successful risk-taking could produce far more value for untaxed workers—through increases in lightly taxed employment, wages, and standards of living—than the value of the lost tax revenues. The middle class should gladly trade swelling tax revenues for real increases in their standard of living.

It is easy to see the benefits of increased competition, risk-taking, and growth in practice. A slowdown in risk-taking in the aftermath of the financial crisis has had a profoundly detrimental impact on employment, median family incomes, and growth. Median family incomes (adjusted for inflation) have fallen 7 percent from 2000 to 2014.[35] Workforce participation has fallen from 67 percent to 62 percent of the working-age population, a historic low.[36] And productivity growth has fallen to a paltry 0.7 percent a year since 2011, far below its 2.2 percent annual long-term average (see Figure 4-3, "U.S. Productivity Growth").

In the long run, the tax revenues collected on success are small compared with the enormous value of success to the rest of society. Despite the political appeal, it is a fool's errand to tax success heavily for the sake of a few extra dollars of tax revenue—an increase that is likely only temporary. Sadly, few people look far enough into the future to see the truth. Advocates of income redistribution take full advantage of voter myopia.

## The Ferocity of Competition Accelerates Growth

The success of America relative to its peers, as well as the evidence that high taxes on the successful hurt everyone, pushes advocates of the incentives-don't-matter myth into a narrow corner, one where only relative differences matter. Cornell economist Robert Frank, for example, argues that successful people seek money for the sake of status, that status is relative, and therefore that redistribution won't affect work effort and risk-taking as long as relative levels of success—that is, percentage differences—are maintained.[37] Of course, Frank doesn't use his argument to advocate for a flat tax, only for steeply progressive taxes.

Frank is surely correct that many highly successful people seek money for the sake of status and that status is relative. And he is right that competition drives us to wear unnecessarily expensive clothes to job interviews (his example), which wastes resources. But he ignores the fact that competition also drives us to get valuable training and to take entrepreneurial risks that drive progress, and that those efforts produce value for others. So while there are costs to society, there are also enormous benefits, which he ignores. Growing world prosperity, for example, has reduced the share of the world's population living on $1.25 a day* from 52 percent in 1981 to 17 percent in 2011.[38] Surely, those poor people don't care if America's middle class gets a greater share of the spoils if greater equality comes at the expense of slower growth for them.

Frank's argument is akin to claiming that the ferocity of the lions doesn't drive the rate of evolutionary change in the antelope—that we could dial ferocity back with no effect on the rate of change—or that the relative difference between a peashooter and a flyswatter would still get Russia to behave without the need for nuclear weapons. Fat chance.

Competition drives evolution to maximize the absolute size of relative differences, if for no other reason than to minimize the cost of randomness. Ferocity is a by-product of the value of maximizing the absolute size of the relative difference. As such, ferocity is an evolutionary trait that drives the rate of evolutionary change.

Business competition similarly forces producers to differentiate themselves by maximizing their advantages and rate of improvement. They can't afford to take chances by throttling back. Samsung and Apple race to outdo each other to the maximum extent possible. Consumers benefit.

* Constant 2005 dollars.

The same is true of individuals. The need for status drives status seekers to maximize the absolute size of the relative difference between their income and the income of others, which is even more important because the high-status way to display status is to display it subtly rather than ostentatiously. Maximizing the absolute size of the relative differences also increases the probability that one's success was not merely randomly achieved, as it is in many cases. Earned success—to gamble prudently and win—is obviously more prestigious than blind luck.

As well, even though relative payoffs matter, many costs are absolute. Restricting the size of gains to minimize the absolute size of the differences makes many investments uneconomical because of their costs. If the payoff for inventing something is only half as much, then investors can afford to invest only half as much. Reduced investment diminishes the rate of progress.

Bigger potential gains motivate larger investments, whether to capture gains or to avoid losses. In turn, larger investments produce bigger gains for investors and losses for their competition. This positive feedback loop drives the ferocity of competition. Ultimately, the ferocity of competition drives the rate of progress.

While it is true that higher payoffs drive up the pay for properly trained talent, which in turn increases the cost of the investment, ultimately, the unwillingness of talented people to get the training and perform the tedious tasks that customers value most sets the pay for properly trained talent. The only reason customers or innovators with competitive advantages agree to accept a lesser share of the value created by an innovation, which is available to be divided, is to motivate more talent to get the training and make the efforts necessary to harvest value on their—the customers' and innovators'—behalf.

It should come as no surprise, then, that Frank's theory that relative status is the only motivation people need flies in the face of the evidence. The highest-paid U.S. workers have worked longer hours, taken more entrepreneurial risks, and produced more innovation than their counterparts in other high-wage economies.[39]

Europe and Japan had access to the same technology as Americans and similarly educated workforces needed to capitalize on that access but failed to produce anywhere near their proportionate share of innovation. In fact, their growth rates would be substantially slower and their wages lower without the disproportionate benefit of American innovation. Given the large differences in the probability and payoff for success in the United States relative to Europe and Japan, it is hard to believe monetary rewards aren't predominantly responsible for the differences.

## Income Redistribution Slows Growth

Let's face facts: high-wage economies that diminish incentives to produce innovation by taxing success more heavily, increasing government spending, and distributing incomes more equally have grown more slowly with lower median incomes. No fewer than nine highly credible cross-country comparisons provide the evidence.

Two important long-term multicountry studies by MIT's Kristin Forbes and Harvard's Robert Barro find empirical evidence that unequal distribution of income accelerates growth in high-wage economies. Forbes finds that "in the short and medium term, an increase in a country's level of income inequality has a significant positive and robust relationship with subsequent economic growth."[40] Barro finds "higher inequality tends to . . . encourage growth in richer places."[41]

A pair of studies by the Organisation for Economic Co-operation and Development (OECD)[42] finds significant evidence that higher marginal tax rates reduce productivity over the long term. The studies compare the tax structures of twenty-one countries over the last thirty-five years, including industry-by-industry comparisons between countries. The studies find that "a strong reliance on income taxes seems to be associated with significantly lower levels of GDP per capita than the use of taxes on consumption and property [which spread taxes more broadly to lower income groups]. . . . High top marginal rates of personal income tax reduce productivity growth by reducing entrepreneurial activity. . . . Industry-level evidence covering a subset of OECD countries suggests that there is a negative relationship between top marginal personal income tax rates and the long-run level of total factor productivity."*[43]

---

* Total factor productivity (TFP) is innovative know-how.

A recent International Monetary Fund (IMF) study, often cited by advocates of redistribution*—whose headlines insisted that redistribution does not slow growth—admits that "when redistribution is already high (above the 75th percentile†), there is evidence that further redistribution is indeed harmful to growth, as the Okun 'big trade-off' hypothesis‡ would suggest."[44] Guess which country lies at the seventy-fifth percentile? America.

A study by Harvard's Christopher Jencks finds that "after 1960 . . . a one percentage point rise in the top decile's income share is associated with a statistically significant 0.12 point rise in GDP growth during the following year."[45] Using these findings, Jencks calculates that by 2001, "the growth promoting effects of [the higher level of inequality in the United States] . . . had pushed the mean income of the bottom nine deciles above what it would have been if their share of total income had not fallen from 68 to 58 percent over the previous thirty years."[46]

A 2013 study of billionaires by University of Michigan economist Sutirtha Bagchi and Columbia University economist Jan Svejnar finds that the causes of rising inequality have a significant impact on the resulting growth of the economy. If a country's billionaires earned their success, the economy grows faster. If their success stems from political cronyism, it slows growth.[47] The study finds that only a tiny fraction of America's billionaires earned their wealth through political cronyism.[48]

As well, two cross-country studies by Aart Kraay and David Dollar for the World Bank find that "When average incomes rise, the average incomes of the poorest fifth of society rise proportionately."[49] No surprise, richer countries can and do spend more helping their poor. Ironically, America's poor are some of the richest people in the world.[50]

It's surely the case that single motherhood, dropping out of high school, drug addiction, and crime, for example, increase income

---

* Ironically, Nobel Prize winner Joe Stiglitz, in the postscript to his recent book *The Great Divide*, calls me out by citing the IMF study to oppose my arguments. Joe and I have publicly debated inequality on multiple occasions.
† That is, above the 75th percentile of countries in the study's sample
‡ Refers to Arthur Okun, an influential economist and adviser in the Kennedy and Johnson administrations, who argued income redistribution reduces efficiency and slows growth in his famous book, *Equality and Efficiency: The Big Tradeoff.*

inequality and slow growth. So advocates of redistribution can use clever rhetorical strategies to misleadingly claim that inequality slows growth. The question is not whether single motherhood slows growth; surely it does. It is whether income redistribution reduces single motherhood enough that the benefits outweigh the cost of slower growth. It is likely that redistribution produces no such reduction in single motherhood; probably even the opposite. The Jencks study suggests that the benefits of redistribution do not outweigh the costs.

Redistribution—whether achieved though taxation, regulatory restrictions, or social norms—appears to have large detrimental effects on risk-taking, innovation, productivity, and growth over the long run, especially in an economy where innovation produced by the entrepreneurial risk-taking of properly trained talent increasingly drives growth.

# Conclusion

A shift in resources to innovation has produced powerful, compounding, long-term beneficial effects on America's institutional capabilities. In turn, these capabilities have accelerated U.S. growth relative to other high-wage economies. Successful innovation creates companies that provide valuable on-the-job training and communities of experts, which increase the expected value of risk-taking that produces innovation. It puts equity into the hands of successful risk-takers more willing and able to underwrite risk. And it raises the bar for success, which increases risk-taking and work effort by the most productive workers. Together they raise the payoff and certainty for risk-taking substantially.

Advocates of redistribution ignore these beneficial effects. Instead, they make far-fetched assumptions—that payoffs have little effects—and make misleading apple-to-orange comparisons that ignore large circumstantial difference, like those found in the 1950s and 1990s. If they had stronger arguments, they would make them.

Contrary to what the mythmakers tell you, the outsized payoff for success is the true cause of growing income inequality. The most credible reason the pay for successful risk-taking has grown is that their discoveries are highly valued by customers.

Cross-country comparisons repeatedly show a correlation between greater income inequality and faster growth in advanced economies like America's. Successful innovation increases living standards and the demand for middle- and working-class workers. This puts upward pressure on their wages. Rather than curse America's success, we should embrace it.

# Chapter 4

# THE MYTH THAT SUCCESS
# IS LARGELY UNEARNED

Instead of denying that pay motivates people to earn their success—a concession that undermines the case for income redistribution—many advocates of redistribution deny that success is earned. If income is unearned, then we can redistribute it without slowing growth or reducing middle- and working-class incomes, even if incentives motivate effort, risk-taking, investment, and innovation. If pay is unearned, it's fair to take it away.

Pay may be unearned for a variety of reasons. The price of talent—the wages of the successful—may rise for no other reason than talent is in short supply and cannot expand to meet the growing demand for it. In that case, a shortage merely redistributes pay from the rest of the economy to talent without talent doing anything more to earn its increased pay. If talent has done nothing to earn their increased pay, then taking away the increase will similarly have no effect on their behaviors.

There are other ways for pay to increase without the increases being earned. CEOs may raise their pay by engaging in faux negotiations with their cronies on their boards of directors. Competitors may cooperate in oligopolies to increase profits by reducing competition in order to raise prices or lower employee pay, which would be impossible if competitors truly competed with one another. Companies may use asymmetrical information to sell unsuspecting customers products they don't need, increasing the companies' returns. Hedge fund managers may use inside information to fleece naive investors. Political contributors may use the government to gain unfair legal advantages. Regardless of the means, when companies or workers increase their pay without serving customers more effectively than their competitors, we can redistribute their increased pay without detrimental consequences to the rest of the economy.

Whether advocates of redistribution show how much the 1 percent's share of GDP has increased over time, calculate how much more the middle class would have earned if the 1 percent had earned less, or compare the faster growth in overall productivity to the slower growth in median incomes, the implied argument is the same. We can redistribute the success of the wealthiest without consequence because their success is unearned and comes at the expense of others. Otherwise, such calculations are misleading.

Purveyors of the success-is-unearned myth blame three different targets for taking what they haven't earned: individuals, businesses, and political contributors. Each line of attack takes a different form. But all of them hinge on the same underlying premise—that growing success is unearned.

Ultimately, advocates of redistribution who believe inequality stems from rising cronyism advocate for using cronyism—minimum-wage laws, unions, and the political process—to take back what was allegedly taken unfairly by the 1 percent. The proponents of these policies mean well, but both their diagnoses and their prescriptions are wrong. Ironically, their solutions make matters worse for the very people they are intended to help. In the long run, they slow middle- and working-class employment and wage growth.

# Evidence Shows the 0.1 Percent Earned, Not Unfairly Negotiated, Their Pay

Thomas Piketty has spearheaded the attacks on individuals who comprise the 0.1 percent by insisting their growing success is unearned. In his book *Capital in the Twenty-First Century*, Piketty rejects claims that income inequality results from skill-biased technological change, globalization, low-skilled immigration, or growing returns to skill that have driven up the pay of the most successful Americans. He fears that these views, whether true or not, legitimize inequality.

Instead, he insists the rich are "rentiers" who earn money solely from passive returns on investment, or "supermanagers" who "by and large have the power to set their own remuneration, in some cases without limit and in many cases without any clear relation to their individual productivity." They earn unfair wages by using nepotism, corruption, and corporate politics, or by conspiring with "hierarchical superiors."[1] According to Piketty, corporate managers are simply the beneficiaries of gradually eroding social norms that previously held their pay in check.

Piketty's supporting arguments, however, are woefully at odds with the evidence. Piketty claims that "recent research, based on matching declared income on tax returns with corporate compensation records, allows me to state that the vast majority (60 to 70 percent, depending on what definitions one chooses) of the top 0.1 percent of the income hierarchy in 2000–2010 consists of top managers."[2] But according to Stockholm School of Economics researcher Tino Sanandaji, the only research Piketty cites neither matches tax returns with corporate compensation nor covers the 2000–2010 period.[3] In the study Piketty cites, only 20 percent of the 0.1 percent were "executives, managers, and supervisors" of public nonfinancial companies.[4]

In a 2013 study that does match tax returns to corporate compensation records for the 2000–2010 period, the approximately seven thousand CEOs and other top corporate executives of the S&P 1500 collectively earned $18 billion in 2010, including equity and stock options—a pittance compared with the $800 billion per year earned by America's 0.1 percent.[5] Clearly, the vast majority of pay earned by the top 0.1 percent is not, as Piketty claims, pay earned by managers who are able to work the corporate system and convince their "hierarchical superiors" to compensate them unfairly.

While it is true that some financial managers have earned extraordinary pay, they have not earned this pay by negotiating with hierarchic supervisors. Rather, they have attracted customers in a highly competitive sector of the economy.

Piketty's claim that eroding social norms have allowed CEOs to raise their pay relative to those they manage is similarly mistaken. A recent study published by the National Bureau of Economic Research (NBER) using extensive tax records from the Social Security Administration directly contradicts Piketty's claim that CEO pay has risen relative to the workers they lead.[6] The study begins:

It is frequently asserted that inequality within the firm is a driving force leading to an increase in overall inequality. For example, according to Mishel and Sabadish (2014),[7] "a key driver of wage inequality is the growth of chief executive officer earnings and compensation." Piketty (2013)* (p. 315)[8] agrees, noting that "the primary reason for increased income inequality in recent decades is the rise of the supermanager." And he adds (p. 332)[9] that "wage inequalities increased rapidly in the United States and Britain because U.S. and British corporations became much more tolerant of extremely generous pay packages after 1970."[10]

The study concludes:

Contrary to the assertions made by Mishel and Sabadish (2014),[11] Piketty (2013),[12] and others, we find strong evidence that . . . individuals in the top one percent in 2012 . . . are now paid less, relative to their firms' mean incomes, than they were three decades ago. . . . Almost the entirety of the increase in individual inequality can be accounted for by the increase in cross-firm inequality. . . . Wage dispersion between firms is increasing, while dispersion within firms has been stable.[13]

In other words, the success of new businesses is driving the increased pay of the 1 percent, and not the 1 percent's ability to negotiate greater pay relative to their employees.

Piketty also argues that the wealthiest simply inherited their wealth. He disputes the claim that most billionaires are self-made entrepreneurs despite the fact that only 30 percent of the *Forbes* list of the richest 400 U.S. billionaires inherited their wealth.[14] Instead, Piketty insists *Forbes*'s estimates are biased because billionaire entrepreneurs are

---

* English version published in 2014.

easier to identify than heirs and heiresses.[15] For Piketty to be correct, the *Forbes* list must suffer from a massive bias that misses the majority of billionaire heirs. But the Internal Revenue Service compared the *Forbes* list of billionaires with the agency's estate-tax data and found only twenty-six additional names that should have been listed.[16]

A seemingly more credible version of the argument that the 0.1 percent have not earned their wealth is the notion that talent is limited. If that's true, and if we've tapped into all the talent that is available, then when the demand for talent grows, pay increases without additional effort expended by the talent. Economists contrast "collecting rent" with actually *earning* pay. If we have indeed tapped into all possible talent, and higher pay can't incentivize untapped talent to enter the marketplace, then high pay could be considered "rent," since it is not based on effort. Ergo, we can take away talent's pay increases and the talent still won't behave any differently.

In truth, America's talent is underutilized. It is not a binding constraint on economic growth. There are armies of students at the most prestigious universities studying literature, art history, psychology, and so forth—curricula that are hardly valued by customers who eagerly pay others to satisfy their needs. There is a shortage of talent willing to get the training and perform the tedious tasks—computer programming, engineering, accounting, among others—that customers value most.

There is also a shortage of properly trained talent willing to take the entrepreneurial risks necessary to produce innovation. But for the right price, there is a near-unlimited supply of talent available to be trained, and already trained talent available to take the necessary risks. That doesn't describe "rent collecting." Quite the contrary—it describes prices motivating an increase in supply.

Ironically, it's the reluctance of talent to suffer the training and pursue the careers necessary to serve customers' demands that sets the price for properly trained talent and successful entrepreneurialism. If more people with talent and privilege stepped up to meet the demands of customers, their wages would be lower. If only a few stepped forward to become teachers or journalists, pay in those fields would be higher.

The evidence points overwhelmingly to the fact that the richest Americans are neither rentiers nor managers but rather entrepreneurs and other innovators who earned their pay by persuading customers, not hierarchical superiors, to pay them more. In 2010 self-employed business owners accounted for 70 percent of the wealth of the top 0.1 percent and 50 percent of their total earnings.[17] With the rise of information technology and the Internet, the share of self-made Forbes 400 billionaires has risen. Today less than 10 percent of the billionaires on the list in 1982 are still on the list.[18] At the same time, CEO turnover has accelerated.[19] Income mobility—the probability of earning more than your parents earned—at all levels of income has risen, despite the wider dispersion of income at the top of the wage scale.[20] All these trends run contrary to the notion that rising cronyism explains the growing share of pay earned by the 1 percent.

Consistent with the evidence that America's highest-paid workers earned their pay rather than having misappropriated it, U.S. growth has accelerated relative to other high-wage economies. Had the economy misallocated resources on a scale necessary to produce the rise in income inequality we have witnessed, growth should have slowed relative to high-wage economies with more equally distributed pay.

Given the weight of the evidence, even Paul Krugman called Piketty's argument on cronyism "an intellectual sleight of hand that detracts from his intellectual achievement."[21] If Piketty had a stronger argument, wouldn't he make it?

## Pay Motivates CEOs to Take Risks

Despite evidence that the 0.1 percent are not managers who earned pay increases by negotiating with cronies, one may nevertheless ask why CEOs are paid so much. Although evidence shows that CEO pay has not risen substantially relative to their own company's median pay, proponents of the-rich-negotiated-their-pay theory—like Joe Stiglitz—argue that companies overpay CEOs. They believe that CEOs would "give it their all" even if they were paid less.[22] Were this true, it would be an indication of crony capitalism, since boards are presumably responsible for negotiating the lowest possible CEO pay and are failing to do so if their CEOs would do their jobs for less than they are paid. Stiglitz argues, "So C.E.O.'s must be given stock options to induce them to work hard. I find this puzzling: If a firm pays someone $10 million to run a company, he should give his all to ensure its success."[23]

Ironically, Stiglitz argues that we needn't pay CEOs to "give it their all" because they will do so regardless—that is, that pay does not incentivize CEO behavior. At the same time, Piketty argues that higher pay motivated CEOs to break social norms and game the system in pursuit of even higher pay.[24] Which is it? Do incentives motivate behavior or not? Apparently, pay only motivates behavior when it suits the argument.

Stiglitz begins with the mistaken assumption that CEOs are paid to work hard (or in some other extreme manner) and then doubts that paying them more could possibly induce them to work any harder than they already are. He doesn't realize that companies don't pay CEOs for what they can do; they pay them for what they are *willing* to do.

Boards pay CEOs to compel them to take the risks necessary to improve the company's performance. Risks that disrupt the status quo put a CEO's own career at risk. Even when a CEO can't work any harder, he can take bigger risks.

These risks are summarized well in *Leadership on the Line,* an important book warning CEOs and other leaders:*

People do not resist change per se. People resist loss. The toughest problems . . . are hard precisely because the group . . . will not authorize anyone to push them to address those problems. Leadership becomes dangerous . . . when it must confront people with loss.

People cannot see at the beginning of the . . . process that the new situation will be any better than the current condition. What they do see clearly is the potential loss. People frequently avoid painful adjustments in their lives if they can postpone them, place the burden on somebody else, or call someone to the rescue.

[People] don't want to be told that they will have to sustain losses; rather they want to know how you're going to protect them from the pains of change. People rarely elect or hire anyone to disturb their jobs or lives. Generally, people will not authorize someone to make them face what they do not want to face. Instead, people hire someone . . . with solutions that require a minimum of disruption.

---

* I have taken the liberty of rearranging quoted sentences into paragraphs.

Though they ought to blame themselves for sticking their heads in the sand and pressuring you to sanction their behavior, it's much more likely they'll blame you. Embodying an issue in your authority role ties your survival, not just your success, to that of the issue. That's a dangerous platform on which to stand.

Rather than focus on the content of your message, taking issue with its merits, they frequently find it more effective to discredit you. Through trial and error, they will find your Achilles' heel. They will come at you where you are most vulnerable. Tacitly, or perhaps explicitly, your own people will instruct you to get the job done by having the people from the other factions make the tough trade-offs.[25]

CEOs are logically reluctant to take unnecessary risks. After all, a CEO's primary personal objective is to maximize the value of his or her career by remaining CEO for as long as possible. Failed risk-taking often ends an executive's career. Compared with diversified investors, CEOs have all their eggs in one basket. Risk-taking jeopardizes once-in-a-lifetime careers. As a result, a CEO can easily become satisfied with satisfactory underperformance if given the opportunity. "Satisfactory underperformance" is difficult for investors to assess.

The magnitude of CEO pay reflects the level of incentive needed to motivate CEOs to take risks. Companies pay CEOs for more than just reactive change. They pay for proactive change—for CEOs to disrupt the status quo prudently, whenever and wherever they can. The differential pay for success must be large enough to compel CEOs to find and take prudent risks proactively.

This incentive structure seems to have served America—namely, employees, customers, and investors—better than the alternatives. America has been at the vanguard of incentive pay that better aligns CEO pay with stock price performance, and the U.S. economy has grown faster than the other high-wage economies. Even if growth hasn't translated into robust income growth, at the very least it has created a better life for America's 40 million foreign-born adults, their 20 million native-born adult children, and the 20 million young children of those 60 million adults.[26]

Besides the need to incentivize risk-taking, the growing value of entrepreneurial success has also increased CEO pay. To attract top talent, CEO pay must be competitive with the pay for other similarly talented endeavors. For companies to hire and retain a stable of managers with CEO-quality talent, they must offer those managers pay comparable to alternative careers—a one-in-a-hundred chance at entrepreneurial-like pay. Otherwise, it would be illogical for a manager with the talent to be a successful entrepreneur—talents similar to those needed to be a successful CEO—to suffer through a corporate career with a similarly slim chance of becoming CEO.

University of Chicago economist Steve Kaplan provides supporting evidence. His research shows that CEO pay has risen comparably with the pay of the 0.1 percent and other high-paid professions such as elite professional athletes. His research also shows that public-company CEO pay has not risen relative to private-company CEO pay where owners, and not cronies, control pay. Nor has the value of CEO pay risen relative to the value of the companies they manage.[27] And boards seem to exert more control over CEOs than in the past, as evidenced by the shortened tenure of CEOs.[28]

While Stiglitz's argument that CEOs are overpaid rings true for many, it simply does not withstand scrutiny. We live in a world filled with disruptive technological threats that can transform stalwarts like IBM and AT&T, and put Kodak out of business. Hedge funds compete with banks on the opposite side of even the largest trades. It's foolish to think that institutions critical to the success of our economy, such as JP Morgan, can run without CEOs as talented and motivated as Jamie Dimon. The economy has already seen a large drain of talent from corporations to more entrepreneurial ventures. We can't afford to lose more.

# Business Has Grown More Competitive Despite Higher Profits

Recognizing the flimsiness of the crony capitalism argument formulated by Piketty, which claims individuals have not earned their success, Larry Summers, Joe Stiglitz, Robert Reich, and others have independently endeavored to argue that rising business profitability is unearned and merely indicates reduced competition between firms (see Figure 4-1, "Corporate Profits Relative to GDP").[29] Corporate profits have risen significantly since the 1990s. They argue that the government should tax and redistribute profits derived from reduced competition or find other ways to restrict the power of companies in order to increase competitiveness.

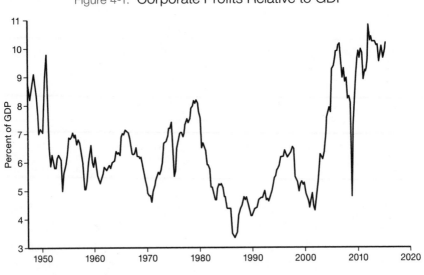

Figure 4-1: Corporate Profits Relative to GDP

Source: Federal Reserve Bank of St. Louis

Summers et al. are correct in their belief that competition is the secret sauce that keeps self-interested capitalism moral. Competition drives companies to strive continually to serve customers more effectively than their competitors. One company's successful innovation or investment takes business and profits away from its competitors. In turn, competitors must respond by investing to avoid losses rather than to increase profits. Competition forces companies to invest continually while driving the benefits of these investments from investors to customers. It prevents producers from fleecing customers and underpaying employees.

In the absence of competition, businesses can take advantage of customers and employees by raising prices and lowering wages. Advocates of redistribution claim this is occurring with increasing frequency. If they can undermine the credibility of competition in today's market, they can argue that increased profits are unearned and therefore can be redistributed back to their rightful owners without adverse consequences to the rest of the economy.

At the Brookings Institution, Summers showed his cards rather plainly. He believes that high profits are evidence of reduced competition and implies these profits can be redistributed without diminishing the prosperity of the rest of the economy:

> One of the puzzles of our economy today is that on the one hand, we have record low real interest rates, ones that are expected to be record low for 30 years if you look at the index bond market. And on the other hand, we have record high profits. . . . The way to think about that is there's a lot of rents in what we're calling profits that don't really represent a return to investment.
>
> The question then is who's going to get those rents? Which goes to the minimum wage, goes to the power of unions, goes through the presence of profit sharing, goes to the length of patents and a variety of other government policies that confer rents and then when those [rents] are received, goes to the question of how progressive the tax and transfer system is. That has got to be a very, very large part of the picture.
>
> If we had the income distribution in the United States that we did in 1979, the top 1% would have $1 trillion less today, and the bottom 80% would have $1 trillion more.[30]

Essentially, Summers claims higher profits provide evidence of reduced competition. He argues that unused savings should lead to increased investment and subsequent competition between firms. The combination of the two—high profits and unused savings—allegedly provides further evidence of reduced competitiveness. If Summers is right, corporate taxation could be used to redistribute income to U.S. middle- and working-class workers.

Were Summers correct, there would be evidence of an increasing number of oligopolies, monopsonies, and asymmetrical negotiations in our market—the three ways companies limit competition and earn income unfairly. Instead, we find evidence to the contrary.

Unfairly reduced competition chiefly occurs for three reasons:

Companies can form oligopolies by cooperating with one another to raise prices. In some cases, where a company is the only employer in a town, it may have monopsony power over labor that allows it to hold down wages. Or it may be able to use asymmetrical information in a negotiation to gain an advantage. For example, an auto mechanic may charge you for unneeded repairs. In each case, such a producer would have an ability to earn profits by controlling prices and wages beyond what competitive markets would otherwise allow.

The case for significantly rising oligarchical pricing power in the case of any company other than Google is slim. While it is true that a company like Google has created a seemingly insurmountable advantage in the market for search because of the scale advantages of user-generated information, even Facebook—second only to Google in the amount of content its users generate—faces a host of competitors for the sale of advertising. LinkedIn, Instagram, Pinterest, and a blizzard of others create user-generated content that competes for advertising dollars linked to views. Given the enormous fragmentation of content, it is hard to believe that any of them, even Google, has much pricing power over advertisers.

Aside from Google, traditional oligopolies, like content providers and aggregators such as television networks and newspapers, have fragmented. So has the communication infrastructure. We now communicate through phone landlines, cable TV lines, fiber-optic lines, cell towers, and satellites—more options than in the past. Google, cloud computing, a revived Apple, and mobile devices now threaten the dominance of Microsoft. The old communication oligarchies are gone.

Most of the manufacturing oligarchies of the past are gone, too. Offshore manufacturers threaten what remains. Dominant U.S. automotive manufacturers and steel producers are things of the past. Expansion of the world's energy sources has reduced Exxon's market share to 3 to 4 percent of world production.[31] U.S. money center banking was quite fragmented until the Fed chose to consolidate banks during the financial crisis.

The case for businesses' rising monopsony power over labor—the ability to hold wages below the market equilibrium—is similarly unconvincing. Were businesses in fact suppressing wages, large companies would have more power to control wages relative to smaller mom-and-pop retailers. But according to a study recently published by the National Bureau of Economic Research, the opposite is true—larger firms and establishments pay more when all other statistically significant characteristics are held constant. The study concludes, "The growth in modern retail, characterized by larger chains of larger establishments . . . is raising wage rates relative to traditional mom-and-pop retail stores."[32]

There's likewise little evidence that business has increasingly benefited from using asymmetrical information to gain price advantages. It is true that companies like Google have proprietary information, which gives them an advantage relative to their competitors. But it's hard to see how it uses that information to the net disadvantage rather than the net benefit of the vast majority of its customers. Customers freely give their information to Google to gain the benefits Google provides. It's hard to believe they would do that if the costs outweighed the benefits.

Given the vast quantities of information Google and the Internet provide to the public, it is hard to believe that the asymmetrical informational advantages of sellers over buyers are growing rather than declining. Today customers are able to use the Internet to second-guess doctors, car salesmen, auto mechanics, real estate brokers, and lenders—the transactions where the middle and working classes have traditionally faced significant asymmetrical informational disadvantages. The Internet allows us to check the fair price of nearly everything.

That's not to deny the existence of isolated cases of oligopolistic pricing power, asymmetrical informational disadvantages, or even monopsony. They exist, to be sure. Rather, it is hard to believe that the frequency and scope of these misallocations have risen to the trillion-dollar scale necessary to account for the increase in income inequality that we see today. Were that the case, it is doubtful that the growth of the United States would be accelerating relative to other high-wage economies as it has.

While it's true that U.S. industries have consolidated, and that this could reduce competition, with so many other factors likely affecting profitability, it is hard to believe suboptimal antitrust enforcement alone accounts for growing corporate profitability.[33] For starters, rising profitability has occurred almost entirely in IT-related businesses where competition is fierce, technology has been highly disruptive, and competitive advantages have proved to be short lived. These are hardly characteristics of an increasingly entrenched status quo—quite the contrary.

A comprehensive 2015 McKinsey study of corporate profitability, for example, finds that the rise in North American profitably largely stems from a shift to idea-intensive companies. According to McKinsey, the share of Western country profits generated by idea-intensive companies has grown from 17 percent in 1999 to 31 percent today. The study shows these firms are twice as profitable as capital-intensive companies, where emerging market competitors squeeze profit margins. The study notes the variability in the profitability of traditional firms "is much smaller than the spread in idea-intensive industries."[34]

The McKinsey study notes that networks may provide economies of scale that "drive marginal costs to almost zero" in some industries. Rather than describing companies that profit from these economics by using their scale advantages to minimizing competition, the McKinsey report describes idea-intensive firms as "brutal competitors" run by founders and venture capital investors "who often prioritize market share and scale at the expense of profits." The study notes, "Among NASDAQ-listed software and Internet companies, founder-controlled firms have 60 percent faster revenue growth and 35 to 40 percent lower profit margins and returns on invested capital than widely held firms"—the opposite of anti-competitive oligarchic behavior.[35]

The study concludes, "The disruption unleashed by tech and tech-enabled firms often plays out in the consumer's favor. Using their cost structure advantages, tech firms often go after a market-leading position [by providing] free or low-cost products or services where traditional businesses have charged fees for years. . . . [These platforms] also serve as launching pads that give thousands of small and medium-sized firms immediate global reach."[36]

It's true that the most successful Internet businesses—for example, Google, Facebook, Instagram, and Twitter—enjoy economies of scale from networks of user-generated content. But, so far, they have been unable to derive much pricing power from these advantages. Instead, they have given their products to users for little more than the reciprocal use of their information. Their profits have predominantly come from the unusual structure of IT-related economics—near-zero incremental costs spread over enormous economy-wide scale.

While patents on intellectual property provide many successful high-tech companies with valuable competitive advantages, patents are short lived relative to the useful lives of innovations and don't reduce competition in the long run. The polio vaccine, for example, lasts forever, or at least until something even better comes along. And the next generation of technologies builds off the prior generation to provide lasting value to consumers.

Moreover, the sustainability of success in information technology, at least so far, has proved extremely fragile. Again, the fifteen largest technology companies in 2000, at the peak of the Internet bubble, have lost 60 percent of their market value—$1.35 trillion as of December 2015. Meanwhile, fifteen companies with combined market capitalization less than $10 billion in 2000 are now worth over $2 trillion today.[37] If the past is any guide to the future, the sustainability of competitive advantages derived from patents and other means appear to be risky and short lived indeed.

Even if the winners' advantages prove to be sustainable, it is hardly obvious that the return on investment before the fact—the relevant measure of profitability—is truly high. Numerous Internet investments are hit-driven businesses where only a handful of start-ups succeed from an enormous sea of failures. Survival bias washes away the true cost of investment that creates success—the cost of the many failures needed to produce a handful of fortunate successes.

A study by the Kauffman Foundation, for example, found, "[Venture capital] returns haven't significantly outperformed the public market since the late 1990s . . . despite occasional high-profile successes."[38] And those were the start-ups funded by large high-profile venture funds—the funds with access to the most promising investments. Nor do the investments of venture capital funds include the lost pay of employees working in failed start-ups whom investors largely paid with now-worthless equity, which represents further unaccounted-for investment. So while the profitability of successful start-ups may appear to be high after the fact, it is a misnomer to assume that returns on investment are high when all the costs are properly considered.

In addition to a shift to innovative information-intensive businesses with hidden costs of failure, economy-wide scale when successful, and near-zero marginal costs—a prescription for profits *when* successful—traditional businesses have also taken a variety of steps to increase returns without necessarily increasing profits. Business now recognizes it makes all its profits on narrow sets of competitive advantages that are the impetus for valuable customer relationships. Business has aggressively outsourced and, in many cases offshored, nonessential tasks. When an electronics manufacturer, like Apple, outsources the manufacturing of the iPhone to Foxconn, it retains its well-deserved profits, without the economy retaining undifferentiated low-margin job-shop manufacturing. Profits increase relative to GDP.

Similarly, companies use information to identify and eliminate unprofitable business and unneeded costs. Unprofitable business can be serviced by better-suited suppliers. And unneeded costs can be redeployed by the rest of the economy into more profitable endeavors. That doesn't hurt consumers.

A large share of the supposed consolidation of business comes from retailers like Williams-Sonoma with successful national and international retail concepts consolidating the highly fragmented retail sector.[39] Despite some consolidation, this sector remains highly competitive with many options for customers to choose from. Consolidators make profits with better concepts and more skillful management than marginally profitably mom-and-pop establishments. And mom-and-pop businesses are notorious for avoiding taxes by hiding profits with unnecessary expenses. The success of companies like Williams-Sonoma has been beneficial to consumers.

Consolidation has also occurred in transportation, where it has been notoriously difficult in some subsectors—airlines and trucking, for example—for competitors to produce sustainable profitability.[40] Policy makers allowed consolidation in these subsectors to help them better weather highly cyclical and unnecessarily damaging booms and busts. It is hardly obvious that reduced competitiveness and increase profitability hurt the economy in these subsectors. Profits were previously too low.

Policy makers also consolidated the financial sector during the financial crisis, albeit perhaps mistakenly. Consolidation of the financial sector is another major cause of the increased consolidation of American business.

None of these major drivers of consolidation and increased profits are indicative of business growing more profitable at the expense of consumers. A telltale sign of oligopolistic behavior is cooperation among competitors that slows investment. Investment spurs competitors to react. This escalating chain reaction drives the return on investment into the pockets of customers at the expense of investors. But, an economist at JP Morgan finds no inverse correlation between the relative growth rate of investment and increased business concentration within business sectors.[41]

There are also reasons to believe business profits are currently lower than they appear to be and that advocates of income redistribution are misinterpreting the apparent rise in corporate profits and mistakenly concluding that they are observing unearned success. In the wake of the financial crisis, companies cut back on investment, which appears as cost reduction that boasts profitability in our information-intensive economy. Competiveness subsequently lulled, further increasing profits. Increased regulations also contributed to a lull in competitiveness. As unemployment rose, the negotiating leverage of labor likely declined relative to capital. All these effects are likely to increase profits temporarily.

Today business increasingly invests by hiring properly trained talent to engineer a more profitable future rather than by building plant and equipment. Companies cut investment not by laying off hard-to-replace talent, but by cutting back their less-costly-to-replace support staff. Cutting back support staff loads talent with administrative work, which reduces the time they have to devote to investment-related activities, such as designing new products or solving problems.

We saw a parallel pattern with more easily measured traditional business investment (see Figure 4-2, "U.S. Private Business Investment (Net of Depreciation)"). It also contracted sharply and recovered slowly after the recession. Why should we expect people-related business investment to have followed a different path?

Accounting largely expenses people-related investment as an intermediate cost of production rather than as investment. Unlike cutting investment, cutting people reduces cost, which appears to increase profits. No surprise, corporate profits and productivity growth appeared to soar in the aftermath of the recession (see Figure 4-1, "Corporate Profits Relative to GDP," and Figure 4-3, "U.S. Productivity Growth").

Figure 4-2: U.S. Private Business Investment (Net of Depreciation)

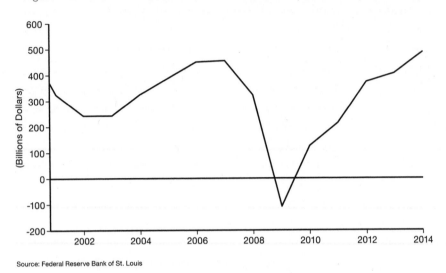

Source: Federal Reserve Bank of St. Louis

If business had cut traditional investment, profits would not have been affected nor would productivity growth appear to have soared. But as happens in traditional investment, as soon as people-related investments were cut, productivity growth slowed (see Figure 4-3, "U.S. Productivity Growth").

Figure 4-3: U.S. Productivity Growth

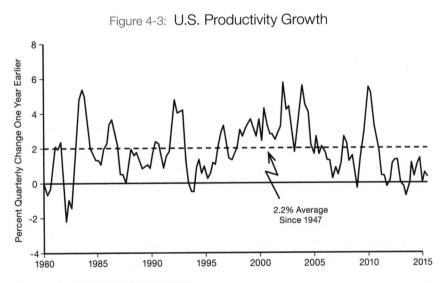

Source: Department of Labor, via *Wall Street Journal*, 2015

A dial-back in investment runs the risk of creating a self-reinforcing feedback loop that reduces competitiveness. Like CEOs, established companies and their investors prefer the status quo. Investment and innovation forces them to compete. Competition begets more investment and innovation.

When competitiveness slows, the overall rate of investment also slows. Profits grow; productivity growth slows; investors capture a greater share of the value they create; and stock prices rise accordingly—exactly as we have seen. The last thing investors want is a fiercely competitive environment where competitors compete away profits and customers, not investors, capture a greater share of the value companies create.

A slowdown in competitive intensity, however, is certainly temporary. Equilibriums that depend solely on cooperation are unstable. Eventually, opportunity, greed, or unexpected innovation and investment disrupt the status quo and competiveness flares. At least, it always has.

Ironically, the Obama administration's successful efforts to disrupt the status quo with extensive regulatory changes likely prolonged this dial-back. Over time, companies gradually test the limits of regulation to search for competitive advantages and new sources of profitability. When lawmakers write and enforce new regulations, it seldom pays to be the test-case guinea pig. Instead, companies take a wait-and-see posture. Reducing regulation in order to unbridle competition might have increased investment, diminished profits, and accelerated growth.

As well, when unemployment is high it is common for negotiating leverage to shift temporarily from workers to employers and their customers. Wages are slow to rise because unemployed workers are eager to take employment, even at lower wages. At the same time, producers may be reluctant to cut prices because it may be difficult to raise them later without unnerving customers. When producers are reluctant to cut prices, profits margins may rise until labor markets tighten and wages rise.

For a variety of reasons, the apparent increase in corporate profits seems unlikely to stem from a permanent decline in competitiveness due to a rise in oligopolistic pricing power, monopsony, or asymmetrical information. In fact, there is little reason to believe competitiveness has permanently declined but for rising profitability. The long-term rise in profitability seems confined to the IT-related sector, where survival bias hides the true return on investment and disruptive turmoil, near-zero incremental costs, and free products indicate fierce competition and anything but business as usual. Moreover, the long-term rise in profitability is likely overstated by a temporary rise in profitability in the aftermath of the financial crisis.

Misdiagnosis of these trends can lead to solutions that do more harm than good. If asymmetrical information, oligopolies, and monopsony are not the source of rising corporate profits, then the policies that would solve those issues will do harm to the economy. For example, if increased risk-aversion in the aftermath of the financial crisis explains both the rise in corporate profits and the apparent surplus of savings relative to demand, then Summers's recommendations would make matters worse. Taxing, redistributing, and consuming returns to equity would reduce risk-taking rather than increase it, slowing the economy further. And if increased regulation diminishes competition, risk-taking, and growth, it would be counterproductive to increase taxes and regulation to solve the problem.

# Efforts by Investors to Influence Economic Policy May Accelerate Growth

A third variation of the success-is-unearned argument concedes that success is earned but fears that if rising income inequality is left unchecked, eventually the 0.1 percent will use their money to influence the government to bend the rules in their favor so that they can garner unearned income. Of course, anything is possible. But the emerging consensus of academic research is that money in politics exerts surprisingly little influence, far less than opponents and the media sensationalize.[42] So far, Democrats and Republicans have fought each other to a draw on political funding.[43] And, if anything, the success of the 1 percent has created a growing political backlash that seeks to redistribute their income.

Moreover, rising marginal tax rates and the continual increase in transfer payments as a share of GDP (see Figure 4-4, "Growth in Federal Spending on Means-Tested Programs and Tax Credits for Low-Income Households") from the top 20 percent of income earners to the bottom 80 percent (see Figure 10-1, "Federal Government Expenditures and Taxes by Household Type") hardly indicates a rise in the success of the rich to influence government at the expense of the middle class. It indicates the opposite.

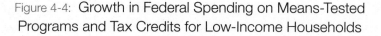

Figure 4-4: Growth in Federal Spending on Means-Tested Programs and Tax Credits for Low-Income Households

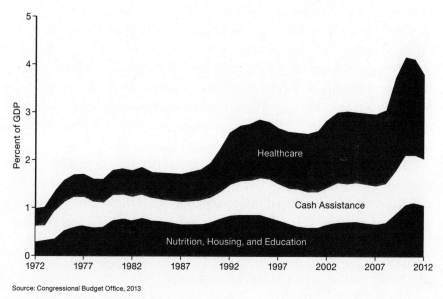

Source: Congressional Budget Office, 2013

That's not to deny the existence of cronyism—far from it. We know from steroids in sports that there is plenty of cheating, at least at the level of misdemeanors. Whether a large share of successful people are willing to risk jail for further success is an entirely different matter. To account for the significant increase in income inequality, the evidence must indicate a *rise* in the success of cronyism, whereas the evidence indicates the opposite: increasing disruption of the status quo.

Even if cheating is rising, it doesn't necessarily transfer money from the middle class to the wealthy. In sports, if competition drives every athlete to use steroids, no one gains an advantage. The competitors largely inflict damage on themselves. Similarly, oil companies may successfully lobby the government for tax breaks, but when all producers pay the same tax rates, competition forces producers to pass these breaks to consumers.

At the same time, democracy gives rise to a second system for allocating resources: democracy, where one person has one vote, versus the economy, where one dollar has one vote. This gives rise to two competing political advocates. The rich—who pay more taxes than they receive in government benefits—largely seek political influence in order to lower their taxes by lowering spending. On the other hand, the majority of voters—who receive more government benefits than they pay in taxes—often seek to increase their government benefits.

On their own, each of these opposing efforts to influence the government may reduce prosperity. Consumers are prone to consume the seed corn, which stunts growth. Private investors are prone to underinvest in public goods, like education, if they are unable to earn a profit. But taken together, these two countervailing efforts to influence the government often mitigate one another. In competition with one another, they drive the process to beneficial compromises.

If higher levels of redistribution ultimately hurt the middle class, then the political power of the rich, which slows the growth of redistribution, while suboptimal on its own, may push the economy toward greater prosperity. Were that not the case, growth would have slowed in the wake of *Roe v. Wade,* which brought Ronald Reagan and pro-business Republicans to power after they formed a winning coalition of odd bedfellows with the Christian Right.

Instead, U.S. growth gradually accelerated relative to other high-wage economies after Republicans used their newfound political influence to slow the growth of business regulation and lower federal marginal tax rates from 70 to 29 percent. Since then, they have lowered capital gains tax rates and fought to keep federal marginal tax rates lower than they had been previously. In the wake of these changes, America's growth, innovativeness, and median wages have gradually accelerated relative to its high-wage peers—evidence that economic policy has moved closer to optimality.

# Raising Wages by Fiat Does More Harm Than Good

Those who claim the 1 percent unfairly negotiated a higher share of income typically make proposals for increasing the negotiating leverage of the middle and working classes by strengthening unions and raising the minimum wage.[44] In this mind-set, the middle and working classes take back what the 1 percent took from them.

Advocates base their proposal on two faulty assumptions: that businesses set wages and that higher mandatory wages would improve the lives of the lowest-skilled workers rather than making it much harder for them to find work.

Most people overlook the fact that employers don't hire workers, customers do. Employers hire workers on behalf of customers. Customers can easily hire different workers to serve them by buying from competitors. At the same time, the market sets the price for labor of various skill levels, not employers. Each employer pays a fraction more than the employee's next best alternative.

To attract customers, employers who hire lower-wage workers must make those employees as attractive to customers as somewhat-higher-wage employees hired by competitors. On average, low-wage workers are less reliable, turn over more frequently, and engage in more unproductive behaviors like theft, drinking, and fighting than somewhat-higher-wage employees. Were these workers more productive, they would garner higher wages like the rest of the workforce.

To make less-productive workers competitive, employers must incur additional costs—for example, more supervision, training, automation, and task design—to bring their productivity up to the rest of the workforce. To remain competitive, the difference in the wages of lower-skilled and somewhat-higher-skilled workers must cover these additional costs. In effect, the wage of a lower-skilled worker should equal the wage necessary to compel an additional somewhat-higher-skilled worker to join the workforce less the cost of increasing the productivity of the lower-wage worker to that of the higher-wage worker. Were that not the case, in the long run, employers would hire more of one skill level and less of another until their wages equilibrated. If anything, the persistently higher unemployment rate of lower-wage workers indicates that many low-wage workers are more expensive to employ than higher-wage workers when all costs are considered.[45]

A mandatory increase in the minimum wage above this market equilibrium level has several effects. First, employers hire somewhat-higher-wage-but-now-relatively-cheaper workers instead of minimum-wage workers until wages once again equilibrate the supply and demand for workers of various skill levels. As a result, many lower-skilled workers lose their jobs to somewhat-higher-skilled workers who join the workforce because wages are higher. Given that there are relatively more potential somewhat-higher-skilled workers,* a small increase in their wage can lead to a large increase in their supply relative to lesser-skilled workers. That does not bode well for the employment of lower-skilled workers.

The minimum wage also sets a hurdle for work. If a worker can't produce \$7.25† an hour of value that customers are willing to buy, the minimum wage bars them from working. When lawmakers raise the minimum wage, workers that can't reach the now-higher hurdle become unemployable.

In addition to the harm raising the minimum wage causes to low-skilled workers, it can also do some good. Markets are not perfectly efficient—they don't price everything perfectly—far from it. Prices are set on average by producers who feel their way in the dark. So when wages are raised by fiat, some workers do receive pay raises rather than lose their jobs. They discover their employer is willing to pay them more—no different than if they had demanded a raise and received it.

Workers who receive increases often receive them because employers discover customers who are willing to pay them more for their products and services. Those employers can therefore afford to pay employees higher wages.

But to the extent wages and prices truly increase in one part of the economy, they must be offset by decreases in other parts. Were that not the case, we could increase prosperity simply by mandating higher wages without the need for investment, risk-taking, and innovation. If only it were that easy!

Ultimately, consumers and investors spend a given amount of income on a basket of different products. If they pay more for one product, they must pay less for another. To the extent real wages rise by fiat, overall employment must decline. At best, an increase in the minimum wage reallocates production. It can't increase production. Production per worker must increase to increase wages overall.

Empirical studies that claim employment does not decline when

---

* Somewhat-higher-skilled workers are closer in skill level to the quasi-normally distributed mean skill level—that is, the skill level with the most workers.
† The current federal minimum wage is \$7.25 per hour.

minimum wages are raised have narrowed their analysis to short time frames, subsets of low-wage industries, namely the fast-food sector, and limited geographies. They have also ignored compositional shifts in the workforce to higher-skilled workers.[46]

Credible empirical studies of minimum-wage employment that take these factors into account show that if employers are forced by law to pay higher wages, they simply hire employees with higher productivity who are worthy of higher wages.[47] These studies show "higher minimum wage drawing those enrolled in school and working part-time into full-time work, while pushing those working full-time and not enrolled in school out of jobs into 'idleness' (neither working nor employed)," and "substitution from low-skilled adults to possibly higher-skilled teenage students (in food-service occupations)."[48] This harms, rather than helps, the low-skilled workers it seeks to help.

A 2014 study published by the National Bureau of Economic Research tracked—for the first time—the employment and earning histories of individuals most affected by increases in the minimum wage and found that increases in the minimum wage over the last ten years reduced employment among low-skilled workers 6 to 9 percentage points.[49]

Similarly, the Congressional Budget Office estimates that 500,000 workers will lose their jobs if the federal government increases the minimum wage from $7.25 an hour to $10.10 an hour, and cautions that the loss among the lowest-skilled workers—namely, African American workers between the ages of twenty and twenty-four, where unemployment rates are twice as high as their white counterparts—will be three times greater than adults generally.[50] In other words, if higher-skilled workers replace lower-skilled workers, the job loss among lower-skilled workers could be substantially greater than 500,000.

Cities with high real estate prices, such as New York, Boston, San Francisco, and Seattle, which have been at the vanguard of raising minimum wages, fail to recognize that low-wage workers in these cities don't earn higher wages. Landlords extract them from employers and customers by charging employees higher rent. Wage increases will result in rent increases in those cities unless the supply of housing expands. The supply of housing won't expand, even though the market prices of real estate are greater than its replacement costs, because the supply is limited by geographic or legal restrictions. If they could expand, they already would have expanded. The rents would be lower and so would worker pay.

While it's true that low-wage workers who hold on to their jobs would garner higher wages, the Congressional Budget Office finds that raising the minimum wage is a very inefficient way to transfer money to the poor. The CBO estimated that transferring a dollar of income to a family in poverty requires transferring almost $7 of income through the minimum wage versus $1.70 using the Earned Income Tax Credit.[51] The CBO finds that aside from the layoffs, "just 19% [of income transferred from an increase in the minimum wage to $10.10 per hour] would accrue to families with earnings below the poverty threshold."[52]

Unions, which increase wages by monopolizing the supply of labor, are similar to minimum-wage laws. Ultimately, they reduce employment and slow growth. Unionized automobile manufacturers, for example, can pass the higher cost of union labor to consumers through higher-priced cars if consumers are unable to buy lower-priced cars made with cheaper labor. The higher cost of labor, however, drives investors to substitute capital for labor domestically and to hire employees elsewhere. The high price of cars reduces both the demand for cars, which reduces employment, and the real wages of car buyers.

Once car buyers can buy lower-priced cars, prices fall and squeeze the profit margins of high-cost unionized producers. With lower profit margins than lower-cost competitors, they can no longer reinvest enough to remain competitive. Consequently, they gradually lose market share. As a result, unionized cities, like Detroit and Cleveland, became hollowed-out shells of their former selves.

Unionized employers can temporarily mitigate the adverse effects of high-cost labor by trading lower labor cost today for greater pension benefits tomorrow. But this simply pushes the cost and consequences onto future generations.

Who really bears the brunt of higher-cost union labor? Younger workers, of course. Go to Detroit or France and look. The unemployment rate of young adults in countries like France and Italy with strong unions and inflexible labor laws, for example, is 25 percent and 40 percent, respectively.[53] Unionized economies raise pay by eating their young.

By mistakenly concluding that the pay of the most successful Americans is unearned, advocates of income redistribution seek to increase the negotiating leverage of lesser-paid workers in order to level the playing field. Because pay is earned by serving customers more effectively than competitors—across the entire spectrum of pay—efforts to increase the pay of lower-paid workers by fiat, whether through unions and minimum-wage laws, are no different than crony capitalism. They misallocate resources and subsequently slow growth and reduce wages. Rather than enlarging the economic pie, they make it smaller than it would otherwise be—smaller still in the long run, especially for the least-skilled workers.

## Conclusion

Efforts to deny the earned success of the 1 percent and link their success to the stagnant wages of the middle class in the long run simply do not withstand scrutiny. A massive misallocation of resources necessary to account for rising U.S. inequality—whether from cronyism, oligopoly pricing, asymmetrical information, monopsony, a shortage of talent, or any other form of unfair negotiation—should have slowed growth relative to other high-wage economies with more equally distributed incomes. Instead, U.S. growth accelerated.

There is a far more plausible explanation for both America's relatively faster growth and rising income inequality: American innovators were more successful than their counterparts elsewhere. Simply put, they *earned* their success.

## Chapter 5

# THE MYTH THAT INVESTMENT OPPORTUNITIES ARE IN SHORT SUPPLY

Recognizing the weaknesses of both the incentives-don't-matter and the-successful-didn't-earn-their-success arguments, proponents of redistribution, chiefly Larry Summers, have put forward a third argument for redistribution. They claim slow growth leaves the economy with a shortage of investment opportunities—so-called secular stagnation. If they are correct, then presumably we can shrink income inequality by taxing, redistributing, and consuming income that would otherwise be invested—namely, business profits and the income of high-income households—without slowing growth and reducing employment.

Fear of secular stagnation—the supply of savings permanently exceeding the demand for investment—assumes investment waits for demand. After all, why would producers add more capacity until growing demand fills their existing capacity? The theory also assumes that unused savings are indicative of a dial-back in consumption stemming from a lack of confidence, which diminishes the need for investment. From this narrow perspective, confidence-driven demand is the only constraint to growth.

Some advocates of this view want the government to borrow and spend idle savings. Others want the Federal Reserve to expand the money supply until prices rise and real interest rates drop below zero in order to discourage saving.

With bank deposits sitting unused despite near-zero interest rates and a history of banks making reckless subprime mortgages, these arguments seem reasonable on the surface. But the facts and circumstances do not fit the conclusions.

There is no evidence of a long-term decline in investment—quite the opposite. When intangible business investment has been counted properly, investment has risen as a share of GDP (see Figure 1-4, "U.S. Investment in Intangibles as a Percentage of GDP").[1] With Silicon Valley on fire and a world full of "capital deepening" opportunities—that is, the opportunity to increase productivity by investing more capital per worker—it seems unlikely that a lack of investment opportunities constrains growth.

An imbalance of unused savings stems chiefly from large and persistent trade deficits where exporters, like China and Germany, loan America the proceeds from the sale of goods to Americans rather than using those proceeds to buy American-made goods that employ Americans. Taxing successful Americans and American companies won't mitigate this imbalance.

Today, with savings sitting unused in a world full of investment opportunities, the economy's capacity and willingness to bear risk—namely, the economy's equity—constrains growth. The shift from exogenously driven growth to endogenous innovation-driven growth, a flood or risk-averse offshore savings that demand equity bear the risk of putting those savings to use, and the now-recognized inherent instability of the financial system put additional strain on the economy's capacity and willingness to bear risk. This slows growth despite a surplus of risk-averse savings. Without more equity to bear risk, proposals to redeploy unused risk-averse savings—increased government borrowing and spending, a larger tax burden, and negative interest rates that discourage saving—are unlikely to accelerate growth and will do more harm than good in the long run. Under the current circumstance, the economy will have to grow the old-fashioned way—by earning it. It must gradually take the risks necessary to produce more equity and grow faster.

Theoretically, the government could take risks on behalf of the economy. But, in truth, government risk-taking is unlikely to be successful—far less likely than private sector risk-taking. And the private sector is likely to dial back risk-taking, at least in part, to compensate for the increased risk its government bears.

## Investment Need Not Wait for Demand

During the Great Depression, Harvard economist Alvin Hansen, one of the most influential economists of his time, feared that slow population growth and a resulting lack of investment opportunities would result in chronically high unemployment or slow wage growth. He feared households would continue to save for retirement, down payments for homes, and college for their children, but without faster growth, there would be more savings than investment.

To achieve full employment at the highest possible wage, the economy must deploy all its resources. It must either consume or invest its output. If consumers reduce consumption and increase savings, investors must borrow and invest the additional savings to maintain full utilization of the economy's resources. Otherwise, growth will slow if savings sit unused. When growth slows, unemployment rises and wages fall relative to the economy deploying all its resources.

Wages and unemployment are two sides of the same coin. Theoretically, the economy can always reach full employment by lowering wages. It simply spreads a given amount of GDP over a greater number of workers.

If growth slows and unemployment rises, the value of the output labor would have produced if the economy had employed it is lost forever. Labor has no shelf life, and the economy doesn't have enough storage capacity to continue producing output in a downturn. It shuts down production and lays off workers, and output is lost forever. There really are no unused savings.

Keynes feared that a shock to the economy, like the terrorist attacks on 9/11 or the financial crisis, could send the economy into a self-reinforcing tailspin. A fearful economy would dial back consumption and increase saving. This would slow growth. Slower growth would cause investors to dial back investment, workers to lose their jobs, and asset values to fall. When that happens, consumers and investors save even more. Keynes called this the "paradox of thrift."

With no apparent self-correcting mechanisms, Keynes believed increased government spending, even if it were wasted, would boast demand, raise confidence, and break this vicious circle. Since the output will be lost forever if unemployed, it doesn't matter if the government employs the labor to make candy and give it away—better to consume the lost labor than waste it.

While Keynes saw weak demand as an arbitrary condition, a by-product of unexplainable "animal spirits"—namely, confidence that ebbed and flowed—Hansen feared slowing population growth could make weak demand a permanent condition. To redeploy idle resources, Hansen believed the economy should permanently increase government investment until the economy finds new investment opportunities. Summers has made the same proposal.[2]

Summers fears savings had grown increasingly difficult to deploy in the lead-up to the financial crisis. He speculates that the economy needed both the real estate bubble in the 2000s and the tech bubble in the 1990s to drive investment beyond their logical levels in order to employ savings fully.[3]

In addition to slowing population growth, Summers also fears the rapid decline in the cost of capital goods reduces the need for savings.[4] But the cost of investment increasingly skews toward high-priced, properly trained talent rather than low-cost plant and equipment (see Figure 1-4, "U.S. Investment in Intangibles as a Percentage of GDP").

In another version of Hansen's argument, President Clinton's former labor secretary, Robert Reich, fears that the tendency of the rich to save rather than to consume all of their income leads to idle savings that slows growth and reduces wages or employment.[5] Reich's argument, like Summers's, runs counter to the evidence. America, with more income inequality than other high-wage economies, grew faster before the recession and has recovered faster since—the opposite of his conjecture. A recently published study by the Organisation for Economic Co-operation and Development (OECD) on the impact of inequality on growth finds that "drawing on harmonised data covering the OECD countries over the past 30 years . . . no evidence is found that those with high incomes pulling away from the rest of the population harms growth."[6] Rather than letting savings sit idle, it is clear that America's rich have invested more productively than investors elsewhere. Neither Summers's nor Reich's added concerns seem credible.

Fears of secular stagnation rest on a number of assumptions. Chief among them is the notion that investment waits for demand. But the iPhone, for example, created its own demand. Innovation is like mining for gold. It can create value at any time. Once innovation is introduced, competitors must respond or face losses. Investment begets competition and competition begets investment in a self-reinforcing feedback loop that drives further investment with no need for increased demand whatsoever.

No surprise, the evidence runs counter to the notion that investment waits for demand. Despite slow growth, Internet-related and intangible investment has increased as a share of GDP (see Figure 1-4, "U.S. Investment in Intangibles as a Percentage of GDP"). Hansen's fear that the world had run out of investment opportunities in 1939 seems quaint with the benefit of 20:20 hindsight.

The former Federal Reserve chairman Ben Bernanke is also skeptical that investment merely waits for demand. Though he acknowledges there is a surplus of savings, he points out that it is unreasonable to expect a lack of investment opportunities to constraint growth. Bernanke reasons:

It's hard to imagine that there would be a permanent dearth of profitable investment projects. As Larry's uncle Paul Samuelson taught me in graduate school at MIT, if the real interest rate were expected to be negative indefinitely, almost any investment is profitable. For example, at a negative (or even zero) interest rate, it would pay to level the Rocky Mountains to save even the small amount of fuel expended by trains and cars that currently must climb steep grades. It's therefore questionable that the economy's equilibrium real rate can really be negative for an extended period.[7]

Bernanke also reasons that even if America is unable to utilize its savings fully, the demand for investment in the emerging world should consume any surplus savings as less-developed countries work to catch up with America's level of investment per worker and per dollar of GDP.[8] America has one of the highest levels of capital investment per

worker in the world and, correspondingly, one of the highest levels of
GDP per worker. The nation's high productivity has demonstrated the
value of additional capital investment to the rest of the world, and they
are eager to imitate us.[9]

It is true that political risks in less developed countries like China
and Mexico increase investment risks. And economists have claimed
increased risk is the reason other countries have failed to achieve the
same capital per worker as that of America.[10] But with investment
pouring into China, Mexico, and other low-wage economies, it's hard
to believe political risk continues to be a significant risk to investment
in these countries. More likely properly trained talent and the economy's capacity and willingness to bear risk limit investment despite a
surplus of capital deepening investment opportunities.

Rather than blame a lack of investment opportunities for the surplus of savings, Bernanke blames the trade deficit for the surplus of
savings flooding into the United States and "international headwinds"
for temporarily holding back investment.[11]

In China, for example, where households save upwards of 50
percent of their incomes,[12] the economy has more savings than it needs
for productive investment, and subsequently exports savings to the
United States. It does this by running trade surpluses. It saves the proceeds from selling goods to Americans and loans these proceeds to
Americans, chiefly by buying safe government-guaranteed debt,
instead of buying American-made goods that employ Americans.
Germany does the same thing. The United States is consequently
flooded with savings from nations that save more than they invest—
chiefly, China, Germany, and previously Japan (before Japan's population aged and started consuming its savings). Bernanke is surely
correct that an increase in the supply of savings has driven down interest rates.

However, other than "temporary headwinds," which sounds like a
euphemism for saying investment waits for demand and demand waits
for unexplainable animal spirits, Bernanke never explains why, with a
surplus of savings, the global economy doesn't expand to put the available pool of savings to work, as it has in the past, especially at near-zero
interest rates. Clearly, the economy has bumped up against other constraints to growth besides a shortage of investment opportunities.

# The Economy's Capacity and Willingness to Bear Risk Constrains Growth

A variety of constraints can restrict the economy's growth—such as a lack of new ideas, a shortage of labor or properly trained talent, less savings than opportunities for investment, and limits to the economy's capacity and willingness to take risk. As the economy bumps up against one of these constraints, it affects the economy differently. When labor binds growth, wages and inflation rise. When properly trained talent limits growth, income inequality rises. As the economy bumps up against savings constraints, interest rates rise. When the economy stumbles on breakthrough ideas—like the airplane, the telephone, the microchip, or the Internet—growth accelerates as follow-on ideas become easier and, therefore, less risky to find. Similarly, growth slows as breakthroughs grow long in the tooth and the pool of add-on opportunities becomes increasingly "fished out."

The available set of ideas and the amount of properly trained talent change slowly. In the intermediate term, then, the economy typically expands until it bumps up against either its savings or its capacity and willingness to take risk.

Investment is composed of two features—the cost needed to fund an investment and the risk of gains or losses. Typically, these two components come part and parcel with each other. An investor who funds an investment bears the risk and captures any gains or losses.

But this need not be the case. Investors can and often do separate the two components. Savings—namely, production that has not been consumed—can be used to fund investment. The ownership of existing assets—namely, the value of future cash flows—can be used to underwrite risk. Like any insurer, risk underwriters capture any gains from an investment but give up ownership rights to future cash flows to make policyholders whole in the event of losses.

A homeowner, for example, typically makes a down payment equal to 20 percent of the value of the house and borrows the other 80 percent. Homeowners agree to pay back the mortgage first and keep whatever value is left over when they sell the house. The investment is funded with first-to-be-repaid debt and last-to-be-repaid equity, where debt largely funds the investment, and equity largely bears the risk of gains and losses.

To protect the bank's loan, the bank has the right to sell the house, if necessary, to recover its loan. The bank's mortgage loan is "over-collateralized," as the house is worth 20 percent more than the loan. Because of this agreement, the homeowner captures 100 percent of the gain but bears 100 percent of any losses up to 20 percent of the value of the house. Over-collateralization protects the lender from losses unless the value of the house falls more than 20 percent. This arrangement protects the lender from bearing the risk of loss. The homeowner's equity bears almost all the risk, while the bank's depositors fund almost all the investment.

Investors willing to bear risk invest as last-to-be-repaid equity holders either by investing their savings directly or by pledging their existing assets—their ownership rights to future cash flows—as collateral in order to borrow and spend risk-averse savings. In the case of a mortgage, the homeowner sells one asset (a house, bank deposits, or other financial assets) and buys another: the last-to-be-repaid 20 percent ownership in a house.

So, two factors can limit investment in the intermediate term: the economy's capacity to fund investment, chiefly with risk-averse savings, or its capacity and willingness to bear risk—namely, the amount of unpledged collateral owned, and the willingness of its owners to risk losing their ownership of that collateral.

Notwithstanding psychological ebbs and flows, the economy's capacity and willingness to bear risk is largely a function of its equity: its assets—that is, its ownership of future cash flows—less the debt it owes risk-averse savers. While it is true that the lenders' ownership of debt is also an asset of the economy, it's an asset unwilling to bear much risk.

In general, the more equity an economy owns, the more risk it is able and willing to take. It is no surprise that the value of the U.S. stock market is significantly larger than those of Europe and Japan relative to GDP, and the United States' has been the economy most willing to take risk.[13]

The economy has a finite capacity and willingness to bear risk. Obviously the economy has a finite amount of assets and equity. Many asset owners are unwilling to bear the additional risk of borrowing against their assets to invest risk-averse savings. They are already taking as much risk as they are willing to bear. As well, asset owners have already pledged some assets as collateral. And risk-averse savers are unwilling to accept some assets as collateral. Taken together, these constraints limit the economy's capacity and willingness to bear risk.

An economy with an abundant capacity and willingness to take risk will expand until it is constrained by savings. In an economy constrained by savings, interest rates will rise until they equilibrate the supply and demand for savings by pruning unworthy investment projects and encouraging savers to save more.

But that's not the economy we see today. Quite the opposite—we see low interest rates stemming from an economy flooded with risk-averse savings stemming largely from a growing trade deficit.

Debt and equity come from different sources. Deferred consumption—namely, savings—chiefly funds debt. Savers tend to be risk-averse. Many would often gladly stuff their mattress with money and earn little if any return rather than take the risk of losing their money. Parents saving for their children's education, for example, are often unwilling to take much risk. Risk-averse savers invest as first-to-be-repaid lenders—that is, as debt holders—often by depositing their savings in banks and allowing banks to make loans on their behalf with their deposits.

Successful investment and innovation chiefly create expected increases in future cash flows, namely equity. A company like Google, for example, created equity through fortunate innovation without much need for investment funded by savings.

While an increase in expected future cash flows can't fund investment, it can underwrite risk that the economy takes with its current production. Only unconsumed production—that is, savings—can be used to fund investment today. Nothing can be teleported back from the future—for example, Google's future cash flows—and used to fund investment today. Buying and selling ownership of future cash flows doesn't change the amount of production currently available for consumption or investment.

An investor can borrow against their ownership of future cash flows, but only if the owner of current production defers consumption and lends it. Just as buying and selling ownership of future cash flows doesn't change the amount of production currently available for consumption or investment, neither does borrowing and lending. It merely transfers production from one owner to another. These transfers allow the economy to use its production more efficiently, but contrary to popular perception, they don't increase production.

Across a spectrum from least risky to most risky, an economy takes risk in three ways: The economy can consume its production instead of saving it without investing. The economy can save and invest its production rather than consuming it. And it can invest its production in riskier investments. Risk-averse savers take more risk by saving less and consuming more of their income. Investors take more risk by consuming less and investing more and by making riskier investments—searching for a cure for cancer rather than merely waiting for growing demand to fill their factories—or by using their assets as collateral to borrow unused savings and taking the risk of using them.

Imagine winning the lottery but not receiving the money until sometime in the future. You may start spending more of your current income in the interim if you weren't already spending all of it, withdraw your savings from the bank and spend it, or even borrow against your assets to spend more. You may even use the proceeds to start making risky venture capital investments.

You would behave similarly if someone made a legal promise to cover your losses with their ownership rights to their future cash flows. The credibility of the contract would be proportional to the amount of future cash flows they pledged as collateral to cover your losses. If someone with no assets made such a promise, it wouldn't have much value because they would unlikely be able to cover your losses should you suffer them.

An economy that has expanded to the limits of its capacity and willingness to take risk dials back risk-taking after a shock, like the financial crisis in 2008, which caused the economy to recognize the financial system was less stable than it thought it was. Shocked to find its capacity and willingness to bear risk overextended, the economy consequently dialed back risk-taking to compensate. As is typical in recessions, consumers and investors cut consumption and saved without investing.

The economy similarly fell into recession in 2000 after the Internet bubble popped and wiped out $5 trillion of the economy's equity.[14] And the economy was slow to recover when the economy feared catastrophic terrorism was a bigger threat than it thought it was prior to 9/11. As the true value of the Internet and the manageability of terrorist threats grew increasingly apparent and the economy gradually accumulated more equity, consumption, investment, and growth recovered.

In a recession, when savings are no longer the binding constraint, interest rates drop to near zero and savings sit unused. Large changes in interest rates produce only small changes in the supply and demand for savings.

Seen from this perspective, weak demand is not a cause in and of itself. It is a symptom of a shortage of equity willing and able to bear risk. If the economy had an infinite amount of wealth, it would have no fear of risk. There wouldn't be any need for it to dial back investment or consumption after a shock to the economy.

Demand does not ebb and flow randomly due to unexplained "animal spirits." Recessions, recoveries, and growth follow predictable patterns, not wholly chaotic patterns consistent with animal spirits.

Government spending in a recession doesn't cause a miraculous increase in confidence that leads to recovery. The reassessment of risk as less than previously feared and the accumulation of equity cause recoveries. If anything, government spending further misallocates resources that the economy must properly reallocate to accelerate growth. This increases risk when the economy is endeavoring to reduce risk and reallocate resources.

That's not to say that people don't overreact in crises or that Keynes's paradox of thrift doesn't amplify downward business cycles. Under those circumstances, short-term Keynesian stimulus may prevent a temporary lull in demand or an overreaction from permanently damaging the economy. A bankrupt General Motors, for example, can permanently cede market share to foreign manufacturers, which it may never recover. Presumably, consumers and investors will grow more optimistic about their future if they see that the government is successfully mitigating permanent damage that the economy could otherwise avoid.

But the financial crisis represents more than just a temporary lull. There was a permanent reassessment of the inherent instability of the financial system with lasting consequences on growth. That's one reason recoveries are typically slow in the aftermath of financial crises.[15]

If Bernanke is right that near-zero interest rates and a world full of undercapitalized emerging economies create a large set of investment opportunities, then what, other than a lack of equity relative to the need for risk-taking, or a lack of properly trained talent needed to mitigate the risks of investing, holds back investment? Summers's "puzzling" increases in profits and the concurrent decline in interest rates as savings sit idle are not symptomatic of rising rents, lack of competition, lack of demand, or waning investment opportunities, as he claims.[16] They are symptoms of an economy bumping up against its capacity and willingness to bear risk.

Under these circumstances, taxing, redistributing, and consuming economic success dulls incentive for risk-taking that creates equity and slows the accumulation of equity. That slows employment and wage growth. Today the economy needs more equity to grow faster.

# Innovation-Driven Growth Demands Increased Risk-Taking

Historically, savings restricted investment in the faster-growing, capital-intensive, manufacturing-based U.S. economy. Today, however, the balance has shifted. Three factors have converged to make the economy's capacity and willingness to bear risk a binding constraint on growth.

First, the economy is undergoing a broad structural shift from a manufacturing-based, capital-intensive economy, where exogenous factors largely drove growth, to a knowledge-intensive economy where risky innovation largely drives growth. The economy faces a more difficult row to hoe with slower growth and more risk. This transition also obsoletes assets and expertise that reduced risk in the past. Blue chip companies like Kodak and Xerox are gone; AT&T and IBM have been transformed, while General Motors and many other large manufacturers meander along, growing less and less important to the economy as a whole.

At the same time, trade deficits have flooded the U.S. economy with risk-averse offshore savings. To avoid slower growth from leaving resources unused, equity holders must bear the risk of putting these savings to work.

Last, the economy now recognizes both that banking is inherently more unstable than it previously recognized and that this instability is damaging to the economy. The economy has dialed back risk-taking to compensate.

As the economy transitions from an exogenously driven, capital-intensive, manufacturing-based economy to innovation-driven, knowledge-intensive, service-based economy, it taxes the economy's capacity and willingness to bear risk and reduces the demand for risk-averse savings. Self-generated growth is slower, more variable, and less predictable. Investments to find and commercialize innovations are inherently riskier—often one-in-a-million long shots. And much of the assets and expertise that the economy could use to bear or minimize risk are rendered obsolete.

While it is true that diversification minimizes "one-in-a-million" investment-specific risks, most risk-takers—companies, managers, and entrepreneurs, for example—bear very high levels of undiversified risk. To the extent risk-takers are undiversified, investment-specific risks diminish risk-takers' capacity and willingness to bear risk else-where.

Faster exogenously driven growth—population growth, education-driven productivity gains, rural migration to more productive cities, and two decades of pent-up demand from both the Great Depression and the Second World War—reduces economy-wide risks and makes risk-averse savers more eager to fund a larger portion of investment. They demand less collateral. If investors overbuild capacity to satisfy growing demand, in a faster-growing economy, eventually growth will fill unused capacity. When unanticipated circumstances delay growth, it may diminish returns on investment, but eventually growth reduces the risk of losses. That's beneficial to risk-averse savers who are willing to forgo gains to minimize losses.

A shortage of savings further reduces investment risks. When savings limit growth, increases in the interest rate prune less worthy—namely, riskier—investment projects. Previously, when the population was growing faster, a greater share of young consumers, who generally borrow and spend more than they earn, relative to middle-aged savers, who tend to save more than others, limited the supply of savings. At the same time, largely closed trade borders restricted cross-border capital flows.

Structural shifts in the economy—in this case, from manufacturing to services and information—diminish the relative value of assets and expertise that previously underwrote risk. A shortage of risk-reducing assets increases their relative value. These asset include: information, teams of properly trained talent, proven supervision, an infrastructure for commercializing innovations, and synergies with existing businesses. At the same time, as growth transitions to new technology, old assets grow relatively less valuable (see Figure 5-1, "Value of Technology vs. Manufacturing Companies").

The same thing happened when the economy made a structural shift from agriculture to manufacturing. Agricultural technology made a large share of the economy's assets and expertise obsolete. Despite the Roaring Twenties, when the economy was booming as consumers bought automobiles and radios, agriculture faced chronic overproduction and low prices. Farmland became worth much less as collateral.

Figure 5-1: Value of Technology vs. Manufacturing Companies

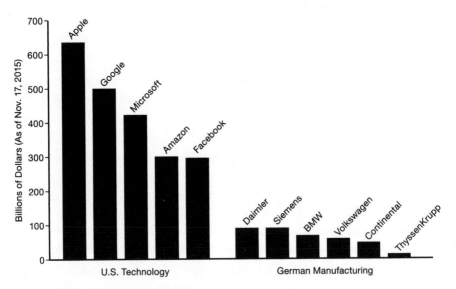

Source: "Does Deutschland Do Digital?" *Economist*, 2015

Nor does innovation create assets that risk-averse savers have typically demanded as collateral, namely assets that are easy to value and sell in the event of a default, such as real estate, inventory, credit card and other accounts receivables, and auto loans. Lenders have been far more reluctant to fund risky venture capital investments or expertise-driven companies with intangible assets—the types of companies that drive growth today—like consulting, accounting, and law firms that are difficult to value and sell.

So far we have not seen diversified portfolios of risky hard-to-value venture investments funded with debt. Instead, we have seen an explosion of subprime mortgages in the United States, the construction of empty cities in China, and the funding of never-to-be-paid-back "government-guaranteed" Greek consumption by German-financed debt. This hardly indicates an adequacy of safe collateral. Quite the opposite: together with low interest rates, they suggest an abundance of risk-averse savings overreaching for traditional collateral. Regardless of the reasons, until risk-averse savings fund innovation, they have sat on the sidelines while equity has funded and underwritten the risks of producing innovation.

At the same time, we see successful faster-growing, high-tech, knowledge-intensive companies, like Google and Apple, generating more cash then they consume and holding cash rather than distributing it to their shareholders or investing it in R&D. In part, they are holding profits offshore to minimize taxes. But it's a misnomer to suggest high-tech companies are accumulating offshore cash simply to avoid taxes as many pundits claim.[17] High-tech companies can and do use intermediaries—namely, banks—to borrow offshore cash and buy back their shares domestically to distribute cash to shareholders. They hold cash regardless. More likely, high-tech companies are holding cash to protect themselves from the risk of unanticipated technological innovations that threaten their businesses.

For a variety of reasons—the broadness of the opportunity set, the fickleness of consumers, the uncertainty of successfully commercializing new innovations, the limited need for capital to scale to economy-wide success, and the difficulty of large slower-growing companies attracting the most productive talent from start-ups with potential for faster growth—technology has grown increasingly disruptive. The time a company remains in the S&P 500 has declined from sixty-five years in the 1920s to only ten years today.[18] And the churn of technological leaders is even greater.[19]

Given the risks, it is imprudent for valuable companies like Google to depend solely on internal development for success despite their valuable assets and expertise. By holding rather than distributing cash, companies maximize their wherewithal to outbid competitors to buy emerging technological threats and opportunities. High-tech companies are likely holding cash to offset risks imposed on them by a capital-light, innovation-driven economy. Pharmaceutical companies are pursuing the same strategy—acquiring and commercializing promising new drug discoveries rather than depending solely on internal development.

One might contend that successful high-tech companies, like Google, are holding cash because they can't find good investment opportunities. But with Silicon Valley teaming with investment, it is hard to believe that Google can't find promising opportunities. More likely, it is keeping its options open because it's too risky not to. To have a significant impact on its market value, Google must acquire and successfully commercialize one-in-a-million breakthrough innovations after the market has revealed their viability rather than merely investing in a portfolio of unproven start-ups.

For all these reasons—a decline in exogenously driven growth, a transition from capital to knowledge-intensity that accelerates obsolescence, innovation-driven growth that increases systematic and unsystematic risks, and a reluctance on the part of risk-averse savers to fund diversified portfolios of risky intangible investments—economic expansion today has less need for risk-averse savings and more need for equity to underwrite risk. Because of these changes, risk-averse savings— which demand others bear the risk of their use—tend to sit unused, even during periods of growth, for lack of equity willing to bear the risk of putting these savings to work.

## Trade Deficits Demand Increased Risk-Taking

In addition to innovation increasing the demand for equity relative to debt, an increase in the trade deficit relative to GDP—which swelled to an unprecedented 6 percent of U.S. GDP prior to the financial crisis—flooded the economy with risk-averse offshore savings and exacerbated the problem of too little equity relative to too much debt.[20]

Trade deficits occur when countries with a surplus of risk-averse savings, like China, Germany, and previously Japan, lend money to the United States to balance trade, instead of buying goods manufactured by producers that employ Americans. These countries export risk-averse savings to import U.S. employment as a matter of strategy.

Risk-averse savings will sit unused unless equity bears the risk of investing or consuming these savings. Without equity to bear the risk of putting risk-averse savings to work, growth slows, unemployment rises, and wages fall relative to what would have been the case if the economy had fully employed all its resources.

To say that borrowing and lending are a problem puts the cart before the horse. The problem is a buildup of risk-averse savings and, worse, that buildup coming at a time when the economy has a shortage of equity willing to bear the risk of putting risk-averse savings to work. Ironically, the solution to a buildup of risk-averse savings, which slows growth if unused, is borrowing and lending.

In part, Americans have compensated for an increase in offshore savings by dropping their own saving rate (see Figure 5-2, "Personal Saving Rate as a Percent of Disposable Income"). As trade deficits mounted, domestic saving rates fell from 12.5 percent of disposable income in the 1970s to 2.5 percent prior to the financial crisis. In fact, many households' saving rates turned negative, as 2.5 percent is the average of rich households with high saving rates and a large share of the income and everyone else, where 40 percent of all households live paycheck to paycheck.[21] With rising real estate values, many households borrowed and spent more than they earned.

While increased business savings partially offset the decrease in personal savings, the decline in personal savings is a chink in the secular stagnation hypothesis, which postulates that savers will continue to save for retirement and other large expenditures regardless of the economy's need for savings. That wasn't true in the lead-up to the financial crisis.

Countries exporting risk-averse savings have found the U.S. government to be an enthusiastic borrower, as lawmakers are eager to

Figure 5-2: Personal Saving Rate as a
Percentage of Disposable Income

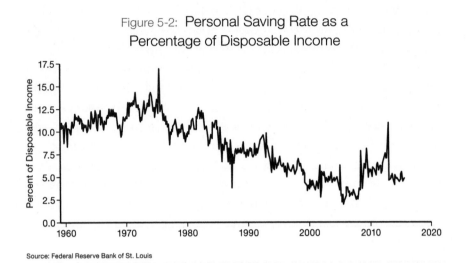

Source: Federal Reserve Bank of St. Louis

spend more and tax less. Increased demand for a somewhat limited amount of government-guaranteed debt pushes risk-averse savers into the private sector who otherwise would have purchased ultra-low-risk government-guaranteed debt. Because of this, a surge in foreign lending indirectly funded an expansion in private-sector lending.

With growing business risk increasing the demand for equity instead of debt, this surge in risk-averse savings chiefly funded subprime-mortgage lending. Ultimately, subprime borrowers borrowed against the rising values of their homes and consumed the proceeds. This spending drove the U.S. economy to full employment despite large trade deficits.

Historically, lenders were reluctant to lend to subprime households. But several confluent events reduced their reluctance. Rising home prices made lenders eager to invest in real estate. This allowed homeowners to withdraw and consume the growing value of their equity.

Homeowners hired Wall Street to find them mortgage financing on the most favorable terms. Wall Street found homeowners no-money-down loans, at below-market interest rates for two years, with the option to refinance if interest rates fell, even if homeowners had poor credit ratings. The banks did this by finding optimistic investors—mainly international investors—who were eager to bear the risk of financing the 20 percent down payment previously financed by homeowners. Investors financed the homeowner's down payment by buying the subordinated tranches of collateralized loans.

Given the opportunity, homeowners logically withdrew their equity by borrowing against the rising value of their homes. Despite popular perceptions, no-money-down mortgages transfer risk from borrower to lender. If homeowners borrow against the rising value of their homes and save rather than consume the borrowed proceeds, they have the option to pay down their mortgage with the saved proceeds if home prices fall, and continue to own their home if that's in their best interest. Or they can default, walk away from their home, rent a near-identical foreclosed house across the street at now-lower prices, and keep their extracted real estate gains.

Ironically, some pundits argue that it was imprudent for poor, financially undiversified homeowners to buy homes in the first place. It's risky for any investors to put all their eggs in one basket. They claim poor homeowners should let rich landlords bear the financial risk of homeownership. That's good financial advice. But for the same reason, poor homeowners should withdraw their at-risk equity—that is, the bank's excess collateral—if given the opportunity.*

The issue is not whether it is prudent for the homeowner to withdraw their equity. It is prudent. The issue is whether it is prudent for the homeowner to increase consumption rather than save their withdrawn equity. It is not prudent to take the additional risk of consuming their proceeds, especially in a real estate bubble.

But, of course, few homeowners saved the proceeds. Most subprime borrowers borrowed against the rising value of their homes and imprudently consumed the proceeds, especially poorer ones with low credit ratings. Poor subprime homeowners behaved as if they had won the lottery and recklessly consumed their windfall.[22]

Falling home prices put a halt to this borrowing and spending. Investors grew reluctant to finance down payments on behalf of homeowners. And the financial crisis led regulators to restrict subprime-mortgage lending, despite senior lenders—chiefly banks—suffering surprisingly small out-of-pocket losses.[23] Subprime-mortgage lending

---

* By and large, a U.S. homeowner only pledges their real estate as collateral. Lenders have no recourse beyond the home.

Figure 5-3:  Mortgage Lending by Credit Score

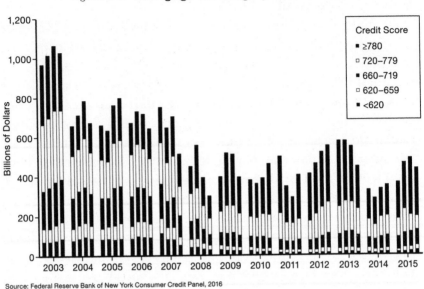

Source: Federal Reserve Bank of New York Consumer Credit Panel, 2016

subsequently ground to a halt and never recovered (see Figure 5-3, "Mortgage Lending by Credit Score").

The economy has yet to find alternative uses for risk-averse savings other than increased government spending. Given the economics of the current information-intensive investment opportunities, companies, on average, have positive cash flows in excess of their need for investment. Risk-averse savers have been unwilling to fund risky innovation and start-ups. Richer families are reluctant to jeopardize their wealth by borrowing to consume or invest more than their incomes will bear. And equity investors are no longer willing to take the risk of making down payments on behalf of subprime homeowners. They have more pressing risks to bear. As a result, risk-averse savings sit unused. Until the economy finds productive alternative uses for risk-averse savings and equity holders are willing to bear the risk of putting those savings to work, the recovery is likely to remain slow.

Slow growth doesn't stem from a shortage of investment opportunities as secular stagnation fears. It stems from the trade deficit flooding the economy with risk-averse savings at a time when the economy needs more equity to bear the risks needed to grow faster. While risk-averse savings sit unused, the subsequent need for businesses and entrepreneurs to create new sources of employment at higher wages places additional demands on the economy's capacity and willingness to bear risk.

# The Instability of Banking Imposes Now-Recognized Risks on the Economy

In addition to a shift in investment from lower-risk capacity expansion to higher-risk innovation that currently requires more risk-bearing equity, and a trade deficit that dumps the world's risk-averse savings into the U.S. economy in exchange for our employment, a third factor now taxes America's capacity and willingness to bear risk. The financial crisis exposed the mistaken belief that the American banking system had grown more stable than it actually is. The private sector has logically dialed back risk-taking to compensate for the now-recognized risk of an inherently unstable banking system.

Since there hadn't been a significant run on U.S. banks since the 1930s, the economy mistakenly came to believe the U.S. banking system was more stable than it was, despite the fact that mathematics proves that banking—borrowing short and lending long—is highly unstable, unlike the rest of the economy. A run on the banks logically cascades to nearly 100 percent withdrawal of deposits.

Banks lend deposits. This maximizes economic growth. Banks don't hold deposits to fund withdrawals. Again, if they did, growth would slow, unemployment would rise, or wages would decline relative to what would have been the case if the economy used all the resources available to it—namely, the risk-averse savings deposited in banks.

When banks must sell assets (portfolios of loans) to fund withdrawals, the price of those assets falls. If depositors panic and run to withdraw their savings from one bank in isolation, other banks can buy that bank's portfolio of loans. This buying supports prices.

But if real estate prices drop 30 percent, as they did in the crisis, and depositors run to all banks, there aren't enough buyers to support the price of loans. As prices fall, banks become unable to sell enough assets at high enough prices to fund withdrawals. Recognizing this dilemma, depositors logically race each other to withdraw their deposits from all banks before asset prices fall and their deposits are worth less. The demand for withdrawals logically cascades to nearly 100 percent.

Because of this well-recognized instability, policy makers created the Federal Reserve as the lender of last resort. In a run, the Federal Reserve prints money and loans it to banks to fund withdrawals, so banks don't need to sell assets, which depresses prices. Once depositors recognize that they can withdrawal their savings, the panic subsides and depositors return their risk-averse savings to the banks. The banks pay off the loans to the Fed and, if it does its job, the Fed burns the newly created money.* *Voilà!* Problem solved.

In the aftermath of the financial crisis, rather than recognizing the effectiveness of the Fed as the lender of last resort, the instability of the banking system shocked the public. The left was eager to blame and punish allegedly reckless bankers.[24] The right was eager to blame the government—namely, the Community Reinvestment Act, which encouraged no-money-down subprime-mortgage lending, and Fannie Mae and Freddie Mac, which drove the implementation of these policies.[25] Neither accepted the truth: banking is inherently unstable.

To rein in the banks, populists on both sides of the aisle agreed to restrict the Fed's ability to function as effectively as the lender of last resort in a panic, as it did in the financial crisis. If banks faced regulatory and political barriers to bailouts, lawmakers presumed banks would compensate by taking less risk. This is true, but at the expense of unused deposits and slower recovery. Throughout history—often when central bankers were nonexistent or less effective—economic recoveries following financial crises have been much slower than recoveries generally.[26]

Unfortunately, many conservatives fail to recognize that, unlike the more robust economy, free market principles that stabilize most markets will not stabilize the inherently unstable equilibrium represented by banking, except at the expense of slower growth. That's why policy makers wisely created the Fed and gave it political independence. Independence makes it easier for the Fed to function as the lender of last resort in panic. Policy makers recognized politicians would likely fight one another to a standstill while Rome burned. Congress, by design, is simply not equipped to act decisively in a crisis.

---

* The Fed did not choose to burn the money.

Shrewd investors recognized that banks were less stable than they had previously believed, and that, despite the Fed's success as the lender of last resort in the financial crisis, regulations and politics had now diminished its effectiveness in a panic. And so, for any given capacity and willingness to bear risk, the economy dialed back risk-taking elsewhere to compensate for the increased risk it now recognized. The economy may not be perfectly rational and dial back perfectly. But we should expect the economy to be quasi-rational and to make some compensating adjustments, no matter how crude its calculations.

It's possible that the Federal Reserve recognizes the risks imposed on the economy when lawmakers restricted its ability to act as the lender of last resort in a crisis. The Fed may have prefunded the liquidity necessary to fund withdrawals as a result. After all, the Fed increased the monetary base from $800 billion prior to the crisis to $4 trillion today.[27] Of that $3.2 trillion increase in the monetary base, $2.6 trillion remains deposited at the Fed as excess reserves—as unlent deposits. These excess reserves are of the same magnitude as the loans made by the Fed to banks to fund withdrawals.[28] In effect, these excess reserves prefund the liquidity banks would need to fund withdrawals in a crisis.

The Fed currently pays 25 basis points (0.25 percent) of interest to banks on their deposits at the Fed. As the economy recovers and banks grow increasingly eager to lend these deposits, the Fed will need to pay a higher and higher interest rate to discourage banks from lending these deposits.

The U.S. banks, however, have seldom needed excess cash to fund widespread withdrawals. Prior to the financial crisis, a major run on the banks hadn't occurred in the United States since the early 1930s. As a result, the Fed may end up paying fifty to one hundred years of interest payments to banks to finance this seldom-used excess liquidity.

Paying fifty to one hundred years of interest is a much costlier method for ensuring liquidity in a crisis than printing money when banks need to fund withdrawals and burning the money when banks no longer need it. At the very least, the economy should recognize the net present value of this increased cost, albeit a cost that merely distorts the allocation of resources because it transfers rather than consumes production.

Perhaps more important, it remains to be seen whether the cost of this prefunding can withstand political pressure if the Fed eventually has to pay banks a high interest rate to discourage them from loaning excess reserves. Politicians and journalists will surely howl. It seems unlikely the Fed can withstand such pressure. Whether it can withstand such pressure reintroduces uncertainty about the Fed's ability to act effectively as the lender of last resort in a future crisis even if it has prefunded liquidity today. This reintroduces more risk for the economy to bear despite prefunding.

Some economists claim that all-equity banking is an alternative that could stabilize the banking system at no cost to the rest of the economy—namely, without the cost of slower growth.[29] This seems highly unlikely. Risk-averse savers are unlikely to accept today's higher returns for funding loans as risk-bearing equity holders instead of ultra-low-risk government-guaranteed depositors. Higher returns are available to risk-bearers today, but risk-averse savers don't accept them. Instead, they accept near-zero returns to avoid putting their savings at risk. Without government guarantees, risk-averse savers would surely just duplicate the ultra-low-risk near-zero returns they currently earn by stuffing their mattresses with savings rather than putting their savings at risk.

If all-equity banks leave risk-averse savers with their savings uninvested, growth would slow—a large cost at the margin. Lost growth could be avoided if equity is currently sitting unused and then steps up to fund loans with equity instead of debt without dialing back risk-taking elsewhere when risk-averse depositors retreated to their mattresses. That might be the case if risk underwriters had let equity sit idle to compensate for the risk of government guarantees of banks that lure risk-averse savings from their mattresses. After all, taxpayers bear those risks.

But why would equity dial back risk-taking in the face of government guarantees of banks? The government made a profit loaning banks $2 trillion to fund withdrawals and making $15 trillion of guarantees (to stop further withdrawals) during the worst bank run since the 1930s.[30] How concerned should risk-bearing taxpayers be about the risk of government guarantees?

While it is true that, to a certain extent, bank guarantees also guarantee loan losses, one way or another the economy already bears that risk. Government guarantees of banks don't change that.

Besides, it's easy to assess and assign loan loss to lenders, as long as we don't try to do it in the thick of the crisis. And if we are more patient than we were in the last financial crisis, there is plenty of time to make the assessment and inflict the losses after a crisis passes.

To believe equity has fully dialed back risk-taking if equity is not sitting idle, one has to believe equity currently has the capacity and willingness to increase prudent risk-taking enough to compensate for the lost growth from leaving risk-averse savings siting idle. That seems unlikely. I argue that the evidence is indicative of a shortage of equity. Summers fears the economy is short on investment opportunities. And with productivity slowing, others are growing increasingly skeptical of the economy's ability to innovate productivity gains.[31] None of those are indicative of large and obvious opportunities to accelerate growth substantially through prudent risk-taking.

Unless equity sits unused in proportion to bank deposits, which seems highly unlikely, all-equity banking merely reallocates equity from underwriting the risk of other endeavors to increasing the stability of banking for no net gain overall, while leaving previously utilized risk-averse savings unused. Unused savings slows growth, which reduces employment or wages. Why suffer permanent recession to avoid intermittent recession?

## Equity Now Constrains Growth

Collectively, a shift from exogenously driven, innovation-driven growth, a structural transition from a capital-intensive to a knowledge-intensive economy, an influx of risk-averse offshore savings, and the now-recognized inherent instability of banking all tax the economy's capacity and willingness to bear risk. Risk-averse savers remain reluctant to fund innovation. And the economy needs more equity to cope with the inherent instability of banking. Meanwhile, the rest of the world dumps their risk-averse savings into the U.S. economy in order to export our employment. Fully utilizing risk-averse savings, which is critical to achieving full employment at the highest possible wages, requires equity to bear risk—namely, collateral that protects lenders against losses. But stretched to its limits, equity remains reluctant to bear more risk. Growth has slowed and risk-averse savings sit unused.

A shortage of equity reduces risk-taking. Less risk-taking slows investment, innovation, and the creation of equity, which are critical for faster growth. Slower growth reduces the demand for middle- and working-class labor, which reduces employment and wage growth. Less risk-taking reduces competition, which shifts profits to investors.

It is also true that the Obama administration's aggressive regulatory posture toward the banks, healthcare, and business more broadly also slows the recovery by further taxing the economy's capacity to bear risk. It can take years for companies to figure out how to operate optimally in a new regulatory regime. In the meantime, companies and investors logically adapt a wait-and-see posture toward the risks associated with untested regulations and new enforcement regimes.

At the same time, greater polarization of the Democrat and Republican parties, growing tension in the Middle East, and a more aggressive Russia and China increase risk by widening the dispersion of potential outcomes and makes them more unpredictable. Compounding matters, the Obama administration lowered the payoff for successful risk-taking by raising marginal tax rates.

Seen from this proper perspective, low interest rates and high corporate profits are not symptomatic of growing rents or a lack of investment opportunities, as some advocates of income redistribution claim. Both are symptomatic of the same thing—the economy bumping up against its capacity and willingness to bear more risk—no different than what we see when the economy falls into recession.

While interest rates may equilibrate the supply and demand for risk-averse savings when savings bind growth, it seems likely the supply and demand for savings grow inelastic (as Summers's secular stagnation also postulates) when the economy's capacity and willingness to bear risk bind growth. In that case, risk-averse savings sit unused in Bernanke's undercapitalized world despite near-zero interest rates.

It is no surprise that one might misinterpreted these circumstances as a lack of viable investment opportunities. Breakthrough innovations like the personal computer, the Internet, or the smartphone open windows of new add-on investment opportunities. These breakthroughs temporarily lower the risk of investing—a welcome break when the economy's capacity and willingness to bear risk limits growth.

Similarly, it's no surprise that properly trained talent restricts growth at the same time as the economy's capacity and willingness to bear risk restricts growth. Properly trained talent is an asset that finds attractive investment opportunities and reduces the risk of pursuing them.

Unlike many recessions, when we often discover risks that shock the economy are not as worrisome as we initially feared and the economy quickly recovers—the fear of terrorism after 9/11, for example—here equity constrains growth with little opportunity for reprieve. The economy can grow only as fast as it creates and accumulates more equity. Unfortunately, this takes time, investment, hard work, and successful risk-taking. There are no shortcuts. No surprise, we have seen a much slower-than-average recovery.

Where success is earned rather than negotiated, the accumulation of wealth is largely driven by the top workers' achievements—which, if successful, increases inequality. The rich create wealth, but use it to underwrite more risk-taking rather than for consumption. When equity binds growth, taxing, redistributing, and consuming income or assets that would otherwise be used to bear risk and increase wealth slows growth by diminishing the economy's capacity for risk-taking. *The more we tax success, the more we slow the accumulation of equity.*

Rather than taxing, redistributing, and consuming success—whether its income or its ownership of future cash flows (i.e., wealth)—we should recognize how difficult and rare the accumulation of equity truly is. It's so rare that it might be uneconomical to produce success systematically. When the economy stumbles upon ideas that produce equity, our goal should be to preserve this equity, rather than taxing, redistributing, and consuming it.

This is why estate taxes make little sense. Successful risk-takers are motivated to build bequests for their children and charity. As a result, they seek to accumulate more equity than they otherwise would if wealth and estate taxes were higher. That unconsumed accumulation of equity is good for the economy. Why de-motivate successful risk-takers from accumulating more equity and consuming less of it? The true cost to society of Bill Gates's or Warren Buffett's owning equity is the cost of their increased consumption, which is tiny in comparison to the value to society of their equity.

Keynes recognized that wealth and inequality accelerate growth. He argued that in the early twentieth century "it was precisely the inequality of the distribution of wealth which made possible those vast accumulations of fixed wealth and of capital improvements which distinguished that age from all others. The immense accumulations of fixed capital which, to the great benefit of mankind, were built up during the half century before the war could never have come about in a society where wealth was divided equitably."[32] The same is true today; the wealthier the economy, the more risk it should logically bear and the faster it should grow.

# Advocates of Income Redistribution Assume an Unbounded Capacity and Willingness to Bear Risk

To avoid acknowledging the critical link between growth and equity, advocates of redistribution postulate a scenario in which the economy's capacity and willingness to take risk far exceeds other constraints. They maintain this unlikely assumption despite the fact that recessions clearly occur when the economy bumps into its capacity for risk-taking, as it did in 2000, 2001, and 2009.

Rather than calling for policies that will accelerate the accumulation of equity, advocates of redistribution, like Summers and Krugman, recommend borrowing unused risk-averse savings to fund increased government spending to increase demand.[33] They insist weak demand is a problem that can be fixed with spending, and not a symptom of a problem that consumption exacerbates.

Advocates of redistribution typically claim the government can assume risk on behalf of the private sector and accelerate growth in a recession—by borrowing and spending, cutting taxes, or buying risky assets such as mortgages.[34] They believe this will pump up demand without the private sector dialing back risk-taking to compensate.

Previously, advocates of increased government spending claimed spending would produce large increases in demand via the so-called Keynesian multiplier effect. But there was no discernible effect on growth after the federal government increased spending from 19 percent of GDP in 2007 to 23 percent in 2011,[35] after cutting taxes from

18 percent of GDP to 15 percent[36] over the same period, and after subsequently increasing publicly held federal debt from 35 percent of GDP in 2007 to over 70 percent by the end of 2012—an approximate $6 trillion stimulus.[37] Instead, we experienced one of the slowest recoveries on record—a permanent drop in demand followed by below-average growth with no rebound typical of other recessions. While it is true that the U.S. economy has recovered faster than Europe's, it has been growing faster than Europe's economy since the commercialization of the Internet, the growth of Silicon Valley, and the differential rise in entrepreneurial risk-taking.

When the economy's capacity for risk-taking binds growth, large increases in unproductive government spending and other schemes that increase risk without creating wealth are likely to result in larger hard-to-recognize dial-backs in private-sector risk-taking than advocates assume. This is especially true when the recession does not stem from a temporary dial-back in risk-taking as is the case today.

While a dial-back may not be perfectly rational—that is, where the private sector fully compensates for any increase in public-sector risk-taking—business leaders who drive long-term growth aren't stupid, either. They surely don't increase investment and risk-taking in the face of increased government spending or a heightened risk of inflation as the logic of Keynesian stimulus demands.[38] In the long run, they dial back.

Krugman, for example, criticizes unconventional monetary policy that calls for printing and distributing money to stimulate growth. He argues: "So why not . . . just drop the [money] from helicopters? . . . A helicopter drop is just like a temporary lump-sum tax cut. . . . We would expect people to save much or most of such a tax cut—all of it, if you believe in full Ricardian equivalence."[39]

David Ricardo, an influential eighteenth-century economist, postulated that if the government borrows to cut taxes or increase spending, taxpayers will save more to pay for future tax increases needed to pay back the debt—that is, that the economy ought to react rationally to what the government does (albeit, in more complex ways than Ricardo imagined). More generally, Nobel Prize–winning economist Robert Lucas's theory of rational expectations postulates economic actors gradually learn to respond rationally to expectations of the future—the expected future effects of economic policy, for example. If policies, like deficit spending and monetary inflation, increase economic risk as the economy nears its capacity and willingness to take risk, the economy will eventually learn to dial back risk-taking.

But then in the next breath, Krugman insists the 2009 fiscal stimulus was too small and called for even more spending, as if the government could take spending risk on behalf of taxpayers, who would not take that risk themselves, without the possibility of an offsetting private-sector dial-back.[40] When the capacity for risk-taking constrains the economy, to assume little, if any, dial-back effectively assumes an infinite capacity for risk. That's far-fetched.

When recessions are brief and temporary, government spending may prevent a temporary lull in demand from permanently damaging the economy. Government spending that avoids avoidable damage may increase private-sector risk-taking.

But when the dial-back in risk-taking is permanent, increased government spending builds a bridge to nowhere. At best, the increased spending has only a temporary effect on GDP. At worst, years of temporary spending to delay an eventual lull in demand further distort the allocation of resources, which reduces long-term growth and slows recovery even more. Under these circumstances, such policies discourage private-sector risk-taking and likely render stimulus far less potent than advocates claim.

Moreover, where offshore economies seek to grow trade surpluses by funding government deficits, as is the case in America today, additional government spending financed by offshore savers may stimulate their economies as much if not more than America's. An increase in the trade deficit to finance increased government spending coupled with an offsetting decline in private-sector spending is unlikely to have much, if any, stimulatory benefits. Advocates of increased government spending simply ignore these hard-to-recognize offsets.

Aside from simply ignoring or denying the possibility of offsetting dial-backs, advocates of redistribution make two proposals to engineer their way around these concerns—increased infrastructure investment and negative interest rates. Infrastructure investment holds out the illusion that the government can make productive investments without incurring much risk—that the government need only pick low-hanging fruit. Productive government investment is no different than productive private sector investment. Both should grow the economy.

Advocates of negative interest rates hold out the illusion that monetary policy can tax risk-averse savers in order to discourage them from saving without inflation having adverse spillover effects on the rest of the economy. Both proposals are designed to contend with trade deficits that flood the economy with risk-averse savings. Expanded infrastructure investment insists the government borrow and use those savings rather than leave them to sit idle. Advocates of negative interest rates seek to tax risk-averse savings out of existence.

A third alternative—restrictions on unbalanced trade, especially when the U.S. economy has no productive use for the rest of the world's risk-averse savings, nor surplus equity necessary to bear the risk of putting those savings to work—is rarely raised by advocates of redistribution. It addresses the problem directly rather than indirectly and, therefore, is less likely to distort the rest of the economy. Distorting the economy increases risk at a time when the economy doesn't have the luxury of spare risk-taking capacity.

Giving lawmakers power over trade may be worse than suffering years of unemployment (albeit perhaps not, if you are unemployed), but such an alternative must be compared with alternatives that also give naive lawmakers more discretionary control over free markets—more infrastructure investment and monetary inflation, for example.

# Increased Infrastructure Investment Is Unlikely to Produce Promised Returns

Recognizing the futility of increased government spending under the current set of circumstances, advocates of government spending have recast unproductive government spending that increases consumption as infrastructure investment that supposedly increases the economy's productivity and subsequent ability to repay borrowed money.[41] Presumably, if the government can make productive investments, it's logical to borrow and spend—no different than the private sector.

While it is true that productive investment is a better use of borrowed offshore funds than unproductive consumption, the same offsetting private-sector reductions in investment likely still apply.[42] This defeats one of the very things advocates of infrastructure spending intend to produce—a large near-term increase in demand.

Moreover, advocates of public investment trump up public-sector returns by ignoring the inefficiencies of using the political process to allocate investment. Free enterprise successfully picks investments by running millions of experiments. Survival depends on producing more value per dollar of cost than alternative products and services. Competition ruthlessly prunes products and services that fail to meet this threshold. Success depends foremost on survival after the fact rather than good intentions before the fact.

The public sector works in the opposite way: it undertakes large investments based on, at best, good intentions before the fact, where investments, once undertaken, face virtually no competition after the fact. Competitors simply can't afford to compete with the unending well of government funding unencumbered by the need to produce profits. Subsequently, there is often no reliable way to define success or failure of government-funded projects and services. Political power, not the economic logic of customer demand, rules the day. Unlike a company, there is no rank ordering of economic priorities. Instead, special interests fight to shape political choices. Ultimately, the political process is a way to garner allocations that Darwinian survival doesn't allow.

Obviously, this process for allocating resources is highly inefficient. The costly wars in Afghanistan and Iraq, the failure of large increases in education spending to boost students' test scores, and the government's inability to rein in the runaway costs of Social Security, healthcare, and municipal labor unions lay bare the inefficiencies of the political process relative to the private sector.

Free enterprise shows us how hard it is to find good investments and how many investment ideas prove unworthy. Rather than taking the difficulty of finding sound investments and the inefficiency of the political process into consideration, advocates for expanding public investment look past these difficulties and inefficiencies by pointing exclusively to specific investment opportunities with theoretically high returns—often projects that are already slated for funding or investments nearing the end of their useful life soon to be on the priority list for funding. This selective focus on success alone assumes infrastructure investments will boost productivity on average despite real-world experience to the contrary.

Moreover, we already invest extensively in infrastructure—on par with other advanced economies. Since the 1970s, U.S. infrastructure investment as a share of GDP has been greater than that of Germany, the United Kingdom, and Italy, for example.[43] So increased investment is at the margin—after we have already funded high-priority projects— where the returns to additional investments are even lower. It's true additional private investment is also at the margin, but the private sector is more likely both to reject unprofitable investments and to cut off funding much sooner.

Given the inefficiency of infrastructure investing, it's no surprise that after Japan boosted infrastructure spending from 4.5 percent of GDP to over 6 percent in 1990 and held spending at that high level for a decade, the increase produced no appreciable gains in productivity (see Figure 5-4, "Government Investment as a Percentage of GDP).[44] Spain's boom in infrastructure spending in the lead-up to the financial crisis left it with a raft of unused airports and other white elephants.[45] A study of 126 countries by the International Monetary Fund (IMF) similarly found "no robust evidence that . . . [public] investment booms

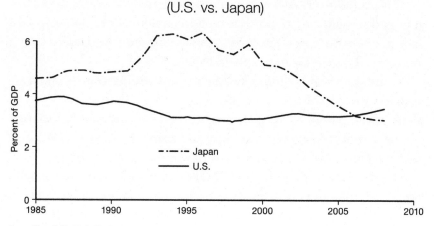

Figure 5-4:  Government Investment as a Percentage of GDP (U.S. vs. Japan)

Source: "Japan's Big-Works Stimulus Is Lesson," *New York Times*, 2009

exerted a long-term positive impact on the level of GDP." The study cautions: "This paper . . . is not about whether in theory public investment . . . could accelerate growth . . . but rather whether in practice, with real governments deciding how to spend the funds and implementing investments, they have in fact accelerated growth."[46]

We already see signs of political compromise that lower already-likely-to-be-low public investment returns. Perhaps subsidizing transportation and subsequent suburban sprawl in a world where carbon emissions are increasing may do more harm than good. And investments in technologies, such as cybersecurity, may produce higher returns than investments in physical infrastructure in an economy where nonphysical goods account for an increasing share of GDP. Nevertheless, advocates of infrastructure spending call for spending more on physical infrastructure rather than nonphysical infrastructure for political reasons—construction employs blue-collar voters rather than a handful of already-in-demand technologists.

Even if the expected returns were adequate, with a limited capacity and willingness to bear risk, the economy would still logically dial back if its government takes more risk. Worse, when the economy has dialed back permanently, government spending just exacerbates and prolongs the misallocation of resources. It consumes resources and risk-taking that the economy would otherwise use to find and commercialize new avenues of growth—alternative uses for risk-averse savings, for example, other than subprime mortgages.

Rather than acknowledging these concerns, advocates of borrowing ignore them and assume rising government debt relative to GDP has no effect on long-term growth, an assumption the Congressional Budget Office, for example, doesn't share.[47]

Ultimately, the economy's capacity and willingness to take risks restricts the size of the economy. If government consumes a greater share of the economy, the private sector will consume a lesser share in the long run. If free enterprise allocates a smaller share of GDP, institutional capabilities critical to growth will evolve more slowly.

If government spending increased demand, all other things being equal, high-wage countries where governments spend more ought to grow faster on average. They do not. On average, they have grown more slowly.

# A Credible Threat of Inflation Is Likely to Slow Growth

An alternative to spending risk-averse saving is to discourage savers from saving. Advocates of this policy recommend taxing saving with inflation. If the cost of saving is high enough, surely savers will stop saving and start spending.

Of course, greater inflation injects more risk into an already over-extended economy. At the very least it makes it harder for decision makers to acquire the information they need to make decisions and distorts the allocation of resources. As such, one should expect the economy to dial back risk-taking, but to do so in ways that avoid taxation via inflation. For example, investors who otherwise may have funded venture capital and innovation may build more real estate instead, which does little to increase productivity and accelerate growth.

Paul Krugman and other like-minded economists blame the inability of interest rates to drop much below zero without a sufficient amount of inflation—the so-called zero lower bound problem*—for the failure of interest rates to equilibrate the supply and demand for savings.[48] Sufficiently negative interest rates—that is, charging savers to save—will presumably discourage risk-averse savers from saving.

Theoretically, the Fed can produce negative interest rates by expanding the monetary base to threaten the economy with price inflation when the economy's capacity and willingness to bear risk grows, the economy subsequently expands, the utilization of labor tightens, and workers can demand higher wages. At that time, if credit growth expands the money supply via the "money multiplier effect"† faster than the economy can add production capacity—whether labor or capital—price inflation will increase.

In the meantime, a surplus of unused savings prevents savers from demanding higher interest rates. With the threat of, say, 5 percent price inflation in the future and a near-zero interest rate today, the real interest rate becomes negative (negative 5 percent in this case). If

---

* Sometimes called a "liquidity trap."
† The money multiplier effect is an undisputed arithmetic fact and is quite different than the disputed Keynesian multiplier effect.

the threat of inflation is large enough—that is, if the interest rate is sufficiently negative—presumably savers will spend rather than save their dollars, and this will accelerate growth in the short run.

While this may be true mathematically, the Fed has been unable to produce price inflation in the aftermath of the financial crisis despite an unprecedented five-fold increase in the monetary base, from $800 billion to $4 trillion.[49] A large portion of that increase in the monetary base, $2.6 trillion of the $3.2 trillion, sits on deposit at the Federal Reserve as excess deposits, neither lent nor borrowed, creating neither growth nor inflation.[50]

Advocates of monetary inflation now insist, "Even though the Fed . . . printed much more money than economists would have thought necessary to offset the impact of the financial crisis . . . it wasn't enough. [Bernanke] balked at taking the next leap: more than doubling the monetary base to $9 trillion."[51] If the Fed recklessly throws the steering wheel out the window and balloons the monetary base to $9 trillion, perhaps it will scare everyone into spending.

But the truth has been revealed: Given the way the Fed currently conducts monetary policy, it takes a massive amount of monetary inflation to produce a minuscule increase in demand—enormous risk for little, if any, benefit. As such, the more relevant question is whether monetary policy can engineer a threat of inflation at a lower cost than the benefit from accelerated growth. Based on recent experience, it appears highly doubtful.

In large part, the Fed has not conducted monetary policy in a way that credibly threatens savers with future price inflation. Quite the contrary—the Fed has repeatedly reassured savers it intends to rein in the monetary base to mitigate credit growth and price inflation when the economy recovers.

Decades of successfully preventing price inflation have given the Fed credibility. Republicans have threatened the Fed's independence if it does otherwise. And frankly, it's hard to imagine the supposedly independent and nonpartisan Fed waging the political battle necessary to tax risk-averse savers with price inflation, much less prevailing. Collectively, these circumstances hardly foster an alarming threat of inflation.

Without a credible threat of future price inflation, loose monetary policy will not stimulate spending in a recession. Such a threat would have credibility only if the Fed had a history of damaging the economy with price inflation after recovery.

And if the Fed had such a history—if it increased the money supply in recessions and refused to rein it afterward—the increased threat of inflation would likely reduce risk-taking elsewhere in the economy, offsetting some or all of its intended effect.[52] For example, rather than merely motivating savers to spend in a recession, monetary policy that inflicted inflation on savers in a recession with certainty might motivate the economy to minimize the risk of recessions. The economy could do this by dialing back investment and risk-taking and subsequently slowing growth and reducing wages for any level of wealth. But again, why suffer permanent recession to avoid intermittent recession?

Advocates of loose monetary policy pretend that expanding the monetary base could have large short-term stimulatory effects through negative interest rates, without long-term consequences—as if we could have our cake and eat it too.[53] In truth, loose monetary policy likely only has short-term effects if it has long-term consequences. Otherwise, when its long-term costs are minimized—that is, if the Fed reins in the monetary base when the economy recovers—monetary policy has only minimal short-term effects in a recession. Even Ben Bernanke now admits that unless quantitative easing is permanent—unless it is guaranteed to inflict inflation on the economy—it is unlikely to have much if any stimulatory effect.[54]

But with the Fed in uncharted waters, never having to have controlled credit growth and price inflation with $2.6 trillion of excess reserves on deposit in the banking system, one has to wonder why there has been little, if any, fear of inflation at all. Surely, the Fed could mistakenly allow inflation even if it intended not to.

One explanation could be that the Fed can't conduct monetary policy in a way that threatens price inflation, even if it wanted to. Borrowing and spending entail risk—by both lenders and borrowers. When the economy's capacity and willingness to bear risk binds growth, savings and money sit unused. Increasing the monetary base just *pushes on a string*.[55] Idle savings, the Fed's inability to produce inflation, and the zero lower bound are all symptoms of the economy's capacity and willingness to bear risk, binding growth.

Krugman agrees that printing money, on its own, won't create inflation. He insists that to produce inflation, the government must increase spending to tighten capacity utilization[56] . . . assuming no corresponding private-sector dial-back, of course!

Rather than admit a real threat of inflation is needed to spark a reduction in saving, some economists point to the 25-basis-point interest rate the Fed currently pays banks to hold unused deposits relative to the 12.5 basis points the government pays on short-term treasuries as the reason banks choose not to lend unused deposits.[57] And this may contribute to the amount of unloaned deposits. But this reason simply begs the question why short-term rates are so low and lenders don't have better alternatives for lending. Rates are low because borrowers are unwilling to use credit by putting collateral at risk that lenders are willing to accept.

Ironically, opponents of loose monetary policy unwittingly lend credibility to its advocates by overstating fears of price inflation prior to the recovery, instead of (long) afterward. When price inflation fails to materialize in the short run, their fears lack credibility. This allows the Fed to continue to expand the monetary base despite its having little, if any, positive effect on growth. In turn, this may hand the Fed and advocates of redistribution the ability to raise taxes on risk-averse savers with price inflation when the economy recovers by failing to rein in the base if they can successfully maneuver politically. Why create this risk unless it significantly accelerates growth?

If the Fed were to unleash price inflation by failing to rein in the monetary base when the economy recovers, price inflation would largely tax the middle and working classes. Middle-income retirees living off their savings and middle-income workers saving for large expenditures like down payments, their children's education, and retirement are predominately risk-averse savers. The wealthy can afford to bear the risk of owning equity, which is largely immune to price inflation, albeit not to other types of losses that middle-income households can ill afford to bear.

While it looks plausible with one eye closed, it seems unlikely that monetary policy can have much stimulatory effect on demand in the short run without slowing growth and diminishing wages in the long run. Despite a four-fold increase in the monetary base, it certainly hasn't produced much benefit so far.

# Conclusion

High corporate profits in the face of low interest rates and unused risk-averse savings are not "rent" that can be redistributed with no effect on the economy, as Summers claims. Nor are they an indication of a shortage of investment opportunities. Quite the opposite—they are symptomatic of increased risk and the economy's limited capacity and willingness to bear it. Weak growth in demand is a symptom of a shortage of equity, not a cause in and of itself.

In the wake of the financial crisis, equity values fell when risk-underwriters, namely equity holders, realized they were overextended. Risk-underwriters dialed back risk-taking by increasing risk-averse savings and leaving them to sit unused. Consumers did this by dialing back consumption; investors dialed back investment. Growth slowed; competitiveness fell; and, once companies cut costs, profit margins expanded. After the economy dialed back risk-taking, equity values rose, and risk-taking gradually resumed, albeit at lower levels and a subsequently slower growth rate. High-tech entrepreneurial risk-taking grew while risk-averse savings sat unused. Faster growth from the former has not been large enough to offset slower growth from the latter.

Meanwhile, slower growth and higher profit margins caused voters to question the status quo. Policy makers responded by raising marginal tax rates on income that would otherwise accumulate as risk-underwriting equity, increasing income redistribution, and tightening bank regulations despite an abundance of unused risk-averse savings that slowed growth. In each case, they did the opposite of what would have accelerated growth in the current circumstances.

Taxing, redistributing, and spending the economy's equity and its returns, whether for consumption or government investment, reduces the payoff for successful risk-taking and slows the accumulation of equity. In an economy constrained by its capacity to bear risk, this diminishes risk-taking, which ultimately slows growth. Slower growth reduces middle- and working-class employment and lowers their wages—the opposite of Summers's good intentions.

Government spending is far less effective at stimulating demand than advocates claim, especially when equity is in short supply—the private sector just dials back. Inflation, which discourages risk-averse savings, is no different. Ironically, if it works, it largely does so by taxing the savings of the middle and working classes or forcing them to take risks they seek to avoid.

Unfortunately, there is no free lunch. With permanent changes to the economy, we must grow the old-fashioned way—by earning it. Today's economy grows through risk-taking, which eventually finds innovations that gradually build institutional capabilities over long periods of time. Rather than crying foul when a large pool of failures stumbles upon success, we should celebrate our good fortune.

## Chapter 6

# THE MYTH THAT PROGRESS HOLLOWS OUT THE MIDDLE CLASS

S ome advocates of income redistribution concede that incentives matter, that the successful predominantly earned their increased success, and that there is no shortage of investment opportunities. Rather than prosecuting these charges, they have instead insisted that success and the progress it creates hurt middle- and working-class wages, whether by destroying their jobs, degrading their values, or competing against them for scarce resources, namely college educations.

The most frequently repeated accusation claims technology hollows out the middle class.[1] Technology, so the argument goes, simplifies semi-skilled jobs while increasing the demand for the most sophisticated skills. Middle-class workers who can do higher-skilled work earn more, but the rest of the workers are pushed into lower-paying jobs. Digital photography, for example, displaced 140,000 Kodak employees, but Instagram had only thirteen employees when Facebook acquired it.[2]

The hollowing-out argument takes other forms. One version of the technology-hollows-out-the-middle-class argument admonishes that robots will eventually replace the middle and working classes.[3] In Thomas Piketty's version, investors collude to keep the return on capital high without restricting the supply of capital—the opposite of how oligopolies operate. He fears high returns—higher than the economy growth rate—will allow capital to accumulate faster than GDP grows, whether or not the capital is needed. Normally, the return on capital exceeds the growth rate only if the economy benefits from more capital, as it has in the past. Otherwise, returns fall to the growth rate, and the amount of capital relative to GDP stabilizes. Rather than making workers richer as the accumulation of capital has in the past, like robots, Piketty fears capital will substitute for labor, eliminate their jobs, and leave them increasingly impoverished.[4]

Liberal economist Brad DeLong complains that Piketty lacks a theory for explaining how returns on capital could remain high independent of the need for capital without restricting the supply.[5] Larry Summers just dismisses Piketty's theory as a "misreading of the literature."[6]

For two hundred years, Luddites have insisted that machinery and technology will reduce employment and wages despite both continuing to grow. Tractors didn't leave starving farmers in their wake. Quite the contrary—the now-lower cost of food made other unfilled jobs more valuable, so valuable that today a Fortune 500 company makes money brewing coffee one cup at a time.

Perhaps robots will finally displace workers rather than increasing workers' prosperity as technology and capital investment has in the past. It's hard to know what will happen when armies of robots build more armies of robots at near-zero cost. One may surmise that even the poor will be rich when the cost of goods is near zero. And so far, wave after wave of robot-like innovation has already rolled in—the agricultural revolution, industrial automation, computerization, and offshoring—with no result other than growing standards of living for everyone.

In another version of the hollowing-out argument, sociologists blame rising income inequality for increasing the unproductive behavior of the working class. For example, the greater uncertainty of employment allegedly makes working-class men less marriageable.[7] Their lower workforce participation allegedly leads to a decline in marriage and a corresponding rise in out-of-wedlock births. The children of single parents are more prone to unruly behavior.[8]

Alternatively, an increase in assortative mating—people with similar levels of education, income, and capability marrying each other—heightens the difference between the children of the haves and the have-nots. The haves devote extra resources—whether money, time, or attention—which allows their children to compete more successfully for an alleged shortage of educational and employment opportunities.[9]

Some sociologists also allege that growing segregation between the haves and the have-nots prevents the have-nots from benefiting from the positive peer pressure of the haves.[10] Ironically, while one school of thought blames the separation of the successful for failing to provide good examples to the middle and working classes, another camp claims that the success of the 1 percent drove an envious middle class to borrow against the rising value of their homes in order to consume too much.[11]

Yet despite these concerns, wages have risen with little change in the shape of their distribution. There has been no discernible hollowing out of the middle class. A closer look at the evidence reveals that wages are growing faster than they appear to be, faster still when we account for shifts in relevant demographics, such as increased immigration and retirement, and that educational opportunities have expanded for minorities and children from lower socioeconomic families.

# There Has Been No Hollowing Out of the Middle Class

The most common of the hollowing-out arguments asserts that technological innovation produced by the success of the 1 percent shrinks the middle class by creating a disproportionate share of high- and low-paying jobs, rather than middle-income jobs.[12] Technology allegedly pushes lesser-skilled manufacturing employees into lower-wage labor, or alternately, into higher-paying service-sector jobs if they are capable to do them.[13] It is true that the U.S. economy has provided lower-paying jobs for a large influx of lesser-skilled Hispanic immigrants. But it has done so with no significant change in the shape of the income distribution of non-Hispanic Americans—both whites and blacks. In fact, median incomes, including those of Hispanic workers, have risen.

While there has been a decline in the percentage of Americans living in middle-income households, it's because the incomes of a large share of non-Hispanic American adults have grown. A recently released Pew Research Center study of America's middle class, for example, shows a decline from 61 percent of adults living in middle-income households in 1971 to 50 percent in 2015.[14] Of the eleven-point decline, four points is from adults in middle-income households moving downward, and seven points is from adults in middle-income households moving upward.

But a closer look reveals that Hispanic immigrants account for three of the four-point increase in the share of adults living in lower-income households. So the rest of America saw a seven-point increase in adults living in upper-income families versus only a one-point increase in adults living in lower-income families—a large upward shift in income.[15]

Were it not for an influx of lower-skilled immigrants, many with limited education and poor English-language skills, America would have seen a disproportionately large increase in the number of high-wage jobs. When the U.S. economy has grown employment two to three times faster than the more manufacturing-oriented economies of Germany, France, and Japan, while providing families with median disposable incomes that are 15 percent to 30 percent higher than that of those countries, it is disingenuous to blame the success of the 1 percent for the lower wages of Hispanic immigrants.

Changes in education patterns also make comparisons with the past misleading. The most logical measure of the economy is a comparison of the work it provides for people with a given level of capability. We cannot compare incomes of current college graduates with incomes of college graduates of the past, when only higher-scoring students attended college. Today 34 percent of young adults earn bachelor's degrees versus only 21 percent in 1980.[16] That's comparing apples to oranges.

An increasing number of retirees also distorts comparisons with the past. Today's average life expectancy is much longer than that of previous generations—but people nonetheless consider sixty-five to be "retirement" age. So a greater share of households are headed by adults who don't work and earn less income, not because they are poorer but because they are richer and can now afford to retire.

Since 1980, for example, the number of families without income earners has grown from 20 percent to 24 percent of all families. This increase largely occurred after the recession in 2008.[17] Almost all of the increase comes from an increase in retirees and disabled workers.[18] Analysis suggests this decline may account for most of the decline in superficial measures of median household earnings.[19]

The income of full-time adult workers is the most relevant measure of the economic health of the middle and working classes. We can't expect adults who don't work full time to garner middle- and working-class incomes.

A real apples-to-apples comparison of white, non-Hispanic full-time workers ages twenty-five to sixty-four shows median earnings—excluding healthcare and other noncash compensation—grew 33 percent between 1979 and 2013, from $37,500 a year to $50,000 a year, excluding inflation* (see Figure 6-1, "Income Distribution, Full-Time White Workers, 25 to 64 Years Old"). The shape of the income distribution curve has *scarcely* changed. There has been no hollowing out of the white middle class.[20] In fact, the portion of full-time workers with low incomes has declined significantly.

There has been no hollowing out of the black middle class, either. The real median earnings of full-time African American workers ages twenty-five to sixty-four—again, excluding healthcare and other noncash compensation—grew even faster: 39 percent, from $26,500 to $36,800, excluding inflation.[21] The portion of full-time black workers with low incomes has also declined significantly (see Figure 6-2, "Income Distribution, Full-Time African American Workers, 25 to 64 Years Old").

While it is true that the earnings of full-time Hispanic workers ages twenty-five to sixty-four (excluding benefits and inflation) have grown more slowly—15 percent, from $26,800 a year to $30,800 a year—this occurred during an explosion in the supply of newly arriving Hispanic

* Inflation adjustments are made using the Personal Consumption Index rather than the Consumer Price Index.

Figure 6-1: Income Distribution, Full-Time White Workers, 25 to 64 Years Old

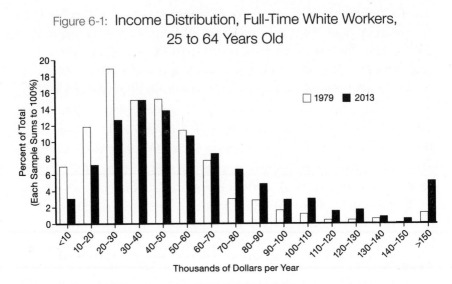

Thousands of Dollars per Year

Source: "Current Population Survey," U.S. Census Bureau, 2013, via Sentier Research, 2015

Figure 6-2: Income Distribution, Full-Time African American Workers, 25 to 64 Years Old

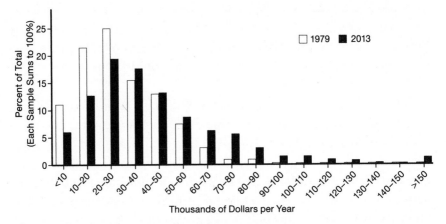

Thousands of Dollars per Year

Source: "Current Population Survey," U.S. Census Bureau, 2013, via Sentier Research, 2015

workers.[22] Rather than bemoaning the fact that today Hispanic incomes are lower than those of other American workers, perhaps we should be amazed that the U.S. economy has been able to provide more than 13 million full-time jobs, with incomes averaging $30,800 a year, to these new job seekers—a third of all the new jobs created by the U.S. economy over that period.[23]

When you add it all up, the truth is clear: The incomes of full-time workers have grown. The portion of full-time jobs has shifted to higher-income work, even more so for non-Hispanic workers. A rapidly expanding population of Hispanic immigrants has taken a disproportionate share of the lower-wage jobs—much to their benefit. Overall, there has been no hollowing out of the middle class (see Figure 6-3, "Income Distribution, All Full-Time Workers, 25 to 64 Years Old").[24] The portion of workers at the middle of the income distribution is virtually unchanged but for an upward shift in incomes.

Figure 6-3: Income Distribution, All Full-Time Workers, 25 to 64 Years Old

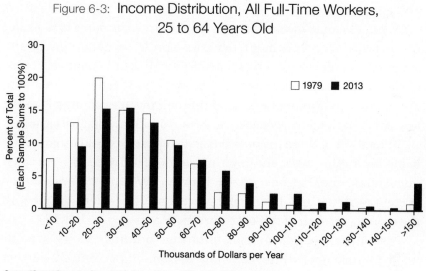

Source: "Current Population Survey," U.S. Census Bureau, 2013, via Sentier Research, 2015

How is it, then, with wage growth of this magnitude that the public believes median household incomes have stagnated? The most frequently cited evidence is highly misleading. The Piketty and Saez data uses tax returns as a surrogate for households despite an explosion of pass-through tax entities in the aftermath of 1980s-era tax reform.[25] These aren't households. As for households, more people live alone and file separate tax returns that support only one person, but, again, Piketty and Saez don't adjust tax returns for the declining number of people the income of each tax return supports.

These basic adjustments, which Piketty and Saez quite shockingly failed to make, have a surprisingly large impact on the accurate measurement of income growth. According to research from the leading income-measurement expert Richard Burkhauser and coauthors, using correct adjustments boosts median household income growth, since 1979, from an apparently stagnant 2 to 3 percent to about 20 percent in 2007—measuring from one economic cyclical peak to another.

Burkhauser's research also shows median household incomes grew an additional seven points because taxable income as measured by tax returns (excluding capital gains) excludes income paid as untaxed healthcare benefits. As the cost of healthcare has increased since 1979, the price of employer-sponsored plans represents a greater share of workers' pay.

Nor does pretax income account for changes to income tax rates and the growth of government benefits—both cornerstones of the government's efforts to redistribute income. It is disingenuous, for example, to pay senior citizens Social Security and Medicare, and then, when they stop working because of this new income, point only to the loss of their formerly earned income as an indication of stagnating wages.

In total, all of these uncontested adjustments—size-adjusted households, healthcare, taxes, and government-transfer payments—increased median household income growth between 1979 and 2007 not from 2 percent to 20 percent, but from 2 percent to 34 percent—in line with the earnings growth of full-time workers.[26]

Applying these adjustments to income quintiles shows virtually identical income growth across the bottom 80 percent: 32 percent growth in the poorest quintile's household income, 34 percent at the median, and 38 percent at the sixtieth to the eightieth quintile. Of course, with the economy growing larger relative to the individuals who compose it, the highest levels of success—which scales with the economy—grew significantly faster, with the top 5 percent growing twice as fast as the median's, and the top 1 percent presumably growing faster still (see Figure 6-4, "U.S. Income Growth by Income Quintile over Time").*

Interestingly, a breakdown of growth by income quintiles into economic cycles shows that virtually all the growth in income inequality occurred in the 1980s and has largely held steady since. No surprise,

---

* The Burkhauser analysis is unable to discern the top 1 percent due to top coding in its data sources.

Figure 6-4:  U.S. Income Growth by Income Quintile over Time

| Income: | 1979–1989 | 1989–2000 | 2000–2007 | 1979–2007 |
|---|---|---|---|---|
| Bottom Quintile | 4.3% | 20.6% | 4.8% | 31.8% |
| 2nd Quintile | 7.0 | 16.7 | 5.2 | 31.3 |
| Middle Quintile | 11.8 | 14.6 | 4.9 | 34.4 |
| 4th Quintile | 15.7 | 12.6 | 6.6 | 38.8 |
| Top Quintile | 29.4 | 13.5 | 4.8 | 54.0 |
| Top 5% | 44.6 | 13.9 | 2.6 | 68.9 |

Source: "Deconstructing Income and Income Inequality Measures," Burkhauser et al., 2013

1980s-era tax reform shifted the reporting of income for tax purposes from corporate to personal tax returns after it lowered personal income tax rates. The 1980s were also a time when women and baby boomers flooded into the workforce and the economy grew relative to the individuals who composed it.*

Demagogues similarly manipulate the commonly cited evidence to claim that wages have stagnated while productivity has soared.[27] This claim also collapses under closer scrutiny. Harvard economist Robert Lawrence, among others, lays out the truth.[28] Four adjustments are needed to compare wages and productivity fairly:

• Income must include all workers, not just production workers.

• Compensation must include health insurance, pension benefits, and other noncash compensation.

• Output and compensation must be deflated using comparable price indices—namely, the Personal Consumption Index, which is used by the Bureau of Economic Analysis (BEA) to compute GDP, the measure of gross output.

• Output net of depreciation, not gross output, is the relevant measure of output. To sustain production, producers must

---

* According to the same study, including realized taxable capital gains has only a small effect on the income growth of the bottom 80 percent. Almost all taxable capital gains accrue to the richest 5 percent of households. Narrowly including only realized taxable capital gains biases the results, however, because a large share of capital gains earned by the middle class is sheltered from taxes. Attempts to include unrealized capital gains, housing wealth, and the growth of tax-sheltered assets such as pension benefits—a more comprehensive measure of capital gains—shows surprisingly large increases in middle and working classes' incomes relative to the highest incomes. But the quality of the data and the ending point—2007, when housing prices were sky-high—makes the analysis hard to interpret.

replace assets as they wear out and grow obsolete. Consuming output is relevant only after companies have replaced assets.

No surprise, when economists make these adjustments, real wages have tracked productivity growth closely just as they have in the past, until the devastating recession of 2009 (see Figure 6-5, "Productivity vs. Wage Growth"). As is common during many recessions, high unemployment temporarily reduces the negotiating leverage of workers who earn less on average until the economy recovers, employment tightens, and wages begin to rise again.

Figure 6-5: Productivity vs. Wage Growth

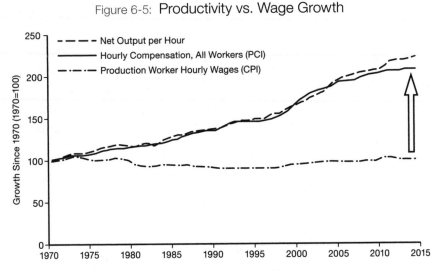

Source: "The Growing Gap Between Real Wages and Labor Productivity," Lawrence, 2015

Demagogues also insist on measuring income inequality despite the fact that consumption is a more logical measure of prosperity than income. With government aid, the poor consume substantially more than they earn. That makes the poor better off. Retirees, similarly, draw down savings and, like the poor, receive income from the government that allows them to consume more than they earn. In both cases, consumption grows without the need for earnings to grow.

At the top of the income distribution, workers and their families consume substantially less than their incomes because they save and invest upwards of 40 percent of their income.[29] Investment benefits others more than it benefits investors. Again, Bill Gates's consumption of resources, which is substantially less than his income, is his true cost to the rest of society.

As such, consumption is a more relevant measure of poverty, prosperity, and inequality. University of Chicago economist Bruce Meyer and the University of Notre Dame economist James Sullivan, leading researchers in the measurement of consumption, find that consumption has grown faster than income, faster still among the poor, and that inequality is substantially less than it appears to be. They conclude:

> After appropriately accounting for inflation, taxes, and noncash benefits . . . median income and consumption both rose by more than 50 percent in real terms between 1980 and 2009. This increase is considerably greater than the gains implied by official statistics.
>
> Similarly, we find strong evidence of improvement in the material well-being of poor families. After incorporating taxes and non-cash benefits and adjusting for bias in standard price indices . . . tenth percentile . . . consumption . . . grew by 54 percent during this period.
>
> Over the past three decades, consumption poverty fell by nearly ten percentage points (a decline of more than 75 percent), indicating substantial improvement in material well-being for the poorest families during this period. Square footage [of bottom quintile housing] rose by over 200 feet . . . since 1989. The share of bottom-quintile individuals with . . . central air conditioning rose . . . from 15 percent to 54 percent. Much of this increase happened after 1999.[30]

Measures of consumption paint a more robust picture of growth than proper measures of income.

Misleading income measures assume tax returns—including pass-through tax entities—represent households. They exclude faster-growing healthcare and other nontaxed benefits. They fail to account for shrinking family sizes, where an increasing number of taxpayers file individual returns. They don't separate retirees from workers. They ignore large demographic shifts that affect the distribution of income. Nor do they acknowledge that consumption is much more evenly distributed than income.

More accurate measures show faster income growth, especially for non-Hispanic workers, and wage growth that parallels productivity growth. In the long run, wages can't grow faster than productivity. Fair measures show that the consumption of the poor is growing faster than median wages. They also show that there is no hollowing out of the middle and working classes.

If advocates of income redistribution had a stronger argument, they wouldn't need to resort to misleading measures of income to strengthen their case.

# The Growing Success of Women Has Reduced the Value of Marriage

While some use superficial measures to claim a hollowing out is occurring, others point to sociological theories. In these versions, technology doesn't hollow out the middle class, nor does it reduce the value of work, per se. Rather, disruptive technologies reduce the certainty and continuity of middle-class employment. As the breadwinning skills of men grow less reliable, men's value as husbands declines. Mothers are less inclined to marry the unreliable fathers of their children.[31] In turn, single motherhood makes sons unruly and daughters prone to single motherhood—that is, prone to unproductive behavior that makes it harder for children to succeed, which reduces their upward mobility. Essentially, advocates of redistribution blame the success of the most successful workers for the failure of marriage among the middle and working classes.

It's an odd conclusion to reach. If work grows less reliable, one ought to expect two-earner families to grow more valuable as a buffer to temporarily lost income. In truth, women's wages have grown faster than men's, and this has made women less dependent on men. That's a good thing.

If technology and the success of the 1 percent create employment opportunities, and women choose to take advantage of those opportunities, only a cockeyed logician would blame technology and the people who create it for the failure of men and women to get married. It would be odd, to say the least, to cap the success of the 1 percent because middle- and working-class women were using their newfound independence not to get married or raise their children to be as productive as they used to raise their children to be.

As women have become more independent, the marriage rate has declined. That may not be a bad thing. It may very well be the case that some men are ill suited to be parents, and that those mothers who choose not to marry the fathers of their children are doing what is in the best interests of their children—banishing low-quality fathers from their families. Years ago, they might not have had that choice.

A different version of the sociological argument, one put forward by Charles Murray[32] and Harvard's Robert Putnam,[33] blames the increasingly unproductive behavior of the middle and working classes on the geographical separation of the wealthy from the rest of society rather than on economic uncertainty. Separation allegedly reduces opportunities for the middle and working classes to see successful examples of productive behavior. Rather than taking responsibility for leading their less successful neighbors, the most successful workers retreat to their private enclaves and leave the rest of the community to behave as they see fit.

There is some evidence that select groups of poor children and families benefit from moving to richer neighborhoods.[34] Nevertheless, one can hardly blame families from running away from communities fraught with unproductive behaviors.

Since 1980, for example, the share of children born out of wedlock has skyrocketed. Today 71 percent of African American children, 53 percent of Hispanic children, and 29 percent of white, non-Hispanic children are born to single mothers; versus 69 percent, 42 percent, and 22 percent, respectively, in 1999; and 56 percent, 24 percent, and 9 percent, respectively, in 1980.[35] One can't help but fear that destructive social behaviors are more contagious than much-harder-to-achieve constructive behaviors, especially among naive and impressionable children. Those who can move are just shielding their children from bad examples.

Given this disparate behavior, is it any wonder, then, that Robert Putnam's own peer-reviewed academic research finds growing resentment in communities where diverse demographics live in proximity with one another?[36] The *Boston Globe* summarizes his unfortunate findings:

> The greater the diversity in a community, the fewer people vote and the less they volunteer, the less they give to charity and work on community projects. In the most diverse communities, neighbors trust one another about half as much as they do in the most homogenous settings. The study, the largest ever on civic engagement in America, found that virtually all measures of civic health are lower in more diverse settings.[37]

Ironically, while some sociologists blame the rich for running away from lower-income neighborhoods and removing their good examples, University of Chicago economist Raghuram Rajan blames the rich for providing a bad example. He argues, with little if any evidence, that the middle and working classes recklessly emulated the rich by borrowing and spending imprudently in the lead-up to the financial crisis—in effect, Rajan claims they were just trying *keep up with the Joneses.*[38]

Mortgages, families, and *keeping up with the Joneses* set many workers on the *straight and narrow*. But it's far-fetched to assume that the growing success of the 0.1 percent—Internet entrepreneurs in Silicon Valley, hedge fund managers in New York, and local entrepreneurs hiding behind their hedgerows rather than living among the poor—drove poorer subprime homeowners in the rest of the country to behave as if they had won the lottery, by borrowing against the rising value of their homes and recklessly consuming their proceeds.

No surprise, work by Rutgers economist Michael Bordo and University of California, Davis, economist Christopher Meissner finds no historical correlation among growing income inequality and increased lending and borrowing—an odd finding if the success of some drives reckless borrowing by others.[39]

Far more likely, subprime homeowners were just taking advantage of circumstances—loose credit in the face of rising home prices—to spend more. If the demand for credit alone had driven increased lending, interest rates would have risen. In fact, they fell. Falling rates in the face of growing demand indicates an increase in the supply of savings leading to an increase in lending and borrowing—and not some exogenous factor, like the success of the rich driving up the demand for credit.

Claims that the rich are to blame for the increasingly unproductive behavior of others are unconvincing. There are too many other, more plausible explanations. Growing prosperity gives people more freedom to do as they please. Erosion of society's respect for authority hurts those who would benefit the most from supervision. The easier-to-achieve status from taking devil-may-care risks is a more contagious role model than the status of hard-earned success, especially for those who can't earn success in more constructive ways. The combination of these trends widens the dispersion of outcomes between those more capable and those less so.

The resulting decline in marriage and religion weakens two important governors of bad behavior. Women rein in men. And religion reins in both.

At the same time, demagogues prey on the naive voters by accusing our leaders—the 1 percent, Wall Street, business, and politicians—of stealing money and slowing growth. Undermining society's leaders by diminishing their moral authority weakens yet another source of governance. It gives people the reason they need to act only in their self-interest, too.

Competition for voyeurs drives the media to set bad examples. TV is full of bad news, scandals, fictional murders, philandering adults, and increasingly dangerous sports. This accelerates the contagion of unconstructive behavior. We scratch our heads and wonder why. And then we have the audacity to blame the growing success of the 1 percent.

# College Credentials Are More Accessible Today Than They Have Ever Been

Yet another line of attack blames the 1 percent for diminishing the middle and working classes by successfully competing against them for the best educations—or, at least, the most prestigious academic credentials—by investing more time and money in their children than those with fewer means are able to invest.[40] The growing resources the rich use to better prepare their children allegedly seize educational opportunities that previously were available to others.

Proponents of this argument ignore the fact that the share of white, native-born students at the most prestigious colleges—where one person's admission comes at the expense of another's—has declined significantly, and that these universities have capped the admissions of Asians at about 15 percent.[41] If anything, Caucasians and Asians are working harder because they are competing for a smaller number of admission slots at the most prestigious schools (see Figure 6-6, "Share of White Students at Select Universities").[42]

Figure 6-6: Share of White Students at Select Universities

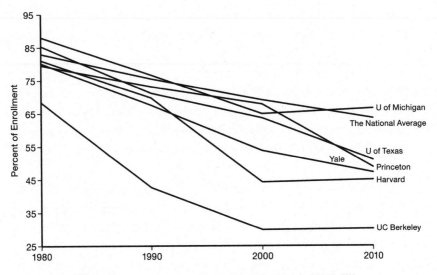

Source: "How America's Top Colleges Reflect (and Massively Distort) the Country's Racial Evolution," *Atlantic*, 2013

It is hard to see how growing income inequality, and not competition for a smaller number of admission slots, is the predominant reason for competition. The 0.1 percent, where incomes have grown disproportionately, aren't large enough to account for many children. And those children were already largely attending the most prestigious schools. More likely, increased competition is coming from upper-middle-class families, where the growth in income relative to the median has been fairly small. Competition for a smaller number of admission slots, not growing income inequality, has driven increased preparation.

Attending college is like running a marathon. It doesn't matter much which marathon you enter. What matters is your time. Work by Princeton economist Alan Krueger finds that, except for the most disadvantaged students—that is, students who are the beneficiaries of affirmative action—students with the same test scores and other characteristics who graduate with a lower class ranking from a top college and those who graduate with a higher ranking from a less prestigious college achieve the same career success.[43]

Enrollment at less prestigious colleges has expanded to meet the growing demand of students with all levels of capability. When there is capacity to educate every student who is ready for college, and to test the capabilities at all skill levels with the most to the least demanding curriculum, it is illogical to complain that the rich are usurping opportunities from others. Quite the opposite—admission rates, enrollment, financial aid, and graduation rates of college students across all socioeconomic backgrounds have increased substantially.

In large part, college is a test of students' preexisting capabilities—both their intellect and their discipline. A degree certifies that its holder is smart enough and diligent enough to graduate with a given class rank. Although separating a person's capabilities from his or her accomplishments is obviously difficult, studies that attempt to separate these characteristics—often by comparing students with similar test scores and other relevant characteristics who graduate to those who fall just short—show that upwards of 50 percent of whatever value college adds comes from this credentialing.[44]

For marginal students graduating from marginal universities, especially if the students have studied marginally useful subjects such as psychology, sociology, English, or history, this credential may be of little value despite student hopes to the contrary. While a recent study shows college may have some value for marginal students,[45] it is generally accepted that it may be of little value for these students, and that if anything, subsidized student loans and financial aid induce far more students to attend college than should (see Figure 6-7, "Value of Education to Marginal Students").[46]

Credentialing is largely a zero-sum game. One person gains the

Figure 6-7: Value of Education to Marginal Students

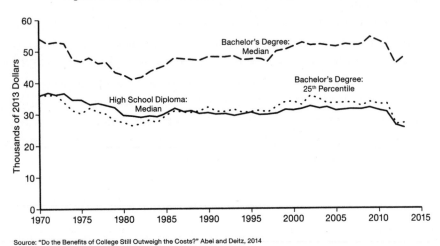

Source: "Do the Benefits of College Still Outweigh the Costs?" Abel and Deitz, 2014

value of a credential at another person's expense. By overemphasizing the importance of college, we now demand average students earn a credential that proves they are merely average. That is, they now need a credential that proves they are not *below* average. That may be good for colleges and professors in the business of conferring credentials, but it is hardly obvious that this is in the best interests of average students.

No surprise, studies estimate that upwards of 30 to 40 percent of college graduates are now in jobs that do not require college degrees.[47] This is an indication that students are earning degrees to prove that they are more diligent than those who don't, but that those degrees aren't providing students much value beyond that.

Larry Summers seems to admit that education has become a zero-sum result. He cautioned, "I think . . . [education] policies . . . are largely whistling past the graveyard. . . . Unless you're doing things that affect the demand for jobs, you're helping people win a race to get a finite number of jobs."[48] If education could truly do for the bottom 70 percent what it did historically for the top 30 percent of students— substantially increase their productivity and ability to add value—it is hard to believe that it wouldn't have a profound effect on employment and GDP, just as it did in the past.

When we pressure every child to prove his or her worth by graduating from college, it no surprise there is a growing demand for help for students who fail to graduate, often students from lower socioeconomic families who are failing to graduate from college at the same rate as students from higher socioeconomic families.[49] Unfortunately, there is an all-too-easy fix for this problem: make the curriculum easier.

But what does it accomplish? Students learn even less, and lowering the bar pressures even more students to earn a credential to prove they are capable enough to earn a degree. Again, who benefits from that, other than the credential-conferring industry? Surely not the increasing number of students who must pay for a de facto rank.

As we pressure more children to go to college, the exclusionary cost of college becomes an increasing concern. The media is full of stories about tuition rising far faster than inflation and students graduating with increasingly burdensome loans. Because of these costs, advocates of redistribution insist that college tuition should be highly subsidized, if not free, for all but the richest students.

The College Board, however, finds that tuition after financial aid for both two- and four-year public colleges is essentially free for students from families with incomes in the lowest quintile. Since 1999 tuition has remained flat, averaging $2,000 to $3,000 per year (in 2011 dollars)—a third of the published tuition rates—for students from families with second quintile incomes.[50] While it's true that room and board adds to tuition costs, it's also true that young people need room and board whether or not they attend college.

According to the College Board, the average student who graduates from a four-year institution borrows $27,000,[51] about the same amount as the average new car loan.[52] Only 4 percent of students incur $100,000 of debt, and 90 percent of those students are doctors, lawyers, business school graduates, and others who have earned graduate degrees in highly paid professions.[53] For those students, payments are limited to 10 percent of their disposable income with the balance forgiven after twenty years—far less onerous than the headlines suggest.[54] Moreover, the Organisation for Economic Co-operation and Development (OECD) estimates the return to an investment in a college education in the United States is more than double that of Germany, France, and Japan.[55] These facts hardly paint a picture of out-of-control costs for middle- and working-class college students.

The more troubling picture is painted by a study published by the New York Federal Reserve, which finds that colleges pocket 65 cents of every dollar increase in government student aid, which they accomplish by raising tuition.[56] Can you imagine how expensive college will be when it's free? We'll need to regulate the cost.

By any relevant measure, college is more accessible today for students from lower socioeconomic backgrounds than it has even been. There are more admission slots available at the most prestigious colleges for non-white students and more tuition aid available for all college students. Credentialing by mastering the toughest majors is available for any student who can earn them. Ironically, the race for credentials is driving a greater share of marginal students to earn degrees of marginal value.

## Conclusion

There is no evidence that technology is hollowing out the middle class. As technology has advanced, every socioeconomic group has grown more prosperous.

The only thing hollowing out the middle class is income growth. When properly measured, median incomes are growing faster than they appear to be, faster still for non-Hispanics. In a ratio of almost 7:1, non-Hispanic workers are moving upward in income rather than downward. Income growth has been slower for Hispanic immigrants, but they have still been the great beneficiaries of this upward income migration of American workers.

By other economic measurements, the middle class is not hollowing out at all. Consumption—the more relevant measure of prosperity—is more evenly distributed and growing faster than average for families with the lowest incomes.

Sociological arguments that the success of the 1 percent is hurting the middle class don't hold water. Claims that the failure of marriage is linked to the success of the 1 percent or that the rich could affect improvements in middle- and working-class behaviors by setting more visible examples are far-fetched. More likely, rising middle- and working-class prosperity is giving people the opportunity to eschew supervision and leadership and to do as they please. Unfortunately, it's easier to gain status destructively with a devil-may-care attitude rather than constructively with hard work and moral fortitude.

While it is true that assortative mating has boosted the incomes of richer households, and that these households have invested more in their children relative to other families, it is doubtful that this trend diminishes anyone's educational opportunities. If anything, the share of rich white children in prestigious colleges, where enrollment is limited, has declined.

College enrollment has expanded to satisfy the growing demand from every socioeconomic group. Government subsidies have restrained the price of college for almost every student, albeit at the expense of driving the cost out of control for the government. Today publicly subsidized colleges offer students the opportunity to test their mettle with curriculum of all levels of difficulty. To the extent some students are poorly prepared to graduate from college, it is not because of the growing success of the 1 percent.

The success of America's 1 percent hasn't hollowed out its middle and working classes. It has increased their prosperity. And it has created enormous opportunities for immigrants. In the face of this success, America hasn't closed the doors of higher learning. It has opened them wider, in part at the expense of traditional college-bound students. Perhaps some people have chosen to use their prosperity unproductively, but it is hard to see how the success of the 1 percent is to blame.

# Chapter 7

# THE MYTH THAT MOBILITY HAS DECLINED

No one argument linking the success of America's 1 percent to the slow wage growth of the middle and working classes is persuasive on its own: not the argument that the 1 percent earned their success at the expense of others; not the argument that the new economy hollows out the middle class and causes increasingly unproductive behaviors; and not the argument that the shortage of investment opportunities slows growth. To avoid having to defend these arguments, some opponents of the growing success of the 1 percent try a different tactic: they claim that the middle and working classes have suffered *death by a thousand cuts.* No one thing holds back the middle and working classes or the poor; it's a little bit of everything. Rather than debate the causes of inequality, this line of attack focuses on the effect of inequality.

Simply put, advocates of redistribution charge growing income inequality with impairing the American dream of upward mobility.[1] Mobility—the opportunity for children to advance to higher income levels than those of their parents—has allegedly declined, or at least it has allegedly declined relative to other high-wage economies with more equally distributed incomes, namely the economies of Scandinavia.

Again, it is an odd argument to advance when the success of the U.S. economy has created an alluring new home for more than 40 million foreign-born adults, their 20 million native-born adult children, and their 20 million native- and foreign-born children. No other high-wage economy has done more to help the world's poor than the U.S. economy. Regardless, advocates of redistribution press on.

If proponents of redistribution are correct, and the success of America's 1 percent comes at the expense of the middle and working classes, we should see mobility declining. Yet, even with immigration, there is little evidence that mobility has declined. Or even that mobility in Scandinavia, the supposed paradise of redistribution, is better than in the United States.

## Mobility Hasn't Declined, nor Is It Much Different Than Mobility in Scandinavia

If mobility hasn't declined or if other high-wage economies with more equally distributed incomes aren't significantly more mobile than the U.S. economy, then how can advocates of redistribution use mobility to indict rising income inequality and the growing success of the 1 percent?

The argument that rising inequality has harmed mobility isn't credible. Economists Raj Chetty, Emmanuel Saez, and others recently completed a definitive study of American mobility. They concluded: "Contrary to the popular perception, we find that percentile rank-based measures of intergenerational mobility have remained extremely stable for the 1971–1993 birth cohorts"—the last cohort of children to become adults with earnings.[2] In fact, "the probability that a child from a low-income family (e.g., the bottom 20%) reaches a fixed upper income threshold (e.g., $100,000) . . . has increased," as has the probability of low-income children attending college.[3]

They go on: "Putting together our results with evidence from Hertz (2007)[4] and Lee and Solon (2009)[5] that intergenerational mobility did not change significantly between the 1950 and 1970 birth cohorts, we conclude that rank-based measures of social mobility have remained stable over the second half of the twentieth century in the United States. . . . If anything, intergenerational mobility may have increased slightly in recent cohorts."[6] Figure 7-1, "U.S. Income Mobility over Time," summarizes their findings.

Figure 7-1: U.S. Income Mobility over Time

Source: "Is the United States Still the Land of Opportunity?" Chetty, Saez et al., 2014

Comparisons with other countries with more equally distributed incomes don't support the argument that rising inequality harms the upward mobility of the middle and working classes, either. An often-cited comparison of U.S. and European mobility reported by the *New York Times* found that U.S. mobility was identical to the most mobile societies in Europe with the most equally distributed incomes—Denmark, for example—for all but the poorest Americans (see Figure 7-2, "Income Mobility: U.S. vs. Denmark").[7]

Figure 7-2: Income Mobility: U.S. vs. Denmark

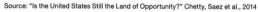

Source: "American Exceptionalism in a New Light," Jantti et al., 2006, via *New York Times*, 2012

The difference in mobility rates between poor Americans and Scandinavians may be overstated. A recent flood of poor immigrants into Scandinavia and the rest of Europe has proved increasingly difficult for these countries to integrate.[8] Unemployment rates and high school dropout rates among these groups are extremely high—hardly an indication of upward mobility.[9] Mobility studies track the success of children after they become adults. Without many grown children, Europe's and Scandinavia's failures to provide mobility to these children is not yet measured by their mobility studies.

The relative lack of mobility among the poorest is concerning, to be sure. No less troubling, a recent Brookings Institution study on U.S. mobility found lack of mobility among the American poor was largely confined to poor African American children (see Figure 7-3, "Effect on Race on Income Mobility").[10] Surprisingly, poor white Americans raised in families with incomes in the bottom quintile had a near-equal chance of advancing to any other quintile of income. The author describes a near-equal chance of advancing to any other quintile of income as "an opportunity utopia."[11] In fact, the study found that the mobility of poor white American children was virtually identical to, if not better than, the mobility of poor Danish children (see Figure 7-4, "Mobility of Poor White Americans Compared to Denmark's Population").[12]

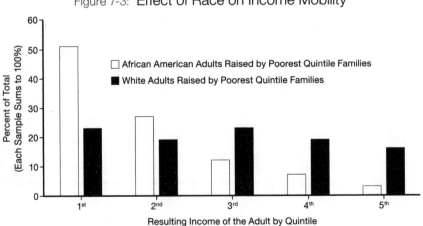

Figure 7-3: **Effect of Race on Income Mobility**

☐ African American Adults Raised by Poorest Quintile Families
■ White Adults Raised by Poorest Quintile Families

Percent of Total (Each Sample Sums to 100%)

Resulting Income of the Adult by Quintile

Source: Brookings Institution Social Genome Model, 2013

Figure 7-4: Mobility of Poor White Americans Compared to Denmark's Population

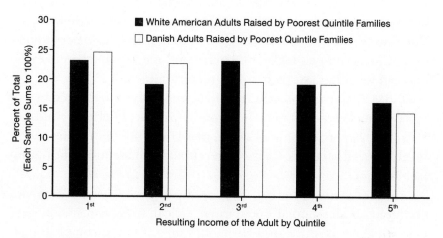

Sources: Brookings Institution Social Genome Model, 2013; "American Exceptionalism in a New Light," Jantti et al., 2006, via *New York Times*, 2012

Figure 7-5: Effect of Marriage on Income Mobility

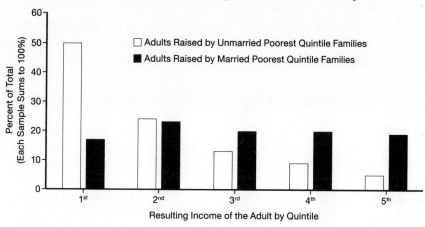

Source: Brookings Institution Social Genome Model, 2013

The U.S. data provides clues for the troubling mobility of poor African Americans. High single parenthood is likely a factor. The Brookings Institution study found that single parenthood has an overwhelming effect on the mobility of poor children.[13] Married parents gave poor children a nearly equal chance to advance to any level of income. In fact, "four out of five children who started out in the bottom income quintile—but who were raised by married parents—rose out of the bottom quintile as adults. Meanwhile, kids raised in the bottom quintile to never-married parents had a 50 percent chance of remaining at the bottom" (see Figure 7-5, "Effect of Marriage on Income Mobility").[14] The Chetty and Saez mobility study also found that single parenthood on its own accounted for over 60 percent of the variability in mobility between the different communities they examined.[15]

Today 50 percent of African American children are raised by unmarried mothers—66 percent of poor African American children. Less than 20 percent of poor white, non-Hispanic children are raised by unmarried mothers.[16] That differential will have a significant impact on mobility.

Another factor affecting the mobility of poor African American children is high school dropout rates. African American students are twice as likely as white, non-Hispanic students not to complete high school on time—30 percent versus 15 percent, respectively—and up nearly 10 percent over the last nine years.[17] The proportions are higher still among poor children. Completing high school on time is a strong indication that a student will be a reliable worker—the kind of worker who is upwardly mobile. Failing to complete high school, even if a student later earns a General Educational Development (GED) certificate, has a significant effect on upward mobility.

Figure 7-6: Effect of Dropping Out of High School on Income Mobility

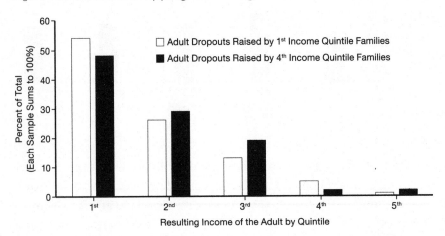

Source: Brookings Institution Social Genome Model, 2013

No surprise, the Brookings Institution study finds that dropping out of high school has the same detrimental effect on mobility for all but the highest-income children (see Figure 7-6, "Effect of Dropping Out of High School on Income Mobility").[18] If the child of rich parents drops out of high school, unlike other children, the rich parents can give the child money to offset the high cost of dropping out of high school.

Based on these results, it seems apparent that the greater prevalence of single motherhood and high school incompletion among poor African Americans likely accounts for the lower mobility of poor African American children.[19] The upward mobility of poor African American children parallels those of children born to single mothers and of high school dropouts (see Figure 7-7, "Comparisons of Causes of Poverty").

Figure 7-7: Comparisons of Causes of Poverty

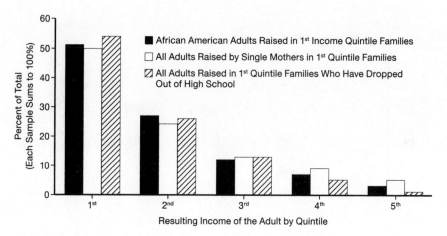

Source: Brookings Institution Social Genome Model, 2013

It's highly unlikely that the rising success of the 0.1 percent has much, if any, effect on single motherhood and high school completion rates. Taxing the rich won't improve mobility per se. To improve mobility, the factors reducing the mobility of poor African Americans must be addressed directly.

For all but the poorest children—children from families who are often plagued by poverty for much deeper reasons than simply low earnings—the key to upward mobility is getting trained properly, putting that training to work, and working hard. The most valuable training by far is on-the-job training. The value of on-the-job training is difficult to measure, however. While college learning may be less valuable than it is often assumed to be, it's the most measurable surrogate of training that we have.

By that measure, the Brookings Institution study finds that, for all but the poorest children, graduating from college has a near-identical benefit to students, regardless of their family's income (see Figure 7-8, "Effect of a College Degree on Income Mobility").[20] Again, the Brookings Institution's study results reflect the findings of the Chetty and Saez mobility study, which found that a child's socioeconomic status explains less than 10 percent of the variation in mobility between the communi-

Figure 7-8: Effect of a College Degree on Income Mobility

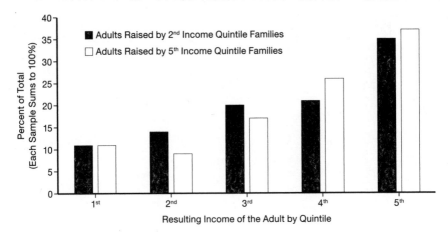

Resulting Income of the Adult by Quintile

Source: Brookings Institution Social Genome Model, 2013

ties they examined.[21] U.S. upward mobility appears to be available to those with the aptitude and determination to earn it.

If America's middle and working classes are suffering death by a thousand cuts, we don't see evidence of it where we would expect to: in decreasing income mobility. Despite a host of efforts that would have increased mobility and the rise of the middle class when they were first initiated—the widespread expansion of education and testing, subsidizing college, and passing laws against discrimination, for example—income mobility has not declined in the aftermath of their implementation. Nor has mobility declined despite an increase in divorce and single motherhood, which are recognized as diminishing the productivity of grown children.

Nor has American income mobility declined relative to other higher-wage economies. In fact, income mobility in America is virtually identical to the most mobile high-wage economies, even those of Scandinavia, for all but the poorest minority children who face an entirely separate set of challenges. And even in Scandinavia there is evidence that mobility among the poor is faltering, too.

Faced with the evidence on mobility, even Miles Corak and his coauthors—whose findings underpinned the Obama admiration's infamous Great Gatsby curve, which purported to demonstrate that income inequality reduces mobility—now admit there are "almost no differences in upward mobility between Canada, Sweden, and the U.S."[22] These three countries, which Corak and his coauthors have studied in detail, were widely dispersed along the infamous Gatsby curve.

## Conclusion

Over and over again, we find that commonly held beliefs that support income redistribution don't stand up to closer scrutiny. Advocates of redistribution, like Diamond and Saez, admit that "long-term responses [to taxes and incentives] are needed to calibrate optimal tax formulas" but nevertheless cavalierly propose redistributive tax policies that assume incentives have no long-term effect.[23] They look at the enormous differences in growth and prosperity between countries like East and West Germany, North and South Korea, Communist and non–Communist China, and the U.S. relative to Europe, along with cross-country comparisons of high-wage economies that indicate the opposite, and have the audacity to assume income redistribution plays *no* role in slowing growth over the long run.

With the S&P 500, Forbes 400 richest Americans, and CEO tenures turning over faster than they ever have, Piketty insists cronyism is rising without even taking the care to make sure his cited evidence adds up.

In the face of this tumult, Summers, Reich, and Stiglitz claim competition is waning. If resources were being increasingly misallocated on the scale necessary to account for growing income inequality—$1 trillion by Summers's estimate—it is hard to imagine why American growth would be accelerating relative to other high-wage economies.[24]

Summers's claims that the American economy has run out of good investment opportunities flies in the face of a steady rise in investment when intangible investments—people who engineer a better future—are properly included. To make his case, he simply ignores risk-averse savings flooding into the U.S. economy because of the trade deficit. More likely, properly trained talent and the economy's capacity and willingness to take risk—namely, equity—and not savings or investment opportunities, now limit growth.

Advocates of redistribution insist that technology and other forces are hollowing out the middle class and incomes are stagnating, when scrutiny of the evidence shows neither to be the case. They blame the success of the 1 percent for destroying middle- and working-class marriages, which seems far-fetched to say the least, and for overpreparing their children to take coveted educational opportunities when the share of rich white Americans in prestigious colleges where enrollment is limited is declining.

Were any of these charges true, upward mobility would have declined. It has not. In truth, we can't find high-wage economies where mobility is better.

What's going on here? We repeatedly find commonly held beliefs widely supported by top academics that crumble under closer scrutiny. Given how often the truth is at odds with popular opinion, one can't help but wonder why this keeps happening.

It's no surprise that advocates of redistribution overreach to attack the status quo. The economy evolves much like biology. A multitude of random experiments finds innovations that prove to be more valuable than existing alternatives. Competition ruthlessly prunes away less valuable alternatives. Economic outcomes are robust because they exist for sound reasons—they have proved to be more valuable than alternatives.

Criticism of the status quo is akin to dismissing wolves and deer as mistaken by-products of biological evolution. Given the complexity of evolution and its results, how could anyone possibly know what the best theoretical alternatives could be? The burden of proof ought to lie with the critics of the status quo. The benefit of the doubt must go to the wolves and deer that have evolved from and survived against real-world alternatives.

That's not to say the economy is optimized, or that ill-conceived manmade restrictions on it couldn't be improved. There is always room for improvement. But one must judge conjectural improvements skeptically and with great respect for the robustness of the existing system.

Unfortunately, few voters have the time or the interest to learn economics. And when they make the time, they look for evidence that reaffirms their views. Brief viewer attention spans require headlines that provoke audiences. So, *all news is bad news.* "Middle-class incomes have stagnated and the rich are to blame" is a lot more provocative than the contrary alternative.

With severe time constraints, there is little time to debate policy or to educate the public, much less to defend the status quo. Mass markets ignore those who try. Complex analysis has a tiny audience. The public is too busy "keeping up with the Kardashians," so the defense of the status quo is weak.

Because of these constraints, leaders must formulate policy for the sake of marketing. They must put forward proposals that get the voter quickly to yes. This reduces every solution to, "If you vote for me, I'll give you more," where "more" is either more government spending or lower taxes. Obviously, this leads to suboptimization.

Rather than using analysis to uncover the truth, leaders are forced to use analysis to maximize the persuasiveness of their proposals. As a result, analysis does little more than promote simple-minded policies, and myths abound. We're told that companies don't succeed by catering to our needs; allegedly, they succeed by stealing from us. If this is true, then there is no cost to redistributing their ill-gotten gains. We're told that payoffs for success don't motivate entrepreneurial risk-taking, innovation supposedly bubbles up randomly, so redistributing lucky gains doesn't slow growth. And we are told that the economy responds to incentives immediately, so cutting taxes at the current spending levels won't blow a multitrillion-dollar hole in public finances. The list of far-fetched assertions—assertions that much of the public takes seriously because our leaders sell them as if they were serious—goes on and on.

Even academics, on whom we depend for the truth, write papers with provocative conclusions intended to garner media attention based on simplifying assumptions overlooked by a time-pressed media and their audience. This is how Piketty and Saez can make headlines with research based on income tax returns, which the public understandably assumes represents household income. Yet scholars have shown there are actually significant differences. Unfortunately, by then, nobody is listening.

Because the academic review process largely focuses on the quantitative findings of a paper, researchers enjoy a great deal of rhetorical latitude when writing introductions and conclusions, which often fail to summarize their papers' objective findings. For example, International Monetary Fund researchers can report that redistribution doesn't hinder growth in the introduction and conclusion of their paper, without acknowledging that their own evidence indicated income redistribution policies more aggressive than United States' hurt growth.[25] A time-pressed media reports no more than the headline.

Critical differences in circumstances are easily overlooked, often intentionally so by propagandists. How else to explain why advocates of income redistribution point to the higher growth in the 1950s when marginal taxes rates were higher as evidence that higher payoffs don't affect the amount of risk-taking? It doesn't take a PhD to understand circumstances in the 1950s were vastly different.

In the 1950s, the economy was recovering from the Great Depression and the Second World War. The value of mass production and related capital investment, education, rural migration, and population drove economic growth more so than today. Corporate investment, where marginal tax rates were lower, drove growth rather than the entrepreneurial success of individuals, where marginal tax rates were higher. The government was much smaller relative to the economy so, ultimately, taxes paid were much lower relative to GDP despite higher marginal rates. Circumstances are very different today.

Winston Churchill understood the problem well. He cautioned, "A lie gets halfway around the world before the truth has a chance to get its pants on."[26] Provocative misperceptions leave truth seekers to sort through the complexities long after the audience has moved on to a continual stream of new provocations. Sadly, lies divide us instead of the truth uniting us.

Critics of the 1 percent are wrong. The 1 percent has not achieved their growing success through cronyism or other uncompetitive practices to negotiate a greater share of GDP at the expense of the middle and working classes. The evidence shows the top 1 percent of income earners have largely earned their success by commercializing successful innovation.

If misallocated resources caused rising income inequality, America's growth would have likely slowed relative to other high-wage economies with more equally distributed incomes. It has accelerated.

Technological innovation produced by the success of the 1 percent hasn't hollowed out the middle class. Despite employing a tsunami of lesser-skilled Hispanic immigrants, the technologically advanced U.S. economy has produced more higher-paying jobs than lower-paying jobs—especially for native-born Americans.

If anything, the success of the 1 percent has *increased* the demand for middle- and working-class labor. U.S. employment has grown two to three times faster than that of Europe and Japan, and provided Americans with incomes that are 15 to 30 percent higher.

Nor is a portfolio of suboptimal economic afflictions, each one difficult to detect on its own, likely to account for growing income inequality. Were that the case, economic mobility should have declined. But U.S. economic mobility is nearly identical to other advanced economies and has shown little, if any, decline over time. In fact, the upward mobility for the poorest North American workers—Hispanic immigrants—has been enormous.

A near-unlimited worldwide supply of lesser-skilled labor—from both immigration and international trade, where the U.S. economy buys lesser-skilled labor and sells higher-skilled labor—holds down the wage growth of the middle and working classes, not the success of the 1 percent. Given a near-unlimited supply of labor, growth manifests itself as increased employment rather than as increased wages.

Meanwhile, as the economy grows larger relative to the individuals who compose it, economy-wide success grows larger relative to the vast majority of workers—doctors, schoolteachers, and waitresses, for example—whose success is limited by the number of customers they have the capacity to serve. Innovation increases the demand for middle- and working-class labor without taking anything away from them.

Fortunately, America has enjoyed unique success producing innovation that benefits the broader economy. This success is an asset, not a liability. At the very least, success increases the tax base and the demand for local services. It also accelerates growth.

Higher payoffs for successful entrepreneurial risk-taking, which is critical to the creation of innovation, have had a large compounding effect that gradually produced the institutions necessary for innovation and faster growth. These assets include companies with valuable on-the-job training; communities of experts; the creation of a pool of highly motivated, properly trained talent; and equity necessary to underwrite risk-taking. Dampened risk-taking and success in Europe and Japan has slowed the production of these assets.

As payoffs for economy-wide success have grown larger, talented workers have flocked to produce information- and technology-related innovation where success requires a minimal amount of capital investment. More resources devoted to lottery-like, all-or-nothing investments will increase income inequality even if the expected value of risk-taking declines on average.

Despite growing demand for properly trained talent, a shortage of talent hasn't restricted growth; a shortage of properly trained talent has. America is full of suboptimally trained talent.

Slower growth, higher corporate profits, lower capital investment, slower productivity growth, and idle risk-averse savings in the aftermath of the financial crisis are not indicative of a shortage of investment opportunities, as secular stagnation postulates. They are indicative of an economy constrained by its capacity and willingness to bear risk. Innovation, the now-recognized elevated risk of bank withdrawals, and an avalanche of new regulations strain our capacity and willingness to take risk. At the same time, large trade deficits dump risk-averse savings from China, Germany, and others into America's economy. Without more equity to bear the risk of using risk-averse savings, these savings sit idle. Unless these savings are loaned and borrowed, idle resources slow growth, lower employment, and pressure wages.

In an economy driven by risk-taking and innovation, the accumulation of equity underwrites risk and accelerates growth. Equity, which bears the risk of losses, restricts growth and competitiveness. With more equity, America took the risks that built institutions needed to accelerate growth. It grew faster than other high-wage economies before the recession and has recovered faster since.

Investment *hasn't* declined as "secular stagnation" postulates. Quite the contrary—when we measure investment properly to include the earnings of people endeavoring to improve the future, it has increased significantly over the long run. If long-run growth has slowed, it is likely due to tougher circumstances.

The question facing America today is not how to defeat the success that brought it here, but how to accelerate growth, employment, and wages in an economy constrained by properly trained talent and its capacity and willingness to take risk.

*Part III*

# THE WAY
# FORWARD

## Chapter 8

# OUR MORAL OBLIGATION TO HELP THOSE LESS FORTUNATE

F inding improvements to the economy is difficult. Like biological evolution, innovators run millions of experiments to find and commercialize new ways to use the economy's resources more effectively. Alternative uses compete fiercely with one another for survival. The surviving alternatives exist because they're better. As such, criticism is cheap, mistakes are costly, and improvements are dear.

That's not to say we can't find and make economic improvements. That's exactly what innovators do. But before someone criticizes the economy and alleges "improvement," he first ought to try to innovate and compete successfully. It's humbling. The robustness of the status quo should be respected. And proposed improvements should be viewed skeptically.

But even if the dubious claims of advocates of greater income redistribution are mistaken, one can still make a strong moral case that the talents of mankind belong to mankind, and not just to the lucky recipients of those talents. It's true that innovation bubbles up from a larger pool of workers who have endured the arduous training necessary to serve customers effectively and have taken the risks needed to find and commercialize hard-to-find innovations. But it is also true that God-given talent amplifies the value of these efforts.

Like all moral arguments, the suggestion that the talents of mankind belong to mankind raises questions. For example, can we coerce the talented into working on behalf of others? Clearly, there is a complicated, perhaps even contradictory hierarchy of values involved in the claim that the less fortunate deserve something from the rest of us. But that doesn't mean the argument has no merit. For the sake of argument, perhaps one need only assume that the talents of mankind belong to mankind and ignore the other complications.

Those who oppose redistribution argue that the goal of equality of outcomes is harmful and that the more desirable goal should be "equality of opportunity."[1] But the opportunity for a person who starts life with a low IQ, emotional problems, or a troubled childhood predominantly means little more than a low-paying job. Surely, they are *entitled* to more.

While growth is critical to achieving and maintaining full employment, it is disingenuous to depend on growth alone to provide less fortunate workers with steady employment and to alleviate poverty, as opponents of redistribution often do. Less fortunate people will be the last workers hired and the first workers laid off in a recession or a downsizing. And when they are hired, they will be paid low wages that compensate employers and their customers for the cost of hiring these workers relative to more productive alternatives.

Nor can we pretend that entry-level jobs are a gateway to higher-paying jobs for every worker. That might be the case for competent workers, but many less fortunate workers will never progress much beyond an entry-level job. We can blame them for being unreliable, irascible, unhealthy, unmotivated, or for whatever else holds them back, but we also have to admit that many people struggle no matter their good intentions, especially when the payoff for their diligence is low.

The poor need help. And public investments should be made where they can be justified. But justification must be based on tough-minded assessments of the truth, and not on the string of myths tossed out by propagandists looking for whatever justification will stick.

Guilt and compassion for poor children drive a never-ending demand for more welfare. Today many poor, able-bodied families are given as much welfare as they could earn by working—$30,000 per year. Freed from the need to work, many people grow irresponsible, and their children suffer the consequences.

Unfortunately, the cost of motivating reluctant but able-bodied workers to work may be prohibitively expensive despite our compassion for their children. Nevertheless, we must continue to search for better alternatives. The current approach abandons the next generation to intractable problems, and that's unfair to them. But as we search for new approaches, we must beware that our compassion can lead us to do more harm than good. We must recognize the limits of our knowledge and capabilities, and strive to do good rather than merely acting to make us feel better about ourselves.

# Our Moral Obligation to Help Those Less Fortunate Is Not What It Seems

Liberals often cast income redistribution as a moral issue, but if it is, whom are the wealthy obligated to help and what is the most effective way to help them—just less fortunate Americans, or the rest of the world, too? America's poor are among the richest people in the world. According to Pew Research, "more than half of Americans who are poor by U.S. government standards would be middle income when compared with the rest of the world."[2] The U.S. poverty threshold of $23,021 for a family of four in 2011, for example, is 50 percent higher than the threshold of $10 per person per day for global middle-income status.[3]

And America's poor achieve middle-income status by world standards with only eight hundred hours a year of work on average, according to the University of Michigan's Panel Study of Income Dynamics.[4] This is far less work than the rest of the world must do to earn the same amount of money.

That's not to say America's poor don't struggle. But there is a very large pool of poor people to help. Do we prioritize the American poor if they are middle income compared with the rest of the world?

It is hard to believe that geography constrains our moral obligations. If the real reason for helping Americans to the exclusion of others is to *keep the revolution down*—that is, to protect the self-interest of the rich, which is really no moral reason at all—then our moral obligation is to accomplish that objective at the lowest cost possible, so we can use the remaining resources to help others who need it more, wherever they are located.

On the other side of the moral issue, does geographic proximity give America's poor (or middle and working classes) the right to tax America's successful workers for their own gain? In effect, Donald Trump and his supporters insist that America's properly trained talent, investors, and risk-takers must work on behalf of Americans only—that they should be restricted from hiring offshore workers, for example. If that's just, and not just political power, then why don't those same rights extend to the rest of the world? With a near-infinite amount of world poverty, where does our moral obligation end? Do we give money to the rest of the world's poor until we drive American consumption down to the median world income?

If Americans aren't morally obligated to give to the rest of the world's poor until they have nothing left to give, are they obligated to give away a certain percentage of their income—a third to a half—to others? If so, when 40 million foreign-born immigrants and their families make America their new home, does a larger population of poor then split the fixed pool of money and accept fewer benefits per poor family?[5] No advocate of redistribution has advocated that.

And if someone takes the risk and makes the effort to bring forward a valuable innovation, what right do we have to take their success away from them beyond what we demand from any other talented person, as if we had imposed something akin to a tax on talent, for example? Don't people have the right to succeed?

The question of whom we are obligated to help raises the question about how best to help. Every alternative has costs and benefits. Common sense obligates us to choose the alternatives that maximize the benefits per dollar expended.

Were we to give money to the poor until the rich's accounts were drained, it would scarcely make a dent in world poverty, and future generations would be poorer still. That wouldn't be effective. Draining America of incentives to take risk and the equity to bear losses would slow growth and innovation. American innovation has arguably been the most important force pulling the rest of the world out of poverty. According to the World Bank, over half the world's population lived on less than $1.25 a day in 1980. By 2011 growing prosperity cut that to 17 percent of the world's population, an enormous improvement.[6]

In comparison, the impact of the entire charitable effort is lost in the rounding. Despite the West's having donating over $4 trillion to developing economies over the last five decades, the general academic consensus is that this aid has had little, if any, impact on growth.[7]

The world's poverty is near infinite. Our only hope of alleviating it comes not from giving charitably, but from making investments and producing innovations that increase prosperity. This is especially true of the cutting-edge U.S. economy, where American innovators predominantly drive increases in standards of living for Americans and the rest of the world. Perhaps investment is the only way to improve the lives of the poor.

For redistribution to make sense, the benefits of redistribution must be greater than the cost of both the diminished incentives and the foregone equity. In a world where entrepreneurs and their investors capture less than 20 percent of the value they create, perhaps even less than 5 percent, if you subtract the investment they make and the taxes they pay from their share of income, tradeoffs favoring redistribution over investment and risk-taking are unlikely to make economic sense.

Yet advocates of redistribution perform few, if any, calculations about the tradeoff between the returns to public investment, which seem to produce surprisingly little at the margin, and private investment that has produced enormous increases in standards of living for everyone. Ironically, it is likely that the moral imperative to help others leads to overreach that drives down returns on public investment at the margin.

Instead of focusing on the dog—talent's moral obligation to get the proper training and bear the risks that grow the economy and increase wages—moralists focus exclusively on the tail, that is, on reducing the resulting consumption of those who succeed. To earn that consumption, the 0.1 percent must overcome slim odds of success by creating five to twenty times more value for others than they capture for themselves. If successful, they must pay taxes on a large portion of the value they capture. And then they predominantly invest and donate what remains.

In light of the value investment, risk-taking, and properly trained talent create for others, it is disheartening to hear well-intended but misguided educators urge our children to take advantage of their privilege and devote their lives to their passion—even work that takes jobs from lesser-skilled workers—rather than maximizing the societal value of their talents. They maximize the value of their talents[8] by getting the training, undertaking the arduous responsibilities, and taking the risks necessary to serve their fellow man, whether through business or some other means.If their work is what will bring success to others, shouldn't talented individuals be working as hard as possible?

When we give money to the poor instead of making investments and producing innovation that increases prosperity, it is important to recognize who foots the bill. By and large it's the middle and working classes who bear the cost. The economist Scott Sumner, author of the blog *TheMoneyIllusion,* summarizes the truth succinctly. He argues:

> You cannot put the burden of a tax on someone unless you cut into his or her consumption. If the Obama tax increases did not cause Gates and Buffett to tighten their belts, then they paid precisely 0% of that tax increase. Someone else paid, even if they wrote the check. If they invested less due to the tax, then workers might have received lower wages. If they gave less to charity then very poor Africans paid the tax. I have no idea who paid, but I'm pretty sure it wasn't Gates and Buffett.[9]

A person's consumption is his or her true cost to the rest of society, not his or her income. To the extent taxes reduce a person's investment and risk-taking rather than his or her consumption, the cost of the taxes are borne by others, namely workers and customers. When the middle and working classes foot the bill in this way, it's critical that they gain more benefits than the costs they bear.

Just as we can't assume that all redistributive taxes increase middle- and working-class prosperity, neither can we evaluate social spending in a vacuum. It's one thing to support greater government spending on the poor, or other investments that help the public—such as infrastructure. But it's quite another to support an increase in overall government spending.

It's disingenuous to debate spending outside of the context of spending priorities. In the long run, increased government spending crowds out the private sector. After all, resources can only be used one way or another. Ultimately, free enterprise, not government, has reduced poverty.

Total U.S. government spending, including federal, state, and local spending, has reached 35 percent of GDP with nothing but projected increases as far as the eye can see.[10] Growth has gradually slowed as spending has increased. The economy faces a wave of retiring baby boomers with ever-expanding medical expenditures, while defense spending as a percent of GDP heads to historical lows. At the same time, publicly held federal debt has reached nearly 75 percent of GDP in the wake of the financial crisis, up from 35 percent prior to the recession.[11]

Does subsidizing the incomes of rich old Americans truly help the poor? If increased government spending slows growth, and if the projected growth in government spending doesn't help the poor, then isn't our moral obligation to reallocate spending rather than to increase it?

It is no surprise that advocates cast redistribution as a moral imperative. It creates a powerful feedback loop that engenders never-ending public support. People eager to help the poor may not feel they have enough money or skill to contribute to the poor, but by voting to redistribute the income of the rich, they believe they are helping. From this perspective, it's their moral obligation to support redistribution, and their vote fulfills it.

This strategy for fulfilling a moral obligation is akin to admonishing a healthy driver not to park in a parking spot reserved for the disabled. The one admonishing fulfills his or her moral obligation, at least in his or her own eyes, by demanding morality from others.

Psychological research shows that people tend to reward themselves after they do a good deed—so-called moral licensing.[12] So if people vote to redistribute other people's money, perhaps they feel less guilty about not giving away their own money, getting the proper training themselves, or taking the necessary entrepreneurial risks that help others. Having taken the moral high ground, they feel less obligated to make their own sacrifices.

Climate-change activists, like Al Gore and Leonardo DiCaprio, provide good examples of this kind of self-deception. They fly private jets spewing carbon dioxide while admonishing the public to limit carbon emissions, as if their crusade for the greater good exempts them from the very thing that they insist is immoral.

Of course Gore, DiCaprio, and others like them buy carbon offsets to soothe their guilt and hypocrisy. But it shouldn't. Again, who really paid for their offsets? . . . the rest of the world of course. They could have flown commercial and bought offsets anyway or used the money they would have used to buy offsets to help the world in other ways—to reduce poverty, for example. In either case, the world would be better off—with either less pollution or less poverty. Instead, they spent the money soothing guilt that they needn't have incurred because they enjoyed the very luxuries they admonish others not to indulge. In their case, the power of moral licensing is beyond the pale.

This desire to help others, which relieves personal guilt, creates a powerful dynamic. It drives people to vote for more redistribution without end, no matter how much the government redistributes income, and how little the further benefits may be. The need to help drives people to find a never-ending supply of needy beneficiaries to receive other people's income. "Poor" becomes a relative term. Advocates of redistribution claim families need 40 percent of the U.S. median income to hold up their heads with dignity.[13] When advocates define poverty as relative, growing median incomes increase the amount of money needed for redistribution. America's poor may be among the richest people in the world, but they are nevertheless poor in the eyes of proponents of redistribution.

Immigrants often risk their lives to come to America for a better life. They may be grateful for the opportunities America has provided. But advocates of redistribution compare their incomes with the rest of America's and insist they need more help. While many immigrants are much richer than they were in their native countries, they are still poor by U.S. standards.

And there is a near-infinite supply of poor to help in the rest of the world. It's like the endless opportunities for good deeds in the movie *Groundhog Day*.

Even advocacy to slow climate change contains an element of this human need to find someone to help. Growing global prosperity is the predominant driver of global warming over the next one hundred years.[14] Imagine someone insisting on investing money to mitigate climate change when horses were the chief means of transportation because the invention of the car and the prosperity it would bring would eventually cause global warming. Surely, the more logical answer would have been to make those investments after the invention of the car, when investments were much more productive and the world was much richer. We cannot only find an abundance of poor in the present to help; we can find them in the future, too, even "poor" in the future who are richer than most people are today!

The never-ending quest to help others without careful regard for the costs drains the economy of investment and risk-taking and slows growth, largely at the expense of those who can least afford it—the middle and working classes who depend on work, and not charity, for their incomes.

All but the most ardent libertarians would agree that we have a moral obligation to help those less fortunate. But in a world where the talented are under no obligation to put their talent to good use on behalf of others, and where many of them don't, what alternative do we have other than to pay them to work on our behalf? When one takes our bait and succeeds, rather than ridiculing them, perhaps we should celebrate their success. After all, free enterprise is the salvation of the poor, not charity.

In truth, arguments for redistribution aren't really the moral arguments they appear to be. They both dismiss the needs of the world's neediest poor while simultaneously insisting the world's richest poor need more. Then they downplay the importance of incentives and the inefficiencies associated with government-allocated spending to trump up the value of redistribution. These are political arguments dressed up as moral ones.

Worse, moral arguments drive demand for redistribution whether or not more redistribution is economically logical. People simply soothe their guilt for not giving by demanding that others give on everyone else's behalf.

The moral obligation of the most talented people is not to give up whatever consumption they keep for themselves—the very thing that motivated them to succeed. It's to serve their fellow man by getting the proper training and by using that training to take the risks that produce a better future for everyone. In the end, the best way to help the poor is to help them in the way that we can help them the most—in the case of a talented person, by finding ways to create more value rather than merely redistributing more and more of the value that has already been created.

# Never-Ending Compassion Has Demotivated Work

Ultimately, questions of morality come down to how much we give the poor. At some level of support, surely we have fulfilled our obligation. No one reasonable would argue that we should give everyone more than the median wage. The math simply wouldn't work. Yet, I'm surprised that advocates of redistribution often don't know how much we give the poor, and are reluctant to offer an amount they consider fair.

The amount America gives the poor is surprisingly hard to come by. In 2013 the Congressional Budget Office estimated that the federal government gave non-elderly households in the lowest-income quintile $15,000 per year not counting government benefits that everyone shares.[15] The U.S. Census estimates 2006 state expenditures added about $4,000 per year.[16] Since 2006 a combination of inflation and increased expenditures has increased this amount to $30,000 per year.[17] Among these heavily subsidized families and households, households with disabilities and single mothers with children received about the same amount of aid on average, albeit from different programs.[18] These estimates are in line with other estimates (see Figure 8-1, "U.S. Spending on Income Support").[19]

To say that we are failing to fulfill our moral obligation when we give poor non-elderly families about $30,000 per year of support is an odd claim to make. This amount is on par with the median income earned by full-time Hispanic or African American workers age 25 to 64.[20] Surely, it is not unfair to give households as much as they could earn in the economy, and more than any other country in Europe gives the poor after taking into account the substantially greater taxes European countries impose on benefits.[21]

If anything, amounts this large may do more harm than good. While there are clearly people who legitimately cannot work and people who briefly stumble onto hard times in a crisis—people for whom we must care—there are also many people who will work less if they

Figure 8-1:  U.S. Spending on Income Support

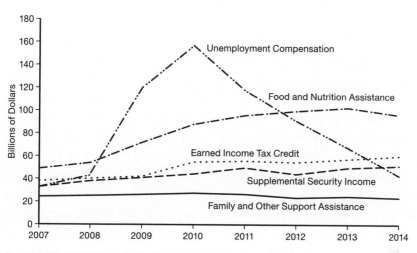

Source: U.S. Office of Management and Budget, "Table 8.5—Outlays for Mandatory and Related Programs: 1962–2020," 2016

earn or receive more. For those people, especially the ones who can't earn much more by working, $30,000 per year will diminish their need to work and sap their motivation to work.

The need to earn a living and hold a job motivates people to act more responsibly. This has large spillover effects that affect the rest of their responsibilities—staying sober, respecting and cooperating with others, and setting a good example for their children, to name a few. Mitigating the need for a large swath of the U.S. population to work will have far-reaching consequences for those who choose not to work.

While many workers will work no matter the disincentives, disincentives to work are in large part a function of one's earnings potential relative to the size of the government safety net on which workers can fall. Workers with high earnings potential and satisfying work logically find welfare less attractive than high-paying work. Conversely, those who are incapable of earning more relative to government alternatives will be less motivated to work, on average.

Advocates of redistribution often point to Scandinavia as evidence that welfare benefits do not reduce incentives to work.[22] Unstated is the fact that Scandinavian wages are high relative to the government safety net.

A Scandinavian economist reportedly told Milton Friedman, "In Scandinavia, we have no poverty," to which Milton Friedman replied, "That's interesting, because in America, among Scandinavians, we have no poverty, either."[23] Scandinavian Americans have median incomes that are $10,000 to $15,000 higher than Americans on average.[24] Their poverty rates are comparable to native Scandinavians, just 6.6 to 7.5 percent in 2010—half the rate of Americans on average.[25] In Scandinavia, high earning potential seems to dampen the effect of welfare on one's work effort, just as it seems to dampen welfare's effects on Scandinavians in America.

There is ample evidence that a worker's earning potential relative to the value of the safety net plays a significant role in many people's motivation to work. The most educated women, for example, have some of the lowest reproductive rates. They seem to prefer work.

The U.S. workforce participation rate of prime working-age Hispanic adult men, ages twenty-five to sixty-four, who, on average, have less access to the U.S. government safety net than American citizens because of their diminished legal status, is higher than that of similarly aged African American men. In 2013 the workforce participation of the Hispanic men was 88 percent versus 75 percent for African American men, despite comparable levels of pay.[26] If the difference between the workforce participation rates of Hispanic and African American men is the result of the demotivating effects of welfare relative to earning potential, then the effects are large, indeed.

Similarly, workforce participation rates rise with educational attainment, which correlates with earnings and earnings potential. Seventy-five percent of male and female college graduates participate in the workforce versus only 57 percent of male and female high school graduates with no further college attendance.[27] The more people can earn from working, the less they value alternatives to work.

The same is true in Europe. The workforce participation rates for men ages twenty-five to fifty-four in the higher-earning Northern European countries are higher than in lower-earning Southern European countries like Italy, where government benefits are high relative to earning potential—90 to 93 percent workforce participation rates in Scandinavia versus 88 percent in Italy.[28]

Consistent with these patterns, the hours worked by Americans and

Europeans have been declining, except among the highest-paid Americans.[29] A recent study by the National Bureau of Economic Research, for example, finds that in America, "the recent increase in long work hours has been concentrated among the highest wage earners: between 1979 and 2006, the frequency of long work hours increased by 11.7 percentage points among the top quintile of wage earners, while falling by 8.4 percentage points in the lowest quintile."[30]

To solve the problem of welfare disincentivizing work, some advocates of increased welfare claim the earned income tax credit (EITC)—which provides government benefits to low-income workers proportional to the hours they work and the money they earn—will increase the motivation of low-wage workers to work by increasing the value of work to them.[31] While surely that's true for some, it will also likely disincentivize others—those who value more leisure over more money—who will work less as they can earn more. As high-wage workers throughout the world have grown more prosperous, all but the highest-paid American workers have worked less.[32]

Money doesn't motivate everyone. Those who are least motivated by money will obviously tend to be poorer.

Today the typical non-elderly household in the lowest-earning quintile works eight hundred hours a year—less than half the hours of a full-time worker.[33] With government benefits, that worker earns more than $30 an hour (see Figure 10-1, "Federal Government Expenditures and Taxes by Household Type").[34] That's far more per hour than the federal minimum wage of $7.25 that advocates of redistribution tout as the true pay of low-wage workers. Thirty dollars an hour is on par with the 2015 U.S. median wage, which was $33.58 including benefits.[35]

Without the prospects of earning substantially more, if they work substantially more, what motivation do they have to work more? Those who can earn substantially more are unlikely to be poor. Only 3 percent of full-time workers, for example, are in poverty.[36]

If an increase in the EITC reduces the motivation for some workers to work more, expanding the ETIC to cover a broader swath of low-wage workers may do more harm than good. Unfortunately, it may be best to keep the EITC limited to those we are most concerned about helping—single mothers with young children and other disadvantaged workers (the handicapped, for example)—rather than expanding it to all workers as some propose. For those for whom we are less concerned, perhaps we just have to accept the fact that they will be poor, often by their own choice.

Many experts, such as the New York University poverty expert Lawrence Mead, are skeptical the EITC will increase work effort overall.[37] Mead bases his skepticism about incentive-based laissez-faire approaches to "workfare," like the EITC, on evidence gathered from field experiments. Mead points to a variety of workfare programs that made welfare conditional on employment—yet very few participated in mandatory employment without high levels of supervision.[38]

In truth, aid to the poor has risen substantially over time with little, if any, increase in work effort. According to the Congressional Budget Office (CBO), means-tested spending and tax credits for low-income households have risen from 1 percent of GDP in 1972 to nearly 4 percent of GDP in 2012 (see Figure 8-2, "Change in Poverty by Source of Income"),[39] with only modest reductions in poverty as measured by market incomes earned. Almost all the reduction in poverty has come from an increase in government aid, not from a corresponding increase in work effort.[40]

Figure 8-2: Change in Poverty by Source of Income

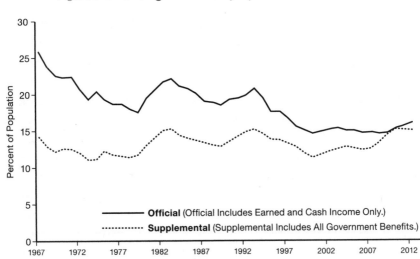

Source: "Trends in Poverty with an Anchored Supplement Poverty Measure," Wimer, et al., 2013

A study of two dozen poor Native American tribes in the Northwest between 2000 and 2010 is quite revealing. Some tribes handed their gambling profits to tribal members, but others did not—a natural, randomized experiment that occurred under fairly uniform economic conditions. Ten out of seventeen tribes that handed casino profits to tribal members saw poverty increase, compared with only two out of seven tribes that did not hand out profits.[41] Poverty among tribes that handed out profits increased four percentage points on average more than Native American tribes nationally—from 25 percent to 29 percent.

According to *The Economist,* the only tribe among the twenty-four that eliminated poverty eschewed per capita payments and instead invested its profits to create new businesses and jobs. A second tribe pursued the same strategy and cut its poverty rate by more than half.[42]

Rather than concede that the availability of work and a low safety net reduces poverty among able-bodied workers, some advocates of redistribution insist that a lack of jobs creates poverty.[43] But if employment opportunities were the primary driver of poverty, poverty rates would have declined significantly leading up to 2007 when the unemployment rate was effectively zero. Instead, during that period, the poverty rate declined only a percentage point or two from its 13 percent to 14 percent forty-year average.[44] Similarly, U.S. Census surveys consistently find that only 10 percent of the non-working poor report being poor because they can't find employment.[45] As well, the continued influx of unskilled immigrants shows that a shortage of work is not the problem.

Others argue that the high cost of childcare makes work uneconomical for low-wage workers.[46] However, the Urban Institute, a credible liberal think tank, finds that the federal- and state-funded Child Care and Development Fund (CCDF) largely subsidizes childcare costs for poor families.[47] The Congressional Research Service estimates that poor families who received childcare subsidies received $4,700 per year on average in 2012 for childcare, not including state funding, which is significant; charitable contributions, such as tuition discounts and scholarships; employer contributions; and tax credits— all of which further reduced the cost of childcare for poor mothers eager to work.[48]

Ironically, childcare subsidies may create a disincentive to work.

There is little to stop two single mothers from caring for each other's children in their own homes and both receiving the childcare subsidy and credit for working.[49] That's a hole so big you could drive a truck through it.

It's hard to look at the macro evidence and not feel deep concern that a safety net, which competes with people's need to work, dulls incentives to work, and that this harms many able-bodied low-wage workers and their children. Differences in the workforce participation rates of able-bodied adults are alarming. Growth in unproductive behavior, such as out-of-wedlock births among lower-wage workers, is worrisome. Lack of increase in the work effort of poor, able-bodied workers, despite increases in social spending, is discouraging. One can't help but wonder if the "War on Poverty" caused more able-bodied poverty than it cured.

## Solutions to Poverty Are Likely to Be Prohibitively Expensive

That said, it's likely to be quite expensive to put able-bodied but reluctant workers to work. It costs far more than just their wages to hire lower-skilled and less-productive workers, especially people who are reluctant to work. The cost of hiring these workers may be so high that many workers may be employable only at wages below zero—thieves and disruptive workers who damage customer relationships and scare off sought-after employees, for example.

The resources that increase workforce productivity—namely, properly trained talent, equity to underwrite the risk of creating new jobs, and, to a lesser extent, capital investment—are in short supply. Alternative uses of these resources with higher returns are economically more logical. To the extent these resources could have been used to increase the productivity and pay of middle- and working-class workers, those workers bear a disproportionate share of the cost.

Employers like Walmart and McDonald's have extensive management systems that increase the productivity of their low-skilled workforce. Similarly, the military invests a fortune in capital investment and technological innovation to make soldiers effective. Soldiers need extensive training and supervision to be effective. Experts estimate employee theft costs American retailers $18 billion a year, for example, in addition to their costs associated with theft prevention.[50] All employers incur employ-related costs far beyond the wages and benefits of their workforces.

In an economy with scarce resources, we can use those resources either to make workers with low productivity more productive or to make the working, middle, or upper class more productive. Scarce resources are logically gravitating toward innovation that grows increasingly more valuable as the economy grows larger relative to the individuals who compose it. And they are gravitating toward serving workers who produce innovation—toward increasing the productivity and motivation of the most productive workers.

Properly trained talent that once supervised the middle and working classes is now engaged in nonsupervisory endeavors—namely, commercializing innovation and supporting those who do. This gradual shift leaves fewer resources devoted to increasing the productivity of the middle and working classes. Frankly, this—increasingly deploying scarce resources to increase the productivity of scarce resources—may be the gravest repercussion of growing income inequality. As the most productive workers increasingly serve the needs of the most productive workers, it runs the risk of leaving everyone else behind.

U.S. capital investment, for example, increasingly funds computerization, not factories that raise blue-collar productivity. The most talented women are no longer schoolteachers. Growing opportunities in engineering and computer programming have stripped factories of critically needed higher-skilled mechanics and foremen necessary for competing with German and Chinese manufacturers. As the economy leaves the supervision of the middle and working classes behind for more productive endeavors, their productivity growth will stagnate.

Given their druthers, what workers really want their productivity increased through supervision? Workers and unions resist greater supervision. And given *their* druthers, companies and their supervisors would rather hire workers who don't need much supervision, especially as properly trained talent and, therefore, supervision are becoming an increasingly constraining resource. It's a Faustian bargain that both sides are eager to make.

The same is true of the poor. If increasing the productivity of able-bodied but chronically poor people requires a great deal of supervision, but supervision can be employed more productively elsewhere—to increase the productivity of innovators or other more-skilled workers—then it may be more cost-effective to do little more than satisfy the material needs of the poor. Perhaps that's what we've already done—acquiesced to generations of intractable poverty.

And who truly pays the opportunity cost of devoting precious supervisory resources to the poor rather than to supervising the middle and working classes or to accelerating innovation? Predominantly it is the middle and working classes, of course, who must forgo supervision to free up the resources. The rich largely dodge the brunt of this cost because supervision of properly trained talent and the people who serve them produce the highest returns.

President Obama recognizes the limitations on America's supervisory capacities to help the poor gain independence. At a summit on poverty at Georgetown University with Harvard's Robert Putnam and American Enterprise Institute president Arthur Brooks, the president said:

> I think it is a mistake for us to suggest that somehow every effort we make [to reduce poverty] has failed and we are powerless to address poverty. That's just not true. . . . In every low-income community around the country, there are programs that work to provide ladders of opportunity to young people; we just haven't figured out how to scale them up.[51]

Wherever we find effective, hard-working supervisors of the poor, we will find ladders of opportunity for eager supervisees. Unfortunately, we won't find many such supervisors willing to do it. And when we do, they won't be very scalable.

This is precisely why reducing poverty has proved to be so intractable. It's more expensive to employ low-skilled, less reliable, and often troubled or reluctant workers than to employ the typical low-skilled worker, especially when supervision is scarce. The resulting low wages reduce the value of work to those workers. Compassion, especially for their children, demands welfare that further reduces incentives to work, especially for those least motivated by money. The high cost of supervising these workers makes it uneconomical to do much more than acquiesce to those people for whom our concerns for their children take precedent—in effect, the current policy.

Where we endeavor to make progress, as difficult as that may be, we should recognize that the organizations that have figured out how to scale up efforts to create independence for the lowest-skilled and least-productive workers are low-wage employers, like McDonald's and Walmart. These employers have successfully provided the engineering and investments necessary to make low-wage workers productive enough to employ. They have found markets where customers are willing to let low-wage workers serve them. And they have found ways to supervise low-wage workers to ensure enough worker productivity and customer satisfaction to make these endeavors successful.

These companies are surely far more effective at putting low-wage workers to work than any government program possibly could be. America is fortunate to have them. The alternative is largely ineffective government-funded make-work programs. Rather than denigrating low-wage employers, as advocates of the poor often do, the government ought to be partnering with them. Whom better to partner with than successful employers?

Employers will be more eager to employ lesser-skilled lower-wage, but ultimately more expensive, workers when workers are in short supply and alternatives are harder to find. That's more likely to occur if growth is robust and low-skilled immigration, low-wage trade, and especially trade deficits are more restricted.

To the extent an earned income tax credit reduces the market wages of workers to the benefit of employers and their customers—in the latter case via lower prices due to competition—so be it. The customers of low-wage workers are largely low-wage workers. And we're fortunate to have eager employers of these workers.

Sadly, well-intentioned but misguided politicians advocate for raising the minimum wage instead of the earned income tax credit. Do they realize that apartheid South Africa raised the minimum wage to prevent black South Africans from competing with lesser-skilled white South Africans for jobs?[52] One can't help but fear that the $15 hourly minimum wage in Seattle, for example, a thriving city with a low share of Hispanic immigrants, isn't intended to do the same thing—eliminate low-skilled jobs and motivate low-skilled workers to settle elsewhere.

Perhaps a high national minimum wage would discourage low-skilled workers from immigrating to America by limiting their opportunities for employment, but it would be detrimental to the low-skilled workers who have already settled here. Meanwhile, advocates of the poor would insist on raising government benefits to meet the material needs of unemployed workers not of their own making. Rather than attracting hard-working immigrants with jobs, we would attract those seeking government benefits.

A low minimum wage with a generous earned income tax credit is more logical. In an economy where supervision and the capacity and willingness to bear risk—ingredients essential for employing the poor—increasingly bind growth, unless we find more effective ways to motivate and supervise chronically poor workers than the failed efforts of the past, we are dooming poor children to certain failure.

For the sake of the children, it may be better to pay the chronically poor not to have children. But here again, the costs likely outweigh the benefits, especially if we endeavor to be compassionate. It would probably require giving every person a lifetime guaranteed income, albeit a low one to minimize disincentives to work and subsidize low-wage work with an earned income tax credit. A guaranteed income and subsidized wages would reduce the work efforts of some workers, many of whom are currently productive. We could deduct the cost of childcare from parents' wages. A working mother would receive these deductions back as child support. If able-bodied workers didn't work, we would subtract whatever support we gave them—money to raise their children, for example—from their lifetime benefits; that is, from their Social Security and Medicare. If such a mother identified the father, we would split the childcare costs between them or pay the mother more.

The cost to society of children raised by irresponsible parents is enormous. Should we care if a father who refuses to support his children lives a life in poverty, or similarly, if a mother who refuses to support her children or identify the father lives in poverty after her children become adults? How else can we better align the incentives for having children with the costs to support those children?

It would hardly be surprising if the costs of such a program outweighed the benefits. But what surprises and disappoints me far more is that for the sake of finding new innovations, the government isn't running a bevy of experiments to find cost-effective solutions for putting irresponsible parents to work and reducing their incentives to have children.

## Conclusion

With properly trained talent and the economy's capacity and willingness to take risk constraining growth, it is not surprising that political factions—America's poor, the middle and working classes, and retirees—are fighting to tax and regulate these constrained resources for their own self-interest. None of these factions recognizes that free enterprise would serve their economic interests far more successfully. The unrecognized benefits of free enterprise lie in the future and are difficult for most people to comprehend.

Unfortunately, once one faction successfully threatens control of these constrained resources, all the other factions must logically follow suit. As Democrats grow increasingly successful taxing and regulating properly trained talent and successful risk-takers for the benefit of the poor—both native- and foreign-born—it's hardly surprising that middle- and working-class workers would fight back, insisting that these resources be used exclusively for the benefit of native-born workers. Each faction proposes taxes and regulations—restrictions on free trade, for example—to coerce constrained resources for their own self-interest. Regardless of each faction's objectives, the value of free enterprise is lost in this struggle and everyone is worse off, on average, because of it.

It is also surprising how coldhearted we can be toward the rest of the world's poor. But compassion, especially for America's poor children, drives a never-ending demand for others to provide welfare, despite welfare payments approaching what a low-skilled worker can earn in the market—nearly $30,000 per year with no end in the demand for further increases in sight. Benefit levels that high demotivate work. Together with the high cost of supervision, it makes the problem of poverty intractable.

Our own actions doom generations of children to poverty despite a growing economy. The success of Hispanic immigrants, who have traveled long distances, shows there is plenty of work for low-skilled, able-bodied workers who are eager to work.

Instead of searching for solutions to this dilemma, we have largely acquiesced to the political demands of the poor and those who feel guilty about not giving them more. In part, we acquiesce because the costs are largely borne, albeit hidden, by the middle and working classes. Income redistribution reduces payoffs for risk-taking, cuts private investment, slows the accumulation of equity, and has large compounding effects on growth, employment, and wages.

We also acquiesce because the cost of poverty may be cheaper than the cost of the solutions we currently have or are likely to find. If there are cost-effective solutions, they likely entail working closely with low-wage employers to create and supervise viable work; using an earned income tax credit to make low-wage work more economical to workers, employers, and, perhaps most of all, customers; and disincentivizing those unwilling to work from having children.

Ironically, as the economy grows more prosperous, poverty is likely to become an increasingly difficult problem to solve. Rather than solve it, we will congratulate ourselves for finding *unscalable ladders of success.*

# Chapter 9

# THE LIMITATIONS
# OF EDUCATION

I n the face of seemingly intractable poverty and slow income growth, both the left and the right frequently hold out education reform as the antidote. It's not hard to see why. If education increases students' earning potential and higher pay motivates them to work, then education will alleviate poverty and accelerate growth.

The question, however, is not whether education reform *can* work; it's whether it *will* work. The latter hinges upon whether there are proven but unimplemented methods for improving test scores. Otherwise, as-yet-undiscovered innovation is needed to achieve sought-after improvements. If innovation is needed for improvements, it's a much tougher row to hoe. In that case, successful strategies for economic growth should assume little change in test scores and grow the economy anyway.

Those who are skeptical that implementation of proven methods alone will produce improvements often blame selfish teachers' unions for preventing competition with government-run schools. They believe competition will spawn as-yet-unfound innovations for improving the outcomes of low-scoring students. Perhaps, but it's impossible to know what value innovation may produce.

Those who believe we need only implement proven pedagogical methods point to the poor test scores of American students relative to their peers in the higher-scoring countries and states, such as Massachusetts, and charter schools. They see poor results as a "national disgrace" that "short changes" students, especially poor students.[1] They often blame a shortfall of educational funding for limiting teacher quality, for preventing teachers from being more effective, and for the lack of effective universal preschool education. They believe effective teachers can improve test scores by teaching smaller classes and that preschool is a critical time for teaching students.

But it's not enough to point only to differences in scores. Differences may exist for a variety of reasons. Theories for such differences lie outside the scope of this book. Evidence that innovation is unneeded must show educational systems that have closed the differences in question and, further, that only a lack of funding stands in the way of successful implementation.

By that standard, the comparisons are far less persuasive than they appear to be. There appears to be little, if any, evidence that other school systems produce higher scores with comparable students and circumstances, or that preschool and smaller classroom sizes are as effective as their proponents claim. If this is true, then innovation, not more funding to implement proven methods, is needed to improve outcomes.

So far, innovation has proved hard to find and harder still to implement. And even if we found and implemented valuable new pedagogical methods, we would not begin to see their benefits to the economy until children joined the workforce twenty years later, longer still before these newly minted students grew to become a significant share of the workforce. That's hardly the panacea for poverty that advocates claim.

In the interim, the country will need to rely on other strategies for growth. When properly trained talent constrains growth, as it does today, it requires persuading a greater share of America's talent to undergo the training and to take the risks needed to be successful employers of the rest of America's workforce.

# Higher-Scoring International Schools Do Not Provide Persuasive Evidence of Inferior U.S. Schools

Claims that America can improve educational outcomes without the need for innovation hinge on the belief that American schools are inferior to the schools of higher-scoring countries—like China, Japan, Korea, and Finland—and that America need only implement their proven methods to achieve similar results. But these claims ignore the fact that there are similarly large and persistent differences between American students descendant from those nations and the scores of other American students. Demonstrating that American schools are inferior requires finding alternate school systems with higher test scores for relevant statistically significant demographics. This simply isn't the case with international schools.

The median test scores of European-American students, for example, are virtually identical to the weighted-average scores of the native-born students in the countries of America's European origins. So, too, are the scores of Asian-American students.[2]

Some critics of American schools counter that because America's population originated with immigrants, Americans represent the cream of the crop of their native-born population—that is, those people best equipped to immigrate—and therefore their scores should be higher than their foreign counterparts. Wild speculation hardly proves that American schools are inferior. And even if it is true in some instances, there is plenty of evidence and counterexamples that dispute these wholesale claims.[3]

In many cases, immigrants come from lower socioeconomic families least equipped to immigrate. And given the sizes and multiple generations of America's demographic populations, it is hard to believe these American subpopulations could deviate much from their origin-country averages. Nor do early age scores, which correlate highly to later age scores, show the alleged superiority of Americans.

Perhaps the higher scores of Caucasian and Asian students both in the United States and abroad are evidence of institutional racism within American schools. If they are, America should endeavor to root it out. Nevertheless, differences in the scores of American students are not evidence of proven methods for rooting out institutional biases.

Moreover, the scores of American students with low socioeconomic status, measured by the number of books in their family's home, are higher than similarly disadvantaged students in France, Germany, and United Kingdom. However, a much higher share of American students have "low socioeconomic status"—20 percent in the United States—compared with 10 to 15 percent in other high-wage economies.[4]

As well, the scores of first-generation U.S. immigrants adjusted for socioeconomic status are the highest in the world. In fact, they are significantly higher than the scores of Finnish immigrants despite the much-touted high scores of native-born Finnish students.[5]

The only school systems with results for immigrants similar to America's are those in Canada and Australia, two countries with explicit immigration strategies for attracting and admitting highly educated or high-scoring immigrants. Today nearly 25 percent of Canadian schoolchildren have an immigrant background.[6]

If comparisons to international test scores reveal weaknesses in American schools, surprisingly, it's among students from families with the most academic resources. Among students from these families—families with top-scoring students—American scores are significantly below those of students from similarly advantaged families in France, Germany, and the United Kingdom.[7] It is possible, however, that Americans with any given level of cognitive capability are richer, on average, than their European counterparts, and therefore have more resources, but that these additional resources do little to increase test scores.

Notwithstanding the possibility that Americans are superior and therefore ought to score higher than their international counterparts, international scores are not significantly different than the test scores of statistically significant demographics of American students, as some critics of American schools are so often quick to assert. Therefore, they cannot provide evidence of proven methods for improving test scores.

Serious comparisons with the rest of the world have lead the Economic Policy Institute, a nonprofit think tank dedicated to advocating for working-class families, to conclude:

> Indeed, from such tests [i.e., comparisons with international test scores], many policymakers and pundits have wrongly concluded that student achievement in the United States lags woefully behind that in many comparable industrialized nations, that this shortcoming threatens the nation's economic future, and that these test results therefore demand radical school reform that includes importing features of schooling in higher-scoring countries.[8]

No surprise, the rest of the world doesn't appear to have any secret sauce that American educators have failed to replicate. The rest of the world appears to have neither superior pedagogical methods nor methods for overcoming the obstacles of implementing these methods in difficult environments—in inner-city schools, for example, where the most effective teachers may be reluctant to teach. Until large-scale alternatives with superior performance indicate otherwise, differences between the test scores of various demographics do not prove U.S. schools are inferior.

That is not to say that we should rest on our laurels and accept wide differences in performance between various demographics—far from it. Rather, we should recognize those differences must be closed largely through harder-to-find innovation, instead of through the implementation of proven methods already successfully implemented by other countries.

# High Massachusetts Test Scores Probably Do Not Result from Superior Pedagogy

Recognizing that international comparisons don't substantiate what they purport to show, proponents of education reform point to Massachusetts—where test scores across all demographics and socio-economic levels are among the highest in the world—as evidence that administrators can easily reconfigure public schools to produce higher scores.[9] While comparisons with Massachusetts are more promising than international comparisons, they, too, are highly suspect.

While Massachusetts's students across all demographics and socio-economic levels score higher than all other states' averages, the Massachusetts scores are higher when the children are first tested and then don't improve relative to other states as the children advance through school.[10] That's hardly clear-cut evidence of superior schooling. If Massachusetts's teaching methods were superior, one would expect to find Massachusetts's students with similar scores as the rest of the country when they started school and their scores advancing relative to the country as they progressed through school.[11] We find no such evidence.

Statistics warns us that the further an outlier is from the mean, the more likely the evidence is unreliable—that it's not what it appears to be. So, if one examines the most promising results from fifty states, one needs to be skeptical about the significance of the results one finds at the tails of the distribution. It is likely the results appear significant for reasons other than the reasons you sought to measure and compare—in the case of Massachusetts, perhaps it has a population with an inherently different capability rather than superior educational methods.

Legitimate comparisons demand assurances of comparability, especially as we choose comparisons further away from the average. If Massachusetts demographics were comparable to the rest of the country, it would provide some assurance. Instead, we find the opposite. Massachusetts—the furthest outlier of fifty states—has demographics very unrepresentative of the rest of the country.

Massachusetts residential real estate prices are much higher. In 2014 the median owner-occupied home was $330,000 versus $175,000 nationally, for example.[12] That makes it more difficult for truly disadvantaged families—whose children score lower on average—to live there.

Other demographic evidence is consistent with this prohibition. Massachusetts has a median household income that's more than 25 percent greater than the rest of America's.[13] And despite having more households where a language other than English is spoken in the home, it has fewer minorities.[14] These differences indicate that comparisons with Massachusetts should be used cautiously and with skepticism rather than as solid proof that America need do little more than implement Massachusetts's proven methods, as advocates of education reform often do.

Demographic differences on their own don't explain why Massachusetts's test scores are higher across all demographics and socioeconomics. But given Massachusetts's prohibitive cost of living, its vibrant knowledge-oriented economy, and its relatively large number of colleges, college students, and recent college graduates, families with low incomes are more likely to be headed by students, recent college graduates, or newly arriving, highly skilled immigrants. The children of those families will score higher on average than truly disadvantaged families, independent of pedagogy.

To its credit, Massachusetts has achieved substantial improvements in scores over time. It was early to test students, to hold teachers and administrators more accountable for results, and to take other steps to improve outcomes. But if Massachusetts truly has methods for improving test scores that other states haven't considered or tried, we should be able to take its methods and repeat the results elsewhere. When someone finds a way to do that, rest assured, it will be headline news. Until then, Massachusetts remains an unexplained outlier.

# The Benefits of Charter Schools Seem Limited

Recognizing that the Massachusetts example is of dubious value, many education reformers turn their attention to the performance of charter schools for evidence that schools can do more to improve the test scores of low-scoring students. Some charter schools, like the Knowledge Is Power Program (KIPP) academies, are having success improving the scores of students from historically low-scoring demographics. While their results, and the results of other charter schools that employ the fierce "no excuses" philosophy of KIPP, hold out guarded hope for implementing large-scale improvements without the need for new pedagogy, the alleged improvements are far less convincing than proponents of education reform would have the public believe.

In any statistical sample, one has to be very concerned that experimental results stem not from the effect of the treatment, but from the selection of participants to receive the treatment—what statisticians call selection bias. This is especially true in education, where conscientious parents work hard to secure the best education for their children.

Given the difficulties of gaining admission to many charter schools—having the interest, making the effort, and often winning one or more of several school lotteries—the pool of students seeking admission to charter schools skews heavily toward students with ambitious and conscientious parents. As a result, the test results of charter schools reported in the press overstate the true effect of charter schools on students, because the pool of students applying and accepting admission is different than the pool of public school students. No surprise, students who lose the lottery for charter school admission and enroll in public schools significantly outperform their public school peers.[15]

Where students face lotteries with long odds to gain admission to sought-after charter schools, conscientious parents logically apply to multiple schools. Less conscientious parents may apply to only one or two schools. So the pool of students seeking admissions will be over-represented by students with very conscientious parents who have applied to multiple schools, no different than other competitive schools where students face long odds and therefore apply to many schools. Under those conditions, lotteries will further skew toward the students of the most conscientious parents.

A positive feedback loop is likely to ensue. Demanding charter schools often have long school days and academic calendars. They have strict, unforgiving codes of conduct. The strenuousness of these standards may scare off all but the most ambitious parents. No surprise, these schools' students score higher on tests, if for no other reason than selection bias.

Higher scores make the schools more desirable to the most ambitious parents. Conscientious parents flock to apply. This further skews the pool to students with parents who apply to a large numbers of schools. No surprise, only fierce, no-excuses, KIPP-like charter schools and schools with lotteries appear to outperform their public school counterparts systematically.[16]

Just as propagandists are quick to overlook alternative explanations for the best results out of fifty states, they are also quick to overlook selection bias. In fact, they often seek out hidden selection bias to add apparent statistical significance to otherwise insignificant results.

Sloppy statistical analysis is the provenance of propaganda, especially in economics, where, unlike in science, it is seldom possible to compare experimental outcomes to carefully designed control groups or other counterfactuals. Selection bias is the scourge of science. Hence, science demands randomized double-blind trials—where neither the subjects nor the researchers know which group is the experimental group and which group is the counterfactual control group. But the very thing scientific experiments endeavor to overcome—selection bias—fiercely drives real-world outcomes.

If I sound too cynical, consider another research area in which natural results are seldom repeatable and where the conclusions are politically charged—climate change. In 2009 hackers revealed e-mails from the Climatic Research Unit (CRU) at the University of East Anglia that raised questions about the institution's objectivity. The British government called upon the independent Science Assessment Panel to investigate these claims. While the panel absolved the university, it found it "very surprising that research in an area that depends so heavily on statistical methods has not been carried out in close collaboration with professional statisticians."[17] These findings are hardly reassuring of wholly unbiased research.

Serious researchers are aware of selection bias and take steps to make adjustments to compensate for its effects. But these adjustments are difficult to make. Students self-select by accepting admission to— and by dropping out of—charter schools. Those to whom charter schools offered admission but turn it down might accept non–public school alternatives more suitable to their capabilities, such as parochial schools. Those denied admission might make similar choices. And public school students who were denied admission are notoriously difficult to track because students from low-socioeconomic backgrounds change addresses often—much more often than their charter school counterparts, for example.

In studying charter schools, careful researchers like Massachusetts Institute of Technology's (MIT) Joshua Angrist, the godfather of selection bias, and his coauthors find the improved results of no-excuses schools may only be "relevant for the set of students who apply"—that is, students with the most ambitious parents. He cautions that the results "may be different for students not interested in attending," and that "no excuses" charter schools "may have little impact on middle-class children."[18]

With charter schools, educational innovators may have discovered an alternative for improving the performance of a select group of students—poor students with conscientious and ambitious parents. However, it is hardly clear that this innovation truly has wide-scale applicability for improving the educations of middle- and working-class students or even a large portion of the poor. And it's important to recognize that the National Association for the Advancement of Colored People (NAACP)—the parents most affected by charter schools—opposes this sorting on the grounds that it removes the role models and leaders from their public schools.[19]

That's not to say that we shouldn't expand charter schools until the supply satisfies the demand of parents and endeavors to give each student the best education we can. But while charter schools may add value through rigorous discipline, a large portion of the value comes from allowing self-selection to separate the most promising students and educating them differently. Let's not kid ourselves—that's hardly a prescription for improving the education of the least-promising students.

If we do expand charter schools, we must not forget that we have a moral obligation to help the least-promising students, too. We must continue to search for and experiment with more effective ways to help these children.

# Replacing the Least Effective Teachers May Be the Best Opportunity for Improvement

Given the limited applicability of charter schools, and the inability to find other proven pedagogy for achieving widespread improvement in test results, advocates of education reform have turned their attention to other avenues to find demonstrated improvement. A Jack Kent Cooke Foundation study, for example, claims students from families in the lower-income half who score in the top 25 percent on nationally normed standardized tests in first grade fall out of the top 25 percent by twelfth grade in greater numbers than their counterparts in the upper-income half.[20] The researchers see this as evidence that school environments and peer groups drag down the academic achievement of lower-income students who may otherwise be successful.

But the study also shows that the same percentage of twelfth graders from families in the lower-income half score in the top 25 percent as first graders from the lower-income half—an indication that environment may have minimal effect on test scores. Differences in the churn of students in the top 25 percent may stem largely from students in the lower-income half scoring closer to the 25 percent cut-off than students in the higher-income half. In that case, random fluctuations in test scores will cause a greater share of the population to cross back and forth over the cut-off line. Unlike the conclusions of the Cooke Foundation study, the Angrist study of charter schools concludes: "Our findings for charter schools provide little support for this theory"—that is, for Richard Rothstein's theory that "ambitions are contagious; if children sit next to others from higher social classes, their ambitions grow."[21]

More promising work by Harvard's Raj Chetty and his team shows that effective teachers can have an impact on the lifetime earnings of students, even though test score improvements achieved by these teachers fade quickly.[22] The study finds that a Herculean one standard deviation improvement in teacher quality—that is, replacing a median teacher with an eighty-fifth-percentile teacher (for one year)—increases the net present value of a student's lifetime earnings by 1.34 percent, or $7,000 in 2010 dollars.*

The authors, however, leave methods for achieving such an improvement in teacher quality to the readers' imagination. In fact, the study finds that because many teachers who would be effective without bonuses will be paid bonuses in order to retain a few additional effective teachers, "the expected benefit of offering a bonus to even an excellent (95th percentile) teacher is only modestly larger than the cost."[23] That's a troublesome finding given the study also finds the benefits of good teachers are substantially greater for students from high-socioeconomic families, and substantially less for students from low-socioeconomic families.[24] That wouldn't improve outcomes for low-scoring students in a cost-effective way that advocates seek.

Instead, the study finds that "replacing ineffective teachers is more cost-effective than attempting to retain high value-added teachers." As a result, it recommends firing teachers whose value-added scores—a measurement of their ability to improve test scores—are in the bottom 5 percent over a three-year period.[25] Unfortunately, firing tenured teachers has proved nearly impossible, at least so far, because of the politically powerful teachers' unions.

One way to implement such a change more cost-effectively might be to pass a constitutional amendment banning teacher tenure in public schools. This may allow schools to replace the least effective

* The study does not address whether such improvements accumulate in subsequent years, or if once a student begins to achieve their full potential, the additional benefit of good teachers declines.

teachers more easily and at lower cost. There may be widespread support for such an amendment. Teachers aren't just union workers in a manufacturing shop. They are custodians of our children. Parents need some say in who teaches their children, when currently they have little. For the sake of our children, it is incomprehensible that schools don't have more leeway to fire incompetent teachers.

That's not to say that teachers' unions cause low test scores or that scores would improve if we fired large numbers of teachers. Without tenure, it is doubtful school systems would fire large numbers of teachers, just as companies rarely fire large numbers of below-average workers. It's just not practical to run organizations that way. But at least we could fire incompetent teachers more easily.

# Preschool Appears to Be Less Effective Than Advocates Claim

Given the difficulty of demonstrating the effect of schooling on test scores, advocates of education now claim that we can achieve substantial improvements in scores by investing in preschool education and by spending more to surround young children with a community of government support outside of school. There is scientific evidence, for example, that the brains of young children are highly plastic. It is presumed this plasticity can be manipulated to produce higher scores and more successful adults. This has led to a concern that three-year-old children from high-socioeconomic families hear as many as 30 million more accumulated words as similarly aged children from low-socioeconomic families, and that this has a large impact on the cognitive capabilities of children later in life.[26]

But here again, the evidence that we need only implement proven methods is discouraging. Head Start—a large government-run preschool program for children from low-socioeconomic families—has produced little, if any, improvement in test scores. Instead, score improvements fade out quickly, just as they seem to in other programs. And the highly regarded Harlem Children's Zone—which provides what it describes as an "unprecedented scale"[27] of support, from the earliest years of childhood through its charter school and into college—seems to achieve no improvement beyond what's achieved in any no-excuses charter school alone according to the Brookings Institution.[28]

The Brookings Institution's report concludes:

> There is no compelling evidence that investments in parenting classes, health services, nutritional programs, and community improvement in general have appreciable effects on student achievement in schools in the U.S. Indeed there is considerable evidence in addition to the results from the present study that questions the return on such investments for academic achievement. For example, the Moving to Opportunity study, a large scale randomized trial that compared the school outcomes of students from poor families who did or did not receive a voucher to move to a better neighborhood, found no impact of better neighborhoods on student academic achievement. The Nurse-Family Partnership, a highly regarded program in which experienced nurses visit low-income expectant mothers during their first pregnancy and the first two years of their children's lives to teach parenting and life skills, does not have an impact on children's reading and mathematics test scores. Head Start, the federal early childhood program, differs from other preschool programs in its inclusion of health, nutrition, and family supports. Children from families enrolled in Head Start do no better academically in early elementary school than similar children whose parents enroll them in preschool programs that do not include these broader services. Even Start, a federal program that combines early childhood education with educational services for parents on the theory that better educated parents produce better educated kids, generates no measureable impact on the academic achievement of children.[29]

This is hardly evidence of proven methods—quite the opposite. It indicates the improvements are hard to produce and that we lack proven methods.

While these efforts may not close test-score gaps, there is nevertheless evidence that early childhood intervention, and intervention generally, improves productive behavior in adulthood. The Perry

Preschool Study—a 1960s study that randomly assigned 58 three- and four-year-old low-income African American children who were assessed as being at high risk of school failure to a high-quality preschool program and then continued to track the children to the present day—often serves as the cornerstone for these claims.[30] While the program achieved significant lifetime results, nearly 90 percent of the program's value to the public came from reducing crime through prevention—hardly a validation of the value of preschool for the vast majority of children who are very unlikely to commit crimes.[31]

Moreover, it is unclear how much of the crime reduction came not from the program but from the well-recognized Hawthorne effect—in which individuals improve aspects of their behavior in response to their awareness of being observed.[32] If the children were singled out on a large scale as children likely to grow up and commit crimes, it's not clear whether the attention would have the same positive effect on behavior.

A recently published study by Vanderbilt University of Tennessee's state-funded Voluntary Pre-K Program, which randomly assigned one thousand economically disadvantaged children to the program and a control group, found that by the end of the third grade, the children attending preschool performed significantly worse on cognitive and behavioral tests than children who did not attend the program.[33]

That's not to say a properly designed preschool program wouldn't be beneficial. But the report concludes:

> It is not at all obvious that the rush to implement pre-k programs widely without the necessary attention to the quality of the program provides worthwhile benefits to children living in those disadvantaged environments. . . . Scaling up pre-k programs quickly could lead to badly run programs that might, in fact, be worse than doing nothing.[34]

A metastudy of 35 high-quality studies of ten much-studied preschool programs found that only half the studies used randomized control trials, the so-called gold standard of research. Of those, only three found statistically significant positive long-term results. But none of those results was linked to school-based pre-K.[35] The study concludes:

We know that parents and early environments play by far the most crucial role in shaping a child's development. . . . At the same time, we do *not* know whether school-based pre-K programs actually affect the outcomes that really matter. . . . Our current knowledge is insufficient to justify a large expansion of pre-K as the best path forward. And the growing pre-K push may well do more harm than good by diverting attention and scarce resources from other more effective approaches.[36]

It is no surprise that advocates of education reform shift the argument from the "known"—college and grammar school education, where there is a growing volume of not very persuasive evidence—to the largely "unknown"—preschool and early childhood development, where evidence is currently scarce. Human nature uses sound reasoning to work backward from one's desired conclusions to a set of defensible foundational beliefs—namely, unprovable beliefs. In effect, people search for unprovable beliefs upon which to build sound arguments that reach their desired conclusions.

Diamond and Saez's assumption that taxes have no long-term effect is an example.[37] They can make an audacious assumption like that because no one can prove otherwise.

Years of research and debate gradually clarifies and narrows the boundaries around unprovable beliefs. Serious economists on opposite ideas of the political divide can legitimately hold opposing views because there are different unprovable beliefs supporting opposing conclusions. People outside of the profession, however, often unwittingly stand outside these boundaries.

Unfortunately, people often cling to whatever unprovable beliefs are necessary to reach the conclusion they seek, no matter how far-fetched those beliefs may be. Ultimately, we must judge the reasonableness of unprovable beliefs without the benefit of more definitive research.

As research gradually disproves education-related myths, it forces advocates of education reform to find new unprovable beliefs upon which to stand. Preschool and early childhood development currently provide such ground in education.

While preschool education may prove to be the key to improving educational outcomes for low-scoring students, currently it is anything but a proven solution that warrants wide-scale investment without equivocation. In truth, it's currently a promising but unproven area for further research.

# We Shouldn't Count on Improvements to Grade School Education for Growth

Despite decades of efforts to improve primary and secondary school educations, and spending per pupil that rivals the highest-spending economies of the world, even for the poorest students, there is little compelling evidence—besides military academy–like, no-excuses charter schools, which the NAACP opposes—that we can significantly improve the academic outcomes of low-scoring students.[38] In *Scientific American,* Grover Whitehurst, now the director of the Brown Center on Education Policy at the Brookings Institution, recalls a call he received in 2002 from the superintendent of a predominantly minority school district asking him to suggest a math curriculum that had been proved effective for his students: "I said, 'There isn't any.'"[39]

Bill Gates, the wealthiest person on the planet, who has rolled up his sleeves and tried to improve education for years through his foundation, recently said:

> The trends are that education hasn't improved much in the United States over the last 50 years. . . . A lot of . . . technology . . . tends to empower motivated students more than unmotivated students. And one thing the U.S. has a lot of, is . . . unmotivated students. . . . People [ask], 'What's the hardest thing our foundation's working on . . . malaria, TB, AIDS?' I always say 'U.S. education.'[40]

Even Paul Krugman recognizes that education is not the panacea its proponents make it out to be. Krugman argues:

> What one still hears from many people inside the Beltway . . . is the continuing urge to make . . . a story about the skills gap, of not enough workers having higher education or maybe the right kind of education. . . . But . . . since [the 1990s] wages of the highly educated have

stagnated. Why on earth are we still hearing the same rhetoric about education as the solution to inequality and unemployment? The answer, I'm sorry to say, is surely that it sounds serious. But, you know, it isn't.[41]

If further investments in education had a demonstrated ability to raise test scores and lead students to more productive behavior in adulthood, surely Krugman wouldn't deride "rhetoric about [improving] education" by saying it "sounds serious. But . . . it isn't."[42] Summers wouldn't be describing it as little more than "whistling past the graveyard."[43] And Gates wouldn't be saying "it's easier to cure malaria."[44]

It's not surprising that large-scale programs have had limited effects on the outcomes of children. Several metastudies of nearly three thousand twin studies published by *Nature* finds that shared environment—the environment we control—currently accounts for less than 20 percent of the variation in cognitive and behavioral traits.[45] That's not to say that some as-yet-unidentified curriculum couldn't have a larger effect on learning, only that modest improvements to current approaches, which have limited effects, will have a small impact.

Harvard economist Greg Mankiw brings the dilemma into sharper focus. He argues:

> One might wonder how much of the income inequality we observe can be explained by differences in the resources that people get because of varying parental incomes.
>
> Let me suggest a rough calculation that gives an approximate answer.
>
> The recent [Chetty] paper [46] finds that . . . 91 percent of the variance [in the income of adult children] is unexplained by parents' income.
>
> I would be willing to venture a guess, based on adoption studies, that a lot of that 9 percent is genetics rather than environment. . . . Conservatively, let's say half is genetics.
>
> If we had some perfect policy invention (such as universal super-duper pre-school) that completely neutralized the effect of parents' income, we would reduce the variance of kids' income to .955 of what it now is. This implies that the standard deviation of income would fall to 0.977 of what it now is.

The bottom line: Even a highly successful policy intervention that neutralized the effects of differing parental incomes
would reduce the gap between rich and poor by only about 2
percent.[47]

And, as Bill Gates fears, any improvements we do find will probably
benefit the children of motivated parents and parents with the resources to take advantage of these improvements the most.

That doesn't mean we shouldn't continue to search for improvements.
Childhood education is surely an area where the private sector will underinvest. Government research and involvement is critical to progress.
Early childhood brain plasticity is real. And no one knows much about it
yet. The world will benefit from running many experiments in an effort
to find new insights in this field of endeavor. That said, we shouldn't roll
out nationwide change for the sake of change by pretending that there
are effective off-the-shelf methods we need only implement.

# There Seems to Be Promising Opportunities to Accelerate Growth with Education

Unfortunately, widespread improvements to America's preschool and
grade school education appears to be difficult and unlikely to be achieve
without innovation. Unlike the rest of the economy, educational innovations have been very slow in the making. Perhaps the government's monopoly on education has slowed innovation. But we see surprisingly little
progress regardless. If educational innovations were easier to find, we
should expect more pockets of success and faster progress.

Regardless of the difficulty, we must strive to find more innovation
and use whatever we find. Education is too important to neglect. Today they are several promising avenues for improvement. Online learning, while nascent, looks very promising. Vocational educations may
prove more effective than traditional education for many students at
all levels of education. At the highest skill levels, for example, it is hard
to see how more history majors serve the needs of America well. And
the evidence seems to suggest that America is squandering some of
the value of high-scoring students from lower-socioeconomic families.

Perhaps fifty years ago, America could afford to waste some of its opportunities—not anymore.

Online learning is one area that may hold great promise for primary, secondary, and higher education. Children miss portions of their lessons for a variety of reasons—boredom, illness, changing addresses, unreliable caregivers, and difficulties with learning. With a classroom full of children, teachers don't have time to go back and teach each individual child who misses a particular point.

As a practical necessity, passing grades allow for plenty of unlearned lessons. But unlearned lessons have a compounding effect, because successive lessons build on prior learning. To catch up, struggling students must often suffer embarrassment in front of their peers when seeking remedial help.

Online learning allows student testing to do more than just rank students and assess teachers. It allows for the delivery of flexible curricula that uniquely adjust to each student's needs. And it can deliver this additional teaching without embarrassing students in front of a classroom.

We should also recognize that on-the-job training likely plays a far greater role in increasing a worker's productivity than formal education.[48] Rather than trying to prepare all children for college—a goal that is out of reach for many students who struggle to graduate from high school—preparing students to succeed at work may be a more logical goal. Perhaps inculcating values that eschew dependency, instill pride in one's work, and increase reliability, cooperation, and sobriety may be more valuable to many workers than math and science. Learning how to do a specific job and how to speak English more effectively might be more valuable than other academic subjects for many students, too.

With 30 percent of African Americans ages sixteen to twenty-four without high school diplomas—nearly double their white peers—at the very least we should be running many experiments to find better alternatives to the current pedagogy.[49] Providing guidance for at-risk students and working with low-wage gateway employers as those students transition into the workforce—perhaps in conjunction with an earned income tax credit that allows employers to lower wages, which makes increased employment more economical while workers earn more—may be a better way to spend money at the margin than traditional education.

Even more important is making sure that talented Americans

are endeavoring to create a robust demand for the work of their less fortunate compatriots. Thirty or forty years ago, America could afford to misallocate a large share of its talent and still grow faster than the rest of the world. Back then, America supplied roughly 30 percent of the world's college graduates—not anymore.[50] Much of the world has caught up. Harvard economist Robert Barro's analysis reveals that over the last decade, America supplied only 10 percent of the increase in the world's college graduates.[51] Continued success in a world with $3-an-hour labor will demand America train its talent more wisely.

Today properly trained talent constrains growth, competitiveness, and wages. Despite the moral obligation of the most talented people to use their talents for the greatest benefit to others, there are armies of top-scoring college students studying curricula where the supply of graduates far outstrips the demand—psychology, sociology, history, and humanities—rather than business, math, and science, which are critical to addressing the needs of others. And there are vast armies of tenured college professors teaching these overdemanded subjects, so shifting supply and demand is likely to be very gradual.

Contrary to popular belief, U.S. employment growth isn't outpacing other high-wage economies because of growing employment in small businesses. Europe has plenty of small family-owned businesses. U.S. growth is driven by small companies that grow large, predominantly successful high-tech start-ups, such as Google, Microsoft, and Apple, which have spawned large industries around them.[52] A combination of business and technical skills are critical to the success of these faster-growing companies.

A Ewing Marion Kauffman Foundation survey of over five hundred engineering and tech companies established between 1995 and 2005 reveals that 55 percent of the U.S.-born company founders held degrees in science, technology, engineering, or mathematics, so-called STEM-related fields. Over 90 percent held terminal degrees in STEM, business, economics, law, and healthcare. Only 7 percent held terminal degrees in other areas—only 3 percent in the arts, humanities, or social sciences.[53] It's true some advanced-degree holders may have earned undergraduate degrees in humanities, but they quickly learned humanities degrees alone offered inadequate training to meet the demands of customers, and they returned to school for more technical degrees.

Other studies reach similar conclusions. A study by Stanford economics professor Charles Jones estimates that 50 percent of the growth since the 1950s comes from increasing the number of scientific researchers relative to the population.[54] A recent study from University of California, Davis, economics professor Giovanni Peri and Colgate economics associate professor Chad Sparber finds the small number of "foreign scientists and engineers brought into this country under the H-1B visa program have contributed to 10%–20% of the yearly productivity growth in the U.S. during the period 1990–2010."[55] Another study finds that as of January 1, 2016, immigrants have started more than half of the eighty-seven U.S. unicorns—privately held U.S. start-ups tracked by the *Wall Street Journal* and Dow Jones VentureSource valued at $1 billion or more.[56]

Despite the outsized importance of business and technology to America's economic growth, colleges awarded nearly half of all recent bachelor's degrees in the 2010–2011 academic year in fields outside these areas of study.[57] Critical thinking is valuable in all forms, but it is more valuable when applied directly to the most pressing demands of society.

At the same time, U.S. universities expect to graduate a third of the computer scientists our society demands, according to a study released by Microsoft.[58] Companies have bridged the talent gap in the information-technology sector with non–computer science majors, according to a report by Daniel Costa of the Economic Policy Institute.[59] The study finds that the IT sector has recruited two-thirds of its talent from other disciplines—predominately workers with other technical degrees. But with the share of top-performing U.S. students earning STEM-related degrees declining sharply over the last two decades, the industry has turned to foreign-born workers and, increasingly, offshore workers to fill its talent needs.[60] While American consumers will benefit from discoveries made in other countries, discoveries made and commercialized here have driven and will continue to drive demand for U.S. employment, both skilled and unskilled, at least indirectly through growing consumption.

University of California, Berkeley, economics professor Enrico Moretti estimates each additional high-tech job creates nearly five jobs in the local economy, more than any other industry creates.[61] Unlike a restaurant, for example, high-tech employment tends to increase demand overall rather than merely shifting employment from one competing establishment to another. If talented workers opt out of valuable training and end up underemployed, not only have they failed to create employment for other less talented workers, they have taken jobs those workers likely could have filled.

Students need not study technology to increase their productivity. The economy also needs armies of salesmen and supervisors who can be more effective with trained interpersonal skills. These skills are critical for increasing the productivity of lesser-skilled workers. But who goes to college with dreams of becoming a salesman or a supervisor, and how many professors are eager to develop expertise in these areas of knowledge so they can impart them?

In large part, the higher pay of highly paid talent stems from the unwillingness of talented people to suffer and endure the arduous training and work that adds value to others. For selfish reasons, talented people with choices often prefer to pursue careers that are more fun and interesting and to avoid taking risks that jeopardize the comfort of their careers. Pay for sought-after talent and risk-taking is set at the price of persuading one more talented person to join these efforts.

Ironically, we complain about growing income inequality by demanding higher taxes on the income of successful workers and risk-takers without ever admonishing talented students who have turned away from higher pay to fulfill their moral obligation to use their talent for the benefit of others. In fact, society tells students that pursing noncommercial endeavors is the higher calling. A better strategy would do the opposite—praise hard work and risk-taking that serves others, especially customers, and rebuke underutilized talent.

In the absence of such a cultural awakening, the government—the largest financer of college educations—could take the lead on driving changes in the studies of students by restricting what educations the government is willing to finance. That doesn't mean the government would stop financing all history degrees. Rather, it would restrict financing to the number of historians demanded by the market, rather than by the students and their faculty influencers.

Free market purists may recoil at the notion of central planning, but the government already largely finances public universities. Naive young students are horrible at matching their studies to the demands of the job market. College professors are largely driven by academic research, not undergraduate job training. Where properly trained talent is one of our economy's binding constraints, perhaps America would benefit from less of a laissez-faire approach to education. Besides, there is plenty of opportunity to attend private schools to pursue whatever students choose.

The availability of faculty to teach a rebalanced curriculum is a major obstacle to implementing wholesale changes to the majors America's universities graduate. But again, online learning may offer a low-cost opportunity to expand the reach of the curriculum, and of the professors most effective at delivering it.

Another large opportunity for harvesting America's underutilized talent and putting it to work creating more productive jobs for others is finding top-scoring students who have not graduated from college and training them to be better job creators. For top-scoring students, the value of additional college-level training is likely greater than mere credentialing.

According to the National Center of Education Statistics' longitudinal study of students in 2002, 74 percent of high school sophomores from families in the top quartile of income who score in the top 25 percent graduate from college with at least a bachelor's degree. Only 41 percent of top-scoring students from families in the lowest quintile earn bachelor's degrees or higher. Similarly, only 53 percent of top-scoring students in the middle two quintiles earn bachelor's degrees or higher.[62] Finding a way to increase the graduation rate of top-scoring, middle- and low-income students to the same rate as the top income quartile would increase top-scoring college graduates by 20 percent.

There may be a variety of hard-to-solve reasons unrelated to education why some low-income families with high-scoring children are unable to earn more money. These reasons may correlate with the lower college graduation rates of their children. Alcoholism and other self-defeating behaviors, for example, are often passed from one generation to the next.

As well, the high scores of lower-income children are likely to be closer to the seventy-fifth percentile, on average, than the high scores of upper-income children. The college graduation rate of lower-scoring, high-income children is lower, too.

For these reasons, perhaps we can capture only half of the apparent improvement in graduation rates—a 10 percent increase in top-scoring college graduates instead of 20 percent. Even half of *that* is still a big increase in the productive capacity of America.

In a world where properly trained talent constrains growth and improving academic scores has proved difficult, investing to train more job creators and helping young at-risk workers transition to work may be a better way to spend money on education, at least at the margin, than the way money is currently spent. Again, running experiments to find ways to improve education may be more valuable than pouring more money into programs that have not been very effective.

## Conclusion

Time and again, we are told that American education is inferior and that improvement is the key to growing the economy, alleviating poverty, and reducing income inequality. Low test scores are troubling. American schools are clearly failing the most disadvantaged students. And higher scores would surely accelerate growth if America could produce them. But despite the higher scores of some other nations, there is scant evidence that America can implement proven off-the-shelf curriculum to achieve better results. Innovation is needed. We should bust our pick searching for it. But improvement via innovation has proved hard to achieve. Wishful thinking, as seductive as it is, is not a strategy. Believing the evidence and making the investments that it supports is the key to success.

The single biggest improvement America could make to grade school education is firing incompetent teachers. To make improvements, we simply have to run schools on behalf of students, and not teachers. Sadly, it may require a constitutional amendment banning tenure. I wouldn't hold my breath if I were you.

Tough, no-excuses charter schools may not be a panacea for every at-risk child, but they are for many of them, especially the ones with conscientious parents. America should expand charter school capacity until any parent who wants their child to attend can do so. Having their child attend an effective charter school ought to be a parent's God-given right, even if the NAACP prefers otherwise.

Rather than pouring more money into America's antiquated education systems, we should be running a multitude of experiments to find solutions that work. Improvements to America's educational practices likely require innovation and not merely the implementation of proven methods that haven't worked well. This may include better preparing lower-scoring students to work more effectively so they create opportunities to learn on the job rather than teaching subjects that seem to do them little good. It may also entail working with low-wage gateway employers to help at-risk students find and hold jobs. Online learning may provide a more cost-effective way to deliver much-needed curricula, especially in a world where the old curricula and teachers may be growing increasingly obsolete.

But even if we do find and implement breakthroughs, it wouldn't begin to have much effect on our workforce for twenty years. Nor will it fully suffuse the workforce until twenty years after that.

While we continue to search for better methods, our strategy today should be to use America's scarcest and most valuable resource—its talent—more effectively. We already know how to do that.

In an economy whose growth is constrained by properly trained talent, training talented students to create productive jobs for their fellow Americans is, by far, the most impactful strategy for using education to improve the economy. The success of America's top students increases the rest of America's productivity and raises standards of living for generations to come.

Perhaps the fastest way to effect change is for the government to stop subsidizing students to study subjects where the supply of graduates far exceeds the demand—history, for example—and pay students more to study curriculum that creates jobs. Currently, there is an enormous mismatch between what students choose to study and what people need them to study.

Nor are talented lower-income students earning bachelor's degrees at the same rate as higher-income students. In today's more technology-driven economy, where the rest of the world's talent grows increasingly competitive, America can no longer afford to waste such an enormous share of its talent.

This education agenda is achievable without the need for innovation. It would accelerate growth, albeit modestly, without budget-busting spending increases of dubious value. It's disappointing that America lacks the will to implement it. And even if it is implemented, America can do more to accelerate growth.

## Chapter 10

# REAL SOLUTIONS

W ithout significant policy changes, the economy is likely to continue growing tepidly as it has since the financial crisis. The impending retirement of baby boomers is a cloud hanging over the success of America. Retirees will inevitably use their political clout to demand promised pension payments that will grow to crowd out private-sector investment and other government spending, and diminish incentives for work and risk-taking. In the meantime, America remains at political loggerheads over the reallocation and reduction of spending. Voters underestimate the compounding value of incentives, risk-taking, and innovation. Political leaders refuse to lead on behalf of the common good. For political gain, everyone points to the greed of others, whether real or imagined, and this drives people to fend only for themselves. Given the intractability of these problems, what can America do to accelerate growth?

In a world where properly trained talent and the economy's capacity and willingness to take risk now constrain growth, America could recruit talent from the rest of the world rather than merely endeavoring to better train its own talent. It could build a climate where business and high-tech entrepreneurial risk-taking thrive rather than undercut success and tax it at every turn. It could take steps to balance trade in order to mitigate the flood of unused risk-averse offshore savings, which slows growth. And it could reduce the inherent instability of banking rather than simply impose a litany of regulations that leave risk-averse savings sitting unused.

In that environment, America's institutional capabilities and its capacity and willingness to take risk would compound and grow at a faster rate. In the long run, American workers of all skill levels and the rest of the world would be more prosperous.

# Ultra-High-Skilled Immigration Would Accelerate Growth

An obvious option for accelerating growth is to increase *high-skilled* immigration dramatically. With 106 million full-time American workers, a 5-million-person increase in ninety-fifth-percentile skill-level workers—the pool of workers who chiefly create technological innovation and drive improvement—would nearly double America's capacity to innovate and grow.[1] Ten million may triple the growth rate.

With over 7 billion non-Americans in the world, there are over 350 million potential recruits in the top 5 percent, albeit many unidentified, too old and too young, or too established to benefit America today. A pool that large makes 5 to 10 million recruits—if not more—look very achievable. If anything, America could probably be even more selective than the top 5 percent.

If more high-skilled workers accelerate growth, it would allow baby boomers to retire with their full benefits, without crowding out other priorities and taxing young workers to death. A large influx of high-skilled workers would likely contribute innovation that creates more value for others than innovators consume themselves. Their success would also increase the pool of equity needed to underwrite increased risk-taking. It would put minimal strain on America's supervisory capacity, as the most talented workers need less supervision. In fact, it may add supervisory capacity that increases middle- and working-class productivity. And, unlike low-skilled immigration, which strains public finances, high-skilled immigrants contribute substantially more taxes than the cost of the government services they consume. In a nutshell, ultra-high-skilled immigration would add to the pool of constrained resources rather than consume them.

In the long run, a large influx of high-skilled workers would also strengthen the U.S. economy and, therefore, its military power relative to China and the rest of the world. Again, the alternative—competing against China with slower growth—is risky, and perhaps even doomed to failure.

Of course, the million-dollar (or trillion-dollar) question is, what effect will a large influx of high-skilled immigrants have on the earnings of America's existing workforce? Surely, there's a significant risk that it would lower earnings relative to what they would have been without the influx. But there are numerous reasons to think otherwise.

If America recruits workers with seventieth-percentile capabilities, those workers will compete directly with American workers. If America recruits workers with ninety-fifth-percentile capabilities, it's debatable whether American workers with seventieth-percentile capabilities can truly fill those jobs. More likely, businesses seeking those skills and not finding them in the United States are simply sourcing these capabilities offshore. If employers were going to fill the jobs offshore anyway, then Americans have already lost those jobs to foreign competition. Ultra-high-skilled immigration retrieves them.

When businesses hire ninety-fifth-percentile workers offshore, middle- and working-class jobs educating the children of those offshore workers, tending to their medical needs, building their homes, transporting their goods, and providing services to those who serve them, move offshore too. It would behoove America to capture some of this employment, since domestic spending by these high-skilled workers would increase demand for lesser-skilled American workers.

To reduce competition with the current workforce further, America could restrict immigration to top-scoring math and science majors. The success of America, relative to Germany, France, and Japan—economies with more high-scoring STEM majors—indicates that a combination of engineering *and* business produces more productivity growth than either expertise alone. No surprise, other high-wage economies are racing to duplicate America's success by substantially increasing their share of business students. America may benefit from the opposite—recruiting overseas math and science majors who complement rather than compete directly with most high-scoring native-born Americans.

Because of the robust demand for business majors, the highest-scoring

Americans have gradually moved away from studying math and science (STEM-related fields) in order to study business, finance, law, communications, and marketing or sales—careers that have proved to be more lucrative than engineering.[2] An increase in math and science majors may increase the demand for higher-skilled, native-born Americans with non-STEM skills. The greater success of the two in combination will likely increase the demand for lesser-skilled workers.

The rising demand for business majors over the last four decades hardly seems coincidental. The demand for highly paid analytical MBAs rose in the wake of personal computers, which helped turn data into valuable information for more optimal decision making. Highly paid analytical management consulting and finance rose at that time. The demand for IT and data rose commensurately. Each one seems to feed off the other. America has a competitive advantage using information for commercial success and ought to capitalize on it.

Despite computerization that increased the productivity and subsequent supply of high-skilled workers, pay rose for ninetieth-percentile workers—that is, for properly trained talent—relative to the median worker.[3] That suggests that the opportunities for high-skilled workers to add value rose faster than the supply. An increase in the supply of high-skilled workers is likely to mine more opportunities rather than reduce pay by dividing the same opportunities among a greater number of miners. More innovation raises living standards for everyone.

To the extent ultra-high-skilled immigrants do compete with lesser-skilled high-skilled Americans, the marginal product of lesser-skilled labor seems to have reached a floor in the American economy despite a near-unlimited supply of lesser-skilled workers. While the large influx of lower-skilled workers may have limited the pay increases of lower-skilled Americans relative to what might have been the case otherwise, it didn't lower their wages. The same might be true of all workers.

As well, high-skilled workers likely enjoyed lower prices due to a near-unlimited supply of lower-skilled labor. It would be fair for high-skilled workers to share some of the benefits they gained with lower-skilled workers who bore the brunt of lesser-skilled immigration and offshore sourcing. Increasing the supply of high-skilled workers shares that benefit by enlarging the economic pie rather than by merely redistributing earnings, although not without risks to the pay of existing higher-skilled workers.

The evolving demographics of America will also help to mitigate downward pressure on wages. Baby boomers will retire over the next fifteen years, opening up promotions for generation Xers. There will be more promotions if demand remains strong. And demand will be stronger if the economy grows.

Increased demand may increase property values for existing homeowners and the revenues of local businesses, such as contractors, doctors, and schoolteachers—at least in the near term when generation X is saving for home purchases, their children's education, and retirement. A substantially lower corporate tax rate may increase the value of the businesses and the stock market as well—assets that pension plans hold as retirement funds.

But what about millennials—Americans born in the 1980s and 1990s—who are reportedly having difficulty gaining traction in the job market, especially in the aftermath of the financial crisis, although the evidence suggests otherwise?[4] Won't they bear the burden of a large influx of high-skilled workers who will compete with them for jobs?

Unlike the small generation X, which inherited an America filled with an enormous population of baby boomers now demanding unsustainable retirement benefits, the relatively large generation of millennials will ultimately inherit an America with a small number of retiring gen-Xers.[5] Demographically, it is a brighter world for American millennials freed from the high cost of retirees.

Perhaps America can trade an expansion in high-skilled immigration for a compromise on low-skilled immigration. Practical limitations on restraining low-skilled immigration have stymied compromise between advocates and opponents of low-skilled immigration. Opponents of low-skilled immigration want to build a wall to keep out Hispanic immigrants in order to prevent them from straining public expenditures. So far, it hasn't worked. Despite wishful thinking, America will never build a physical barrier effective enough to keep out illegal low-skilled immigration. There is simply too much trade crossing the border with Mexico to make such barriers effective.

Nor will illegal immigrants likely ever be deported. The opposition to deporting illegal immigrants is far too great, and the political costs when their children become eligible to vote are even greater. While legal low-skilled immigration could be dialed back, high-skilled immigration is likely the only viable alternative for rebalancing the mix between high- and low-skilled workers. The latter solution is better for growth, too.

And even if illegal immigrants were deported, America is still employing many lower-skilled Mexicans in Mexican factories that supply the American economy. American-owned, Mexican-based manufacturing requires engineering and managerial talent that the American economy could otherwise use to employ and better utilize American workers. High-skilled immigration gives the American economy more capacity to manage both Mexican- and American-based workers, and to put more Mexican-based workers to work on America's behalf.

Perhaps a more practical version of a wall links the number of high-skilled immigrants to the number of low-skilled immigrants—the more of the latter, the more of the former—to hold the mix between high- and low-skilled workers in balance. Increasing the number of highly skilled workers, who contribute more to constrained resources than they consume and pay more taxes than government services they consume, may offset the strain on public finances that opponents of low-skilled immigration hope to mitigate with a wall.

Were Americans to pursue immigration as a strategy for accelerating growth and improving their future—a future sure to be more troubled in the absence of significant growth that will be nearly impossible to produce otherwise—we should recognize that middle- and working-class workers currently consume more government service than they pay in taxes. Before expanding immigration it would be logical to reform Social Security and Medicare, at least for immigrants, by either raising their taxes or reducing their retirement benefits to ensure all immigrants and eventually the vast majority of all workers truly covered their own costs.

Without such a rebalancing of high-skilled workers relative to low-skilled workers, the future looks more worrisome than it otherwise could be. In the future, pension benefits and government spending will become major drags on growth. Despite wishful thinking, education reformers have not found a way to turn low-scoring students into high-scoring students as promised. When we project into the future, a skeptical person can't help but be concerned about the declining share of high-scoring students entering the workforce. Recruiting high-skilled workers solves this concern without relying on unlikely improvements to America's school system. It will accelerate growth and make everyone better off in the future.

# A Lower Marginal Corporate Tax Rate Would Attract Employers and Increase International Competitiveness

As beneficial as an increase in high-skilled immigration could be, it would accelerate growth even more in combination with a lower marginal corporate tax rate.

A strategy based on recruiting high-skilled workers in order to ramp up innovation and grow the economy runs the risk that innovation will ebb and flow somewhat independently of the efforts expended to create it. If corporate jobs don't scale proportionately with the increased supply of workers, additional high-skilled workers would need to pursue entrepreneurial endeavors, supervise others to increase their effectiveness, or compete for lesser-skilled jobs. As such, the share of secure corporate-type jobs may decline, and employment may grow less certain. Typically, corporate jobs are higher paying and more secure than entrepreneurial endeavors, which often fail.

To mitigate this risk, a substantially lower corporate tax rate may gradually increase both the quantity and quality of high-skilled jobs. It would make America one of the most attractive places on earth to locate businesses, especially businesses that need highly skilled workers.

With a very low, even zero, business tax rate, corporations would find it less attractive to locate elsewhere. Other economies simply don't have the depth of assets needed for higher growth—a highly motivated pool of talent, the optimal mix of business and technical expertise, opportunities for on-the-job training at cutting-edge companies like Google, large communities of experts like Silicon Valley, a growing population, and cheap energy (when oil prices are high), for example. America ought to take full advantage of these assets. Given the assets America offers employers, when combined with a low corporate tax rate, it would be difficult for other countries to lure the most talented workers and their employers. Why create large umbrellas under which the rest of the world can compete with America?

A low corporate tax rate should also attract equity that underwrites and profits from risk-taking. In large part, corporate profits represent return on investment. A high corporate tax rate may lower investment returns, especially where companies compete against competitors with lower tax rates. This subsequently drives investment elsewhere. There is widespread consensus that investment (machines, for example) increases employment more than it substitutes for labor, despite what the Luddites feared.* So while automation may reduce the number of workers needed to produce cars, the fact that Germany and Japan have auto factories on their soil gives their citizens jobs. The investment of brainpower instead of capital is no different.

A strategy that lures worldwide businesses to America must recognize that its unlikely high-wage economies can compete with low-wage economies by exporting manufactured goods for consumption by low-wage workers. The growth of intangible exports like software is likely to be more robust. And as populations age, as they are expected to do, they are likely to need more local medical services but fewer consumable goods transported from around the world, although perhaps not fewer intangible goods like software. So it is likely that global trade may not be as robust as it has been. Nevertheless, it is surely better to have the brainpower behind worldwide businesses located in America rather than elsewhere. In today's economy, the success of talented workers fuels growth and expands the local economy.

While lower corporate tax rates may attract employers and accelerate growth, current efforts to reform corporate taxes may be misguided. These efforts chiefly center on lowering the marginal rate, from 35 percent (40 percent including state taxes)—the highest marginal business tax rate in the world—to a more competitive 28 percent, and only taxing profits earned in the United States rather than anywhere in the world.[6] Ironically, that may do more harm than good.

Were the United States to enforce its current 40 percent U.S. marginal corporate tax rate on worldwide earnings of American compa-

---

* Except, perhaps, Thomas Piketty (and other outliers), whose view on this Larry Summers characterized as a misreading of the literature.

nies, U.S. taxes would be highly uncompetitive. Many companies would be inclined to locate elsewhere. As it is, the prevalence of tax inversions—American companies locating elsewhere to avoided onerous U.S. corporate taxes—largely drive efforts to reform the U.S. corporate tax code.

Fortunately, the U.S. tax code as enforced is very different than the code as written. In truth, as enforced, the U.S. corporate tax code is actually highly competitive and may have contributed to the success of America's high-tech industry.

Contrary to popular belief, the American tax system as it is enforced neither taxes worldwide earnings nor prevents repatriation of untaxed international earnings. For high-tech companies that produce intellectual property—where America has built a significant competitive advantage—it also taxes domestic earnings at very low rates.

Unlike most countries, the American tax code as written imposes taxes on U.S. corporate profits earned worldwide but taxes those profits only when companies repatriate offshore profits to the United States, which they seemingly never do. Most countries, in contrast, tax profits only earned within their borders.

Under the auspices of worldwide taxation, the United States largely turns a blind eye to the allocation of profits between countries because it assumes that profits earned offshore will eventually be repatriated. High-tech companies subsequently move ownership of their intellectual property to low-tax jurisdictions. Because the value of high-tech products is largely intellectual property, a company can charge its U.S. subsidiary a high licensing fee for using this asset in the sale of its products. This moves profits to low-taxed jurisdictions. Countries that impose only territorial taxes restrict transactions such as these and insist companies allocate profits to territories largely in proportion to the territory's sales.

To prevent companies from repatriating profits without paying taxes, the United States prohibits companies from loaning rather than repatriating their international earnings back to their domestic parent. It does, however, allow the companies to deposit the funds in banks and borrow money domestically. In effect, companies repatriated international earnings without paying taxes by depositing them in banks and then borrowing domestically. Companies often borrow to buy back shares, which is akin to paying a dividend with international earnings without further taxation.

As a result, there is much less cash on corporate balance sheets than there appears to be once companies net domestic borrowings against overseas cash. Nor is there as much money "trapped" overseas as popularly claimed.

By enforcing the tax code in this way, the U.S. does not tax overseas earnings even if corporations, in effect, repatriate them. Nor does it impose high tax rates on the domestic profits of high-tech companies with intellectual property. This gives high-tech U.S. companies a significant competitive advantage relative to their international competitors. This tax advantage may be one of the reasons for the compounding success of high-tech U.S. companies relative to the rest of the world.

The fact that today's high-tech companies tend to use brainpower to make investments rather than capital gives them additional tax advantages. Unlike capital, which companies must write off gradually over its useful life for tax purposes, tax law allows companies to expense most employee-related costs in the year they incur them. Expensing investments immediately, rather than gradually over years, lowers taxes today rather than in the future. This gives high-tech companies another tax advantage relative to more capital-intensive manufacturers. This tax advantage may be another reason for the success of high-tech companies relative to capital-intensive companies.

Domestic low-tech industries, such as stores and restaurants, do not have access to these tax avoidance opportunities. As such, they face high tax rates. Were it strictly the case that the owners of domestic industries were taxed more heavily, investors would logically invest in low-taxed sectors such as high-tech and offshore manufacturing, rather than these more highly taxed domestic sectors. To a certain extent, they probably have already, and this lowers U.S. employment.

Where domestic competitors all face the same high tax burden, however, to a large extent these competitors can pass high domestic taxes to customers through higher prices. These companies become hidden tax collectors, a fact often overlooked by unsuspecting voters eager to tax investors, rather than wage earners.* Where companies

---

* And these high taxes are passed to companies that compete internationally when those companies buy local services like healthcare.

can pass the cost of taxes to customers, investment returns are unaffected by higher taxes.

If individual competitors in domestic U.S. industries can find ways to avoid high U.S. corporate taxes—by using tax inversions, which move U.S.-based companies to foreign tax jurisdictions, for example—they gain a competitive advantage, in this case lower taxes, that was unearned in the marketplace. This reduces competitiveness overall, which is disadvantageous to consumers and society. It is no surprise that domestic U.S. businesses like Burger King and Walgreens may seek to capitalize on such an advantage, but high tax rates are only sustainable with minimal adverse consequences if all competitors within a domestic industry face the same tax rate.

To prevent tax inversions, many economists have recommended that the United States bring its tax code into alignment with the rest of the world by moving to a territorial system that taxes only domestic profits, and by closing loopholes to lower marginal corporate tax rates while maintaining tax revenue neutrality. This lowers the U.S. marginal corporate tax rate to about 28 percent.

Such a reduction would lower taxes on domestic industries, where taxes are largely paid by customers, and raise taxes on international high-tech companies, whose federal tax rate is often closer to 15 percent and where taxes are largely paid by investors at the margin. Ultimately, this would shift some portion of U.S. corporate taxes from domestic consumers to high-tech companies and their investors. That would lower the competitiveness of international high-tech competitors without producing offsetting gains in the competiveness of the domestic sectors of the economy, where investment returns are less affected by taxes. It's hard to see why that would accelerate U.S. growth in the long run—quite the opposite.

A better business-tax-reform strategy—one that doesn't hurt the faster growing high-tech sector—lowers corporate taxes to at least the approximate 15 percent rate high-tech firms are currently paying if not lower—zero if we could—and collects lost tax revenues elsewhere.

A 15 percent marginal corporate tax rate may seem politically unfeasible, but it would probably be worth trading an increase in the capital gains rate to the ordinary income tax rate to achieve such a reduction in the corporate tax rate. After all, one reason for lower capital gains taxes is the double taxation of business earnings—first as corporate profits and then as dividends and capital gains, when these after-tax profits are distributed to investors and taxed as personal income.

Profits retained by businesses and the resulting unrealized increase in the market value of the company's equity may have a greater impact on growth than profits distributed to households because equity, especially business equity, largely underwrites risk-taking. It also pays off successful risk-takers when existing companies acquire successful start-ups. With a very low corporate tax rate, earnings held for investment would be largely untaxed until distributed. That's more akin to a tax on consumption, which most economists believe would produce faster growth.

In a world where risk-taking and properly trained talent constrains growth, a strategy for recruiting high-skilled immigrants and their employers is America's most feasible opportunity for accelerating growth and lifting middle- and working-class wages. If America can't slow low-skilled immigration, which puts downward pressure on lesser-skilled wages, then it needs to balance the demand on constrained resources by recruiting more high-skilled workers. It can't depend on advancements in education nor the moral obligations of talented but reluctant students to ensure that balance.

To the extent America recruits high-skilled workers, it runs the risk of becoming increasingly dependent on risky entrepreneurialism to grow the economy. Lowering the corporate tax rate may ease that risk by encouraging equity investors and employers to invest in America rather than elsewhere. A low business tax rate coupled with a large, growing, and motivated supply of properly trained talent, an optimal mix of business and technical expertise, and large spillover benefits from on-the-job training at companies like Microsoft and from communities of experts like Silicon Valley, together with other U.S. assets, could make locating elsewhere increasingly uncompetitive.

# Demanding Balanced Trade and Strengthening, Rather Than Weakening, Bank Guarantees Would Accelerate Growth

There are other things America can do to accelerate growth. In my previous book, *Unintended Consequences: Why Everything You've Been Told*

*About the Economy Is Wrong*, I made two additional proposals that are critical to economic recovery and growth—demanding balanced trade with our trading partners and strengthening rather than weakening the Federal Reserve's ability to act as the lender of last resort during a run on the banks. They are difficult to implement politically, but they remain as relevant today as they were in 2012.

International trade is essential to growth. America can't spend twenty dollars to produce something that it can buy for five dollars and remain competitive. It can use the fifteen dollars of savings to hire more schoolteachers, truck drivers, restaurant staff, and doctors.

Trade deficits, however, export employment and flood our economy with risk-averse savings for which we have no productive use. Unless we borrow and spend those savings, we will not achieve full employment—at least not at the highest possible wages. Borrowing and spending risk-averse savings strains the economy's limited capacity and willingness to bear risk. That constrained resource could be used more constructively.

China, Germany, and previously Japan have a glut of risk-averse savings—more than they can logically invest in their own economies. They use the proceeds from the sale of goods to Americans to buy U.S. assets—namely, low-risk government-guaranteed debt—instead of American-made goods that employ Americans. With a limited amount of government-guaranteed debt, an influx of risk-averse savings indirectly floods the U.S. economy with risk-averse savings. This destabilizes our banking system and requires America to lend, borrow, and spend these savings to reach full employment at the highest possible wages.

Unfortunately, our innovation-based economy has little use for risk-averse savings. No surprise—risk-averse savings have sat idle since the financial crisis, and the economy has suffered from mediocre growth off a permanently lower base of economic activity. Workers have paid the price with slower wage growth.

A more logical trade policy demands that our trade partners balance trade by requiring would-be American importers to buy a dollar of American-made goods for the right to import a dollar of goods produced offshore—a plan first proposed by Warren Buffett.[7] Rather than loaning the U.S. economy money to balance trade, trade partners would have to find American-made goods to buy. Economies that ran trade deficits with the United States could freely sell their rights to import to countries with trade surpluses, which would balance trade overall.

This policy may have some costs to Americans, but those costs are likely to be minimal. Countries like China and Germany run trade surplus as a matter of strategy to employ their savings and citizens at America's expense. We should be eager to trade with them, but not for those reasons.

It's costly to do nothing. Employing their workers instead of ours, which is not the case with balanced trade, and using our equity to underwrite the risk of redeploying their risk-averse savings in order to reach full employment at the highest possible wage have real costs to Americans. Allowing Germany and China to trade their unused savings for employment at a time when we have little use for their risk-averse savings slows America's growth. Policies that demand balanced trade with trade partners would accelerate growth, increase employment, and reduce the inherent instability of banking under the current set of circumstances.

The costs of demanding balanced trade are likely to be less than the alternatives for putting risk-averse savings stemming from trade deficits to work in order to reach full employment. Large government deficits in the face of historically high government debt levels decouple voters and lawmakers from constraining government spending and push out-of-control costs onto younger generations. A massive expansion of government-chosen infrastructure projects is unproven and unlikely to be as valuable as proponents claim. Radical monetary policy designed to increase inflation in order to discourage saving is expensive to middle-class savers and destabilizing to the economy more broadly. Subprime-mortgage lending to fuel subprime consumption has proved to be unsustainable.

While it may be true that giving lawmakers control over imports is like taking a shot of malaria to cure a cold—or mononucleosis, in this case—proposed alternatives don't avoid government interference, either. The proposed plan minimizes the need for policy makers to micromanage trade by picking winners and losers, imposing tariffs, or reacting to unfair trade practices that lower the price of goods to American consumers. It simply says to Germany, China, and others: find offsetting American goods to buy. It's hard to believe that in America's vast economy, they can't find something to buy.

At the same time, strengthening the Fed's role as the lender of last resort during a run on the banks would reduce the inherent instability of banking. It is likely the economy has permanently dialed back risk-taking to account for this now-recognized risk. Mitigating this risk would accelerate growth.

We must hold banks responsible for every nickel of their loan losses. If we don't, banks will lend recklessly and make bad loans. There is plenty of time *after* a run on the banks to assess loan losses and charge banks accordingly. But when we hold banks responsible for bank runs, they have no choice but to leave deposits—or worse, equity—sitting idle, available for withdrawal. Idle savings slow growth.

Alternatively, the Federal Reserve as the lender of last resort can simply print money and loan it to the banks to fund withdrawals during a run on the banks. Once people see that they are able to withdraw their savings, panic subsides, deposits return to the banks, and the Fed can burn the printed money at no cost. And this is what the Fed did.* It briefly guaranteed $15 trillion of deposits, loaned the banks $2 trillion to fund withdrawals, and made a profit.[8] The Fed made a *profit* acting as the lender of last resort in the worst financial crisis in nearly a millennium. The Fed took surprisingly little risk despite an avalanche of reckless claims to the contrary.

Rather than strengthening the Fed's ability to act more effectively as the lender of last resort in a bank run, policy makers have done the opposite. They have held banks more responsible for bank runs by intentionally weakening the Fed's ability to act in a panic. Banks pulled back lending by raising credit standards. Risk-averse savings have subsequently sat unused, and the recovery has been anemic.

Other well-intentioned policies would have the same effect. Demanding that banks hold more equity largely just reallocates risk-taking from other sectors of the economy. The risk-underwriting capacity of equity is zero-sum unless the economy has illogically held large amounts of equity idle to compensate for the risk of government guarantees of banks. But why would it do that when the true cost of government guarantees is small if properly managed?

Nor can banks match the duration of loans to the duration of their

* Although the Fed didn't burn the money. Instead, the surplus money sat unused, producing neither growth nor inflation.

deposits. Loans are inherently long term except loans supporting financial arbitrage, which do little to grow the economy. Risk-averse deposits are inherently short term. Banks must provide depositors on-demand withdrawals of guaranteed principal to provide a credible alternative to risk-averse savers stuffing their mattresses with cash and subsequently slowing growth.

These ill-advised alternatives—holding the banks more responsible for bank runs by weakening the Fed's ability to act as the lender of last resort, demanding that banks hold more equity, and insisting on matching the duration of loans to the duration of savings—leave risk-averse savings or equity sitting idle. Why suffer permanent recession to avoid intermittent recession?

In the aftermath of the financial crisis, the economy has dialed back risk-taking to compensate for the now-recognized inherent instability of banking and the damage it causes. Unfortunately, political leaders—on both the left and the right—have successfully persuaded the public to blame Wall Street, the Community Reinvestment Act, Fannie Mae and Freddie Mac, loose monetary policy, a laissez-faire regulatory philosophy, credit default swaps, the failure to save Lehman Brothers, and anyone and anything else they can for the inherent instability of banking. For political gain, lawmakers have done little to address the situation logically.

Instead, lawmakers have undermined the low-cost alternative to a panic by weakening the Fed's ability to act swiftly and without political interference in a bank run. They have threatened the banks with bankruptcy and litigation, which has slowed bank lending and economic activity. They have increased capital requirements on banks, which, at best, just reallocates equity that was underwriting risk elsewhere in the economy. And they have passed a plethora of regulations that do little more than reduce competition and trading volumes, which reduces liquidity in markets. Is it any surprise the recovery has been anemic?

Then to mitigate the resulting weak recovery, some economists have recommended the government borrow and spend idle savings. When spending proved to have little, if any, promised multiplier effect, they now recommend infrastructure investment. But promised returns are unlikely to materialize. Others have recommended permanently inflating the money supply to spark price inflation in order to reduce saving. Rather than borrowing to increase unneeded spending or taxing savings with inflation, wouldn't it be less damaging to demand balanced trade in order to reduce excess risk-averse savings directly? Unfortunately there is little hope that America can make any progress in these critical areas given the divisive leadership and diversity of opinions on the financial crisis.

# A Middle-Class Tax Cut Will Slow Growth

One of the few proposals for reducing inequality and accelerating growth that seems to be gaining traction is a middle-class tax cut led by advocates of redistribution. Given the size of the middle-class voter base and Republican arguments that claim lower taxes alone will accelerate growth, it will be politically difficult for many politicians to oppose such a tax cut. It is doubtful, however, that such a tax cut will accelerate growth.

Tax cuts don't accelerate growth per se. Successful risk-taking that produces innovation and gradually builds institutional capabilities accelerates growth. A middle-class tax cut will have no such effect.

Instead, the lower price of government services will motivate demand for more services. Ultimately, money spent is money taxed—even if the government borrows in the interim. When government consumes a greater share of GDP, even if it merely transfers GDP from workers to other consumers, it reduces incentives to work, invest, and innovate. That slows growth. If successful risk-takers bear a disproportionate share of the cost of increased government spending, growth will slow further.

A more logical approach to taxation than selling government services to taxpayers for less than their cost reduces the middle-class tax rate to zero but charges citizens the true cost of the government services they consume—no different than if they had purchased those services in the private sector. After all, advocates of smaller government should be concerned that free or underpriced services cause voters to consume far more government than they otherwise would. This overconsumption of inefficiently produced goods and services slows growth.

Of course, there are real-world complications. We may insist that people save for their retirement and buy health insurance so they can't take advantage of a society that is unwilling to let freeloaders suffer. Similarly, people may be unwilling to fund defense, aid for the poor, and other common goods unless the government forces them to pay. And we may demand a level of nutrition and education for children that some parents are unable, or unwilling, to buy.

Many of these issues can and are solved with mandates and nontransferable vouchers for services—healthcare subsidies for people with preexisting medical conditions, for example. We could also raise the tax rate to force everyone to save 10 percent of their income for retirement or lower the tax rate to less than zero to subsidize the earnings of the poor via an earned income tax credit. But leaving aside these practical issues, this theoretical exercise provides a baseline for understanding taxation and government spending and its effect on growth.

The true measure of taxation is the amount one pays over and above the cost of the government services they consume—the dollars redistributed from one person's pocket to another's. We don't consider it taxation when we buy food. We should think about taxation for government services in the same way. Taxes are what we pay over and above the cost of the government services we receive.

Interestingly, the Congressional Budget Office (CBO) has conducted the complex exercise of allocating the cost of federal government services directly consumed by the elderly—chiefly Social Security and Medicare—and then separately, for each of the income quintiles of non-elderly workers.[9] With a little more elbow grease, one can also allocate the indirect government services that everyone shares.

For example, military expenditures—60 percent of shared government services—can be allocated to households based on their income.[10] By that, I mean the true measure of their income—not just their earned income, but their earned income plus the value of government services and transfers less taxes. That allocation scheme presumes rich families have more to protect and lowers everyone else's allocation.

The CBO doesn't allocate interest expense.[11] It reasons that interest expense is for government services previously provided, not currently received. While that's true, the argument is hard to buy economically.

If the government borrows instead of taxing you, and you use the tax savings to consume or invest, clearly the government now incurs interest expenses on your incremental purchases, no different than if you had used your credit card instead of the government's. Economically, you should reimburse the government for the interest payments it makes on your behalf.

Interest expense can be allocated based on either government services received or taxes paid. One could argue that interest payments are proportional to services received—that the government borrows to provide more services because it is unable to tax anyone any more than it already is. Alternatively, one could argue that borrowing avoids taxation, so interest should be allocated proportionally with taxes paid. The latter gives the benefit of the doubt to the middle class by heaping the benefits of government borrowing on rich taxpayers, who pay a greater share of the taxes than the government benefits they receive.

Conversely, government deficits should be allocated as additional taxes. Ultimately, money spent is money taxed. Surely, when the government borrows on your behalf, it has a real cost to you. While interest expense is a benefit paid on your behalf by the government so you can consume more than you would if taxes were higher, deficits are really (future) taxes in disguise.

Deficits can also be allocated based on benefits received or taxes paid. Again, the more persuasive approach allocates deficits based on taxes paid, but with one important caveat: the elderly will be dead before we pay off the debt, so it is more logical to allocate deficits to non-elderly households only. That increases non-elderly middle-class taxes. But because the CBO used 2006 for its analysis, the deficit was only $200 billion—small compared with the years afterward.

All other unallocated government services—largely the cost of running the government—probably should be allocated on a per-person basis. For the sake of fairness, surely the true value of some unallocated government services accrues to people on a per-person basis rather than proportional to their income.

From this perspective, the non-elderly middle class paid about $13,000 in taxes in 2006, including payroll taxes paid by individuals and their employers and allocated deficit spending, for the $14,000 of government services they received (see Figure 10-1, "Federal Government Expenditures and Taxes by Household Type"). They received nearly a $1,000-a-year stipend to supplement their nearly $60,000 a year of household earnings, plus they expect to receive about $29,000 a year of retirement benefits in the future, for which, in truth, they contributed nothing.[12] Nor did they pay any assistance to the poor or the elderly.

In 2006 non-elderly working-class households earning between the twentieth and fortieth percentiles of income paid about $7,000 a year in taxes, including payroll taxes, for $15,000 a year of government services. They received an $8,000 stipend on their approximately $36,000 of household income, not including their expected retirement benefits. In fact, they paid about the same amount of taxes as they received in *direct* government benefits.

Households in the top 20 percent paid about $50,000 more per year in taxes than the value of the government services they received. These households paid nearly 90 percent of the $24,000 a year of government benefits received by the 25 million elderly households over and above the taxes paid by those elderly households, and the $20,000 a year (over and above the taxes they paid) received by the 18 million poorest non-elderly households—the bottom 20 percent of non-elderly households. The top 20 percent of non-elderly households also covered 40 percent of the military expenditures and 55 percent of the interest expense.

With publicly held federal debt at 73 percent of GDP—more than double the level prior to the financial crisis—and with baby boomers retiring en masse with no plan or consensus to pay for their promised benefits, at the very least, it's risky to cut taxes without first cutting spending.[13] The middle class isn't even paying for their *own* retirement under the current tax policy.

Even worse, in an economy where workers have worked less over time as they earn more—unless their work is either intrinsically interesting or it enhances their status—lowering the middle-class tax rate from an already less-than-zero level is likely to have worrisomely unintended consequences.[14] It will likely lower work efforts and increase government dependence, which is probably already much higher than it would be if people were properly charged for the government services they consumed.

## Figure 10-1:  Federal Government Expenditures and Taxes by Household Type

| (Dollars per Household) | ELDERLY | NON-ELDERLY BY INCOME QUINTILE | | | | |
|---|---|---|---|---|---|---|
| | | Lowest | Second | Middle | Fourth | Highest |
| Cash and Near Cash Transfers | 16,550 | 10,000 | 4,600 | 2,600 | 1,850 | 1,450 |
| Healthcare | 12,250 | 5,200 | 2,000 | 1,100 | 750 | 550 |
| Direct Transfer Subtotal | 28,800 | 15,200 | 6,600 | 3,700 | 2,600 | 2,000 |
| Military (By Net Income) | 5,150 | 1,850 | 2,650 | 3,750 | 5,350 | 12,800 |
| Interest Expense (By Taxes Paid) | 1,350 | 250 | 600 | 1,050 | 1,800 | 6,200 |
| Other (Per Person) | 3,300 | 5,250 | 5,650 | 5,350 | 5,350 | 5,100 |
| Indirect Government Services Subtotal | 9,800 | 7,350 | 8,900 | 10,150 | 12,500 | 24,100 |
| Total Government Services | 38,600 | 22,550 | 15,500 | 13,850 | 15,100 | 26,100 |
| Taxes Paid (All) | 14,800 | 2,600 | 6,500 | 11,800 | 19,700 | 68,100 |
| Deficit Accrued (By Taxes Paid) | 0 | 250 | 650 | 1,200 | 2,050 | 7,050 |
| Total Tax Expense | 14,800 | 2,850 | 7,150 | 13,000 | 21,750 | 75,150 |
| Net Subsidy | 23,800 | 19,700 | 8,350 | 850 | (6,650) | (49,050) |
| Mean Market Income | 56,200 | 12,600 | 36,100 | 59,500 | 89,900 | 240,800 |

Sources: Congressional Budget Office, 2013; Author's calculations

Perhaps we have already seen what happens when we no longer ask people to feel responsible for setting aside some portion of their income for others (namely, for the poor and the elderly) or even to save for their own retirement, because they assume others will provide it for them. The moral fabric seems to fray when people no longer have fundamental responsibilities for others.

When political leaders insist that the handful of successful entrepreneurs—who took the risks and made the sacrifices necessary to produce innovation in an economy that would otherwise grow more slowly, and who serve their fellow man by serving customers—are nothing more than cheaters who succeeded at the expense of the middle class, moral obligations fray further. Advocates of redistribution insist that these successful leaders refuse to pay their "fair share" of taxes, despite their financing almost all of the aid to the poor and elderly. Rather than uniting society's leaders and followers and calling for everyone to fulfill their civic obligations, advocates of redistribution claim middle- and working-class taxpayers deserve to pay less—when they are already paying less than zero.

And is it any wonder the moral fabric frays when we look to our elders and find that they take more than everyone else, no matter how high their income, when this money could be used to help the poor, lower the deficit, or fund research and development that improves the future? Doesn't it fray even more when political leaders, especially advocates of redistribution, refuse to demand any entitlement reforms whatsoever? Don't most people throw up their hands and justify looking after only themselves?

A better approach would be to set the tax rate for the middle and working classes at zero or less. And then charge them the true cost of the government services they consume. If we did that, people would demand less services. They would get more demanding about the cost of government services. And they would search for more effective private-sector alternatives. They might even grow more appreciative of the benefits they are receiving from others—wishful thinking, I know.

Gradually, government spending would dial back to the services people were willing to buy. That would go a long way toward accelerating growth.

At the very least, we shouldn't open the door to immigrants and then pay them stipends, too. It's hard to see how that benefits America.

## Conclusion

We are wasting precious opportunities to accelerate growth. Growth is constrained by the economy's capacity and willingness to take risk and by properly trained talent that's motivated to find and take thoughtful risks that grow the economy. We need more equity to bear the risks that grow the economy, more properly trained talent to take those risks, and stronger incentives to motivate the talent to take them. The combination of these three factors produces powerful, gradually compounding institutional capabilities that accelerate growth. There is no alternative.

We're not going to fix America's seemingly intractable problems—slowing growth, the retirement of baby boomers whose demand for retirement benefits funded by others will eat us alive, never-ending poverty, low-skilled immigration that strains resources further, and potentially lethal competition with a rapidly emerging China—by ignoring these problems and delaying solutions while we try to push the costs onto others. It's time to act like successful entrepreneurs. Expunge seductive wishful thinking and be tough-minded about what we can truly accomplish. Resources are limited. Ultimately, strategy is deciding what not to do.

We're not going to innovate our way out of these problems. Nor export our way out. And we're certainly not going to redistribute our way out. Europe tried that; others have, too. Income redistribution dulls incentives and gradually slows growth.

We must remain vigilant, because as growth slows, special interests will fight for political control over constrained resources for the sake of their own self-interests. As one faction endeavors to gain control, others must necessarily fight for control, too. This fight leaves few champions of free enterprise. Ultimately, the success of special interests to control constrained resources gradually replaces free enterprise and its Darwinian struggle to create value—a dynamic process that has served mankind far more successfully than all other alternatives—with centralized planning, which has repeatedly slowed growth and diminished prosperity.

To succeed in today's competitive world, we have to recognize that we have to do things differently than in the past. We no longer have the luxury of remaining hostile toward business and investors in an increasingly competitive world. We can't take growth for granted and wait for demand to spur investment. We can't let trade partners dump their risk-averse savings into our economy, when we have no need for those savings. We can't afford to waste talent by paying students to study subjects that taxpayers don't value. We can't keep pretending there is a miraculous cure for turning low-scoring students into higher-scoring students and that school, as it is currently configured, is helping at-risk children compete for jobs and climb out of poverty.

America needs to drive its own talent to get trained, which it can do by reducing subsidies to college students pursing majors far in excess of the economy's demand. It can spend more to ensure top-scoring students from lower-socioeconomic families graduate from college. But that's not enough. America can also recruit properly trained talent from the rest of the world.

More talent combined with a lower corporate tax rate will lure employers of high-skilled workers to America. The success of these companies and workers will accelerate growth and the accumulation of equity that's needed to underwrite further risk-taking. Gradually, this will have large and compound effects on growth, employment, and wages at all skill levels.

At the same time, demanding balanced trade with trading partners is a better way to eliminate excess risk-averse savings, which slow growth, than monetary inflation or increased government spending. Enhancing the Fed's ability to function as the lender of last resort in a bank run, which unnecessarily damages the economy, is far superior to any other alternative. Zeroing middle-class tax rates and charging people the true cost of government services would gradually rein in government spending that crowds out the private sector and slows growth.

Like every successful enterprise, to grow faster, America needs to hire properly trained talent—its own and high-skilled immigrants— and maximize its return on investment by implementing a lower corporate tax rate and reining in unproductive government spending. The rest is little more than wishful thinking and good intentions.

# ACKNOWLEDGMENTS

Without Bruce Greenwald—whom I co-opted through thirty-six years of lunches into being what is, in effect, my thesis adviser—my understanding of the economy would be pedestrian. It was Bruce and Joe Stiglitz's book *Towards a New Paradigm in Monetary Economics* that allowed me to see that risk-averse savings could and would sit unused when equity and the economy's capacity and willingness to take risk constrained growth. Their insight opened my eyes to other unconventional constraints to growth and their effects on the economy, namely, properly trained talent. Kevin Hassett also provided invaluable insights and second opinions.

Steve Levitt's early praise for the rough draft of my first book, *Unintended Consequences,* gave me the credibility I needed to persuade agents and publishers to take me seriously.

Without my wife's agent, David McCormick, I would never have met my agent, Cathy Hemming. And without Cathy Hemming's relationship with my publisher, Adrian Zackheim, there would be no book.

Nor would there be a book without Adrian's right-hand man, Will Weisser. Adrian and Will took a chance on my first book when no one else dared.

It's an understatement to say that my business partner, Mitt Romney, winning the Republican nomination for president generated interest in my first book. That interest gave me a second career.

The American Enterprise Institute's stamp of approval and the endorsements of many top economists—Glenn Hubbard, Greg Mankiw,

Tyler Cowen, Nouriel Roubini, Andrei Shliefer, and others—persuaded some skeptical readers and journalists to take a more thoughtful look at my work.

My research assistant, Steve Bogden, ensured that I considered every relevant economic study. I doubt there is a person who has surveyed as much of the economic landscape as Steve. Matt Rousu and Ben Ho also chipped in with valuable research, criticism, and insights.

Without my editor, Bria Sandford, and her assistant, Vivian Roberson, this book would be harder to read than it is. Having written a book, I thought I knew how to write. I am continually mistaken.

Tara Gilbride, Kelsey Odorczyk, and the publicity team at Penguin/Portfolio, along with Peter Barden and Matt Olsen on the inside and Stephanie Marshall on the outside, all helped with the one thing harder than writing a book—getting someone to read it!

Jessica Gordon, my assistant, catered to my demands with a never-ending smile.

Mitt Romney and my partners at Bain Capital gave me a career opportunity that eventually allowed me the luxury of affording my own time. Like Adrian and Will, if Mitt hadn't bet on me early in my career, it is doubtful that I'd be writing today.

Without my wife, Jill Davis, and our daughter, Campbell, I would be less inspired to write. They are the true source of my motivation—to leave the world a better place than I found it, and to set an example for my daughter to follow, important lessons my parents taught me.

And thank you for investing the time to consider my arguments.

# NOTES

## Introduction

1. Timothy Noah, "Why Edward Conard Is Wrong About Income Inequality," *Huffington Post,* May 29, 2012, http://www.huffingtonpost.com/timothy -noah/edward-conard-inequality_b_1551342.html.
2. "Ed Conard Debates Austan Goolsbee at the Center for American Progress," Edward Conard, n.d., http://www.edwardconard.com/cap/.
3. David Leonhardt and Kevin Quealy, "The American Middle Class Is No Longer the World's Richest," *New York Times,* April 22, 2014, http://www .nytimes.com/2014/04/23/upshot/the-american-middle-class-is-no-longer -the-worlds-richest.html.
4. Pew Research Center, "Modern Immigration Wave Brings 59 Million to U.S. Driving Population Growth and Change Through 2065," September 28, 2015, http://www.pewhispanic.org/files/2015/09/2015-09-28_modern-immigration -wave_REPORT.pdf.

## *Chapter 1:* The Causes of Growing Inequality

1. Joseph Stiglitz, *Rewriting the Rules of the American Economy* (New York: W. W. Norton, 2015).
2. Martin Ford, *Rise of the Robots: Technology and the Threat of a Jobless Future* (New York: Basic Books, 2015).
3. Thomas Piketty, *Capital in the Twenty-First Century* (Cambridge, MA: Harvard University Press, 2013).
4. Alyssa Davis and Lawrence Mishel, "CEO Pay Continues to Rise as Typical Workers Are Paid Less," Economic Policy Institute, June 12, 2014, http://www .epi.org/publication/ceo-pay-continues-to-rise.
5. Bruce Greenwald and Judd Kahn *Globalization: n. The Irrational Fear That Some- one in China Will Take Your Job* (Hoboken, NJ: John Wiley & Sons, 2008).
6. "Modern Immigration Wave Brings 59 Million to U.S. Driving Population Growth and Change Through 2065," Pew Research Center, September 28, 2015, http://www.pewhispanic.org/files/2015/09/2015-09-28_modern-immi gration-wave_REPORT.pdf.
7. David Leonhardt and Kevin Quealy, "The American Middle Class Is No Longer the World's Richest," *New York Times,* April 22, 2014, http://www.nytimes

.com/2014/04/23/upshot/the-american-middle-class-is-no-longer-the-worlds
-richest.html?_r=0.

8. Ibid.

9. Paul Krugman, "The Conscience of a Liberal: Inequality and Economic Performance," *New York Times,* December 2, 2014, http://krugman.blogs.nytimes
.com/2014/12/02/inequality-and-economic-performance/?module=BlogPost
-Title&version=Blog.

10. Gross World Product, Wikipedia (n.d.), https://en.wikipedia.org/wiki
/Gross_world_product.

International Monetary Fund, "Report for Selected Countries and Subjects," World Economic Outlook Database, October 2014, https://www.imf
.org/external/pubs/ft/weo/2014/02/weodata/weorept.aspx?pr.x=67&pr.y=8
&sy=2012&ey=2019&scsm=1&ssd=1&sort=country&ds=.&br=1&c=924&s=NG
DP_R%2CNGDP_RPCH%2CNGDP%2CNGDPD%2CNGDP_D
%2CNGDPRPC%2CNGDPPC%2CNGDPDPC%2CPPPGDP%2CPPPPC%2CP
PPSH&grp=0&a.

11. Organization for Economic Co-operation and Development, *In It Together:
Why Less Inequality Benefits All* (OECD Publishing, 2015), http://www.keepeek
.com/Digital-Asset-Management/oecd/employment/in-it-together-why-less
-inequality-benefits-all_9789264235120-en#page17.

12. Robert H. Frank and Phillip J. Cook, *The Winner-Take-All Society: Why the Few at
the Top Get So Much More Than the Rest of Us* (New York: Free Press, 1995).

Sherwin Rosen, "The Economics of Superstars," *American Economic Review*
71, no. 5 (1981), http://home.uchicago.edu/~vlima/courses/econ201/Super
stars.pdf.

13. "The S&P 500 at Your Fingertips," *Political Calculations,* December 6, 2006,
http://politicalcalculations.blogspot.com/2006/12/sp-500-at-your-finger
tips.html#.VOX1tth0zSc.

"The Top 1% vs the S&P 500," *Political Calculations,* October 27, 2011, http://
politicalcalculations.blogspot.com/2011/10/top-1-vs-s-500.html#.VOXz5dh0zSc.

"The Distribution of Household Income and Federal Taxes, 2011," Congressional Budget Office, November 12, 2014, https://www.cbo.gov/publica
tion/49440.

14. Jan Behringer and Till van Treeck, "Income Distribution, Aggregate Demand
and Current Account: A Sectoral Perspective," Working Paper, October 21, 2013,
http://www.boeckler.de/pdf/v_2013_10_24_behringer_van_treeck.pdf.

15. Ibid.

16. Carol Corrado, Charles Hulten, and Daniel Sichel, "Intangible Capital and
Economic Growth," Finance and Economics Discussion Series, Federal Reserve Board, April 2006, http://www.federalreserve.gov/pubs/feds/2006
/200624/200624pap.pdf.

17. Bart van Ark, Janet X. Hao, Carol A. Corrado, and Charles R. Hulton, "Measuring Intangible Capital and Its Contribution to Economic Growth in Europe," *European Investment Bank Papers* 14, no. 1 (2009), http://econweb.umd
.edu/~hulten/L5/Measuring%20Intangible%20Capital%20and%20Its%20
Contribution%20to%20Economic%20Growth.pdf.

Janet X. Hao and Charles R. Hulton, "What Is a Company Really Worth?
Intangible Capital and the 'Market to Book Value' Puzzle," Working Paper
08-02, Economics Program of the Conference Board, revised December
2008, http://www.nber.org/papers/w14548.

18. Chad Syverson, "Challenges to Mismeasurement Explanations for the U.S. Productivity Slowdown," National Bureau of Economic Research, January 2016, http://faculty.chicagobooth.edu/chad.syverson/research/productivi tyslowdown.pdf.

   David M. Byrne, John G. Fernald, and Marshall B. Reinsdorf, "Does the United States Have a Productivity Slowdown or a Measurement Problem?" *Brookings Papers on Economic Activity*, March 1, 2016, http://www.brookings .edu/~/media/projects/bpea/spring-2016/byrneetal_productivitymeasure ment_conferencedraft.pdf

19. "Frothy.com," *Economist*, December 20, 2014, http://www.economist.com /news/business/21636754-new-tech-bubble-seems-be-inflating-when -it-pops-it-should-cause-less-damage.

20. Eric Newcomer, "Venture Funding of U.S. Startups Last Year Was Most Since 2000," *Bloomberg Business*, January 16, 2015, http://www.bloomberg.com/news/ articles/2015-01-16/it-s-official-startup-funding-last-year-was-biggest-since-2000.

21. Ian Hathaway and Robert E. Litan, "Declining Business Dynamism in the United States: A Look at States and Metros," *Economic Studies at Brookings*, May 2014, http://www.brookings.edu/~/media/research/files/papers/2014/05/ declining%20business%20dynamism%20litan/declining_business_dyna mism_hathaway_litan.pdf.

22. Ian Hathaway, "Tech Starts: High-Technology Business Formation and Job Creation in the United States," *Kauffman Foundation Research Series: Firm Formation and Economic Growth*, 2013, http://www.kauffman.org/what-we-do/ research/firm-formation-and-growth-series/tech-starts-hightechnology-busi ness-formation-and-job-creation-in-the-united-states.

   Jonathan Ortmans, "Deconstructing Job Creation from Startups," Ewing Marion Kauffman Foundation, August 10, 2015, http://www.kauffman .org/blogs/policy-dialogue/2015/august/deconstructing-job-creation-from -startups.

23. Jorge Guzman and Scott Stern, "The State of American Entrepreneurship: New Estimates of the Quantity and Quality of Entrepreneurship for 15 US States, 1988–2014," National Bureau of Economic Research, March 2016, http://static1.squarespace.com/static/53d52829e4b0d9e21c9a6940 /t/56d9a05545bf217588498535/1457102936611/Guzman+Stern+—+State +of+American+Entrepreneurship+FINAL.pdf.

24. Ibid.

25. Chad Syverson, "Challenges to Mismeasurement Explanations for the U.S. Productivity Slowdown," National Bureau of Economic Research, January 2016, http://faculty.chicagobooth.edu/chad.syverson/research/productivi tyslowdown.pdf.

   Byrne, Fernald, and Reinsdorf, "Does the United States Have a Productivity Slowdown or a Measurement Problem?"

   Andrew Smithers, "Executive Pay Holds the Key to the Productivity Puzzle," *Financial Times*, May 28, 2015, http://www.ft.com/intl/cms/s/0/64b73a8e -0485-11e5-95ad-00144feabdc0.html#axzz3n4A85pjM.

26. Author's calculation using Figure 4-2. Assumes $450 billion per year average net investment from 2009 to 2014.

27. Social Security Administration, "The Boskin Commission Report: Toward a More Accurate Measure of the Cost of Living," December 4, 1996, http:// www.ssa.gov/history/reports/boskinrpt.html.

Robert J. Gordon, "The Boskin Commission Report: A Retrospective One Decade Later," National Bureau of Economic Research Working Paper Series, Working Paper 12311, June 2006, http://www.nber.org/papers/w12311.pdf.

David S. Johnson, Stephen B. Reed, and Kenneth J. Steward, "Price Measurement in the United States: A Decade After the Boskin Report," *Monthly Labor Review*, May 2006: 10–19, http://www.bls.gov/opub/mlr/2006/05/art2full.pdf.

28. James Pethokoukis, "Goldman Sachs Says the US Economy Could Be Growing a Lot Faster Than GDP Stats Say. Here's Why," American Enterprise Institute, July 25, 2015, https://www.aei.org/publication/goldman-sachs-says-the-us-economy-could-be-growing-a-lot-faster-than-gdp-stats-say-heres-why.

29. Richard Dobbs et al., "The New Global Competition for Corporate Profits," McKinsey Global Institute Report, September 2015, http://www.mckinsey.com/insights/corporate_finance/the_new_global_competition_for_corporate_profits.

30. Ibid.

31. Ibid.

32. David N. Weill, *Economic Growth* (New York: Prentice Hall, 2005), 252.

33. Ibid.

34. Jon Bakija, Adam Cole, and Bradley T. Heim, "Jobs and Income Growth of Top Earners and the Causes of Changing Income Inequality: Evidence from the U.S. Tax Return Data," Working Paper, April 2012, http://web.williams.edu/Economics/wp/BakijaColeHeimJobsIncomeGrowthTopEarners.pdf.

35. Richard Foster and Sarah Kaplan, *Creative Destruction: Why Companies That Are Built to Last Underperform the Market—and How to Successfully Transform Them* (New York: Crown, 2001), 11. First chapter available at: http://itech.fgcu.edu/faculty/bhobbs/Creative%20destruction%20McKinsey%20Report%20CDch1.pdf.

36. Ibid.

37. Michael Moritz, "The Fall and Rise of Technology Juggernauts," *Financial Times*, December 4, 2015, https://next.ft.com/content/6b859714-99ba-11e5-9228-87e603d47bdc#axzz3tJPF7UAb.

38. Ibid.

39. Joseph Stiglitz, *The Great Divide: Unequal Societies and What We Can Do About Them* (New York: W. W. Norton, 2015), 420.

40. "Keeping Up with the Karumes," *Economist,* October 29, 2015, http://www.economist.com/node/21677223.

41. Ibid.

Ada Ferrer-i-Carbonell, "Income and Well-Being: An Empirical Analysis of the Comparison Income Effect," *Journal of Public Economics* 89 (2005), http://darp.lse.ac.uk/papersDB/Ferrer-i-Carbonell_(JPubE05).pdf.

42. Aileen Lee, "Welcome to the Unicorn Club, 2015: Learning from Billion-Dollar Companies," *TechCrunch,* July 18, 2015, http://techcrunch.com/2015/07/18/welcome-to-the-unicorn-club-2015-learning-from-billion-dollar-companies/#.ttgtoz:1W8T.

"European Unicorns: Do They Have Legs?" GP. Bullhound, June 17, 2015, http://www.gpbullhound.com/wp-content/uploads/2015/06/GP-Bullhound-Research-Billion-Dollar-Companies-2015.pdf.

43. Scott Austin, Chris Canipe, and Sarah Slobin, "The Billion Dollar Startup Club," *Wall Street Journal*, February 18, 2015, http://graphics.wsj.com/billion -dollar-club.

44. Ibid.

45. Alan Greenspan, *The Age of Turbulence: Adventures in a New World* (New York: Penguin Press, 2007), 351.

46. "The Distribution of Household Income and Federal Taxes, 2011," Congressional Budget Office

47. Ford, *Rise of the Robots.*

## Chapter 2: The Reasons for Slowing Wage Growth

1. Bruce Greenwald and Judd Kahn, *Globalization: n. The Irrational Fear That Someone in China Will Take Your Job* (Hoboken, NJ: John Wiley & Sons, 2008).

2. "Modern Immigration Wave Brings 59 Million to U.S. Driving Population Growth and Change Through 2065," Pew Research Center, September 28, 2015, http://www.pewhispanic.org/files/2015/09/2015-09-28_modern-imm igration-wave_REPORT.pdf.

   Paul Taylor et al., "Second-Generation Americans: A Portrait of the Adult Children of Immigrants," Pew Research Center, February 7, 2013, http:// www.pewsocialtrends.org/2013/02/07/second-generation-americans.

3. Claudia Goldin and Lawrence F. Katz, *The Race Between Education and Technology* (Cambridge, MA: Belknap Press, 2008).

4. Eliza Barclay, "Your Grandparents Spent More of Their Money on Food Than You Do," National Public Radio, March 2, 2015, http://www.npr.org/sections/ thesalt/2015/03/02/389578089/your-grandparents-spent-more-of-their -money-on-food-than-you-do.

   "Table 7—Food Expenditures by Families and Individuals as a Share of Disposable Personal Income," U.S. Department of Agriculture, Economic Research Service, accessed April 8, 2016, http://www.ers.usda.gov/data-prod ucts/food-expenditures.aspx.

5. Christian Broda and John Romalis, "Inequality and Prices: Does China Benefit the Poor in America?" European Trade Study Group, 2008, http://www .etsg.org/ETSG2008/Papers/Romalis.pdf.

   Christian Broda, Ephraim Leibtag, and David Weinstein, "The Role of Prices in Measuring the Poor's Living Standards," *Journal of Economic Perspectives* 23, no. 2 (2009): 77–97, http://www.columbia.edu/~dew35/Papers/Poors _Living_Standards.pdf.

   Bruce Meyer and James Sullivan, "Winning the War: Poverty from Great Society to the Great Recession," *Brookings Papers on Economic Activity*, 2012, http://www.brookings.edu/~/media/Projects/BPEA/Fall%202012/2012b _Meyer.pdf.

6. "What Are Poverty Rates Among Working Adults?" University of California–Davis Center for Poverty Research, http://poverty.ucdavis.edu/faq/what-are -poverty-rates-among-working-adults.

   Carmen DeNavas-Walt and Bernadette D. Proctor, "Income and Poverty in the United States: 2014," U.S. Census Bureau, September 2015, http:// www.census.gov/content/dam/Census/library/publications/2015/demo/ p60-252.pdf.

7. David Card, "The Impact of the Mariel Boatlift on the Miami Labor Market," *Industrial and Labor Relations Review* 43 (1990): 245–57, http://davidcard .berkeley.edu/papers/mariel-impact.pdf.

Gianmarco Ottaviano and Giovanni Peri, "Rethinking the Effects of Immigration on Wages," National Bureau of Economic Research, 2006, http://www.parisschoolofeconomics.eu/docs/ydepot/semin/texte0607 /OTT2006RET.pdf.

Ann Harrison, John McLaren, and Margaret McMillan, "Recent Findings on Trade and Inequality," National Bureau of Economic Research, September 2010, http://www.nber.org/papers/w16425.

8. Michael Clemens, "Economics and Emigration: Trillion-Dollar Bills on the Sidewalk?" *Journal of Economic Perspectives*, 2011, http://pubs.aeaweb.org/doi/ pdfplus/10.1257/jep.25.3.83.

9. "Excess Reserves of Depository Institutions," FRED Economic Data, Federal Reserve Bank of St. Louis, accessed February 29, 2016, https://research.stlou isfed.org/fred2/series/EXCSRESNS.

10. Lawrence Summers, "U.S. Economic Prospects: Secular Stagnation, Hysteresis, and the Zero Lower Bound," *Business Economics* 49, no. 2 (February 24), 2014, http://larrysummers.com/wp-content/uploads/2014/06/NABE-speech -Lawrence-H.-Summers1.pdf.

11. Paul Krugman, "The Conscience of a Liberal: Demand Creates Its Own Supply," *New York Times*, November 3, 2015, http://krugman.blogs.nytimes .com/2015/11/03/demand-creates-its-own-supply/.

12. David Card, "Comment: The Elusive Search for Negative Wage Impacts of Immigration," National Bureau of Economic Research, 2012, http://david card.berkeley.edu/papers/jeea2012.pdf.

13. "Real Median Household Income in the United States," FRED Economic Data, Federal Reserve Bank of St. Louis, accessed May 10, 2016, https://re search.stlouisfed.org/fred2/series/MEHOINUSA672N.

14. David M. Weil, *Economic Growth* (Boston: Pearson, 2005), figure 3.1, *GDP and Capital per Worker, 2000,* 49.

15. Matthew F. Cancian and Michael W. Klein, "Military Officer Quality in the All-Volunteer Force," National Bureau of Economic Research, 2015, http:// www.brookings.edu/research/papers/2015/07/20-nber-military-officer- quality-volunteer-force—klein.

16. Federal Reserve Bank of San Francisco, "Is the U.S. Trade Deficit a Problem? What Is the Link Between the Trade Deficit and Exchange Rates?" *Dr. Econ*, June 2007, http://www.frbsf.org/education/publications/doctor-econ/2007/ june/trade-deficit-exchange-rate.

17. Atif Mian and Amir Sufi, "The Consequences of the Mortgage Credit Expansion: Evidence from the US Mortgage Default Crisis," *Social Science Research Network*, December 12, 2008, http://www.nber.org/papers /w13936.

18. "Excess Reserves of Depository Institutions," FRED Economic Data, Federal Reserve Bank of St. Louis, accessed September 3, 2015, https://research .stlouisfed.org/fred2/series/EXCSRESNS.

19. Ottaviano and Peri, "Rethinking the Effects of Immigration on Wages."

20. Lawrence Edwards and Robert Lawrence, "U.S. Trade and Wages: The Misleading Implications of Conventional Trade Theory," National Bureau of Economic Research, June 2010, http://www.nber.org/papers/w16106.

21. Harrison, McLaren, and McMillan, "Recent Findings on Trade and Inequality." Paul Krugman, "Trade and Wages, Reconsidered," *Brookings Papers on Economic Activity*, February 2008, http://www.brookings.edu/~/media/proj ects/bpea/spring -2008/2008a_bpea_krugman.pdf.

22. George J. Borjas, "The Wage Impact of the *Marielitos*: A Reappraisal," National Bureau of Economic Statistics, October 2015, http://www.hks.harvard .edu/fs/gborjas/publications/working%20papers/Mariel2015.pdf.

23. George J. Borjas, *Immigration Economics* (Cambridge, MA: Harvard University Press, 2014).

   George J. Borjas, "Immigration and the American Worker," Center for Immigration Studies, April 2013, http://cis.org/immigration-and-the -american-worker-review-academic-literature.

24. Alisa Priddle and Brent Snavely, "More Car Manufacturing Jobs Move South—to Mexico," *Detroit Free Press*, June 15, 2015, http://www.usatoday .com/story/money/cars/2015/06/15/auto-jobs-mexico/71224972.

25. Gerald Donahoe, "Capital in the National Health Accounts," Health Care Financing Administration, September 2000, https://www.cms.gov/research -statistics-data-and-systems/statistics-trends-and-reports/nationalhealthex penddata/downloads/capital.pdf.

26. "Employed Persons by Detailed Industry, Sex, Race, and Hispanic or Latino Ethnicity," Current Population Survey, Bureau of Labor Statistics, accessed December 17, 2015, http://www.bls.gov/cps/cpsaat18.htm.

27. David Autor, David Dorn, and Gordon Hanson, "The China Shock: Learning from Labor Market Adjustment to Large Changes in Trade," National Bureau of Economic Research, January 2016, http://www.nber.org/papers /w21906.

28. "Excess Reserves of Depository Institutions," FRED Economic Data, Federal Reserve Bank of St. Louis, accessed February 29, 2016, https://research.stlou isfed.org/fred2/series/EXCSRESNS.

29. Christoph Lakner and Milanovic Branko, "Global Income Distribution: From the Fall of the Berlin Wall to the Great Recession," World Bank, December 2013, http://www.umass.edu/preferen/You%20Must%20Read%20This /Global%20Income%20Distribution%20Lakner%20Milanovic.pdf.

*Chapter 3:* The Myth That Incentives Don't Matter

1. Peter Diamond and Emmanuel Saez, "The Case for a Progressive Tax: From Basic Research to Policy Recommendations," *Journal of Economic Perspectives* 25, no. 4 (2011): 165–90, http://eml.berkeley.edu/~saez/diamond-saezJE P11opttax.pdf.

2. Thomas Piketty, *Capital in the Twenty-First Century* (Cambridge, MA: Harvard University Press, 2013).

3. Lawrence Summers, "U.S. Economic Prospects: Secular Stagnation, Hysteresis, and the Zero Lower Bound," *Business Economics* 49, no. 2 (February 24, 2014), http://larrysummers.com/wp-content/uploads/2014/06/NABE-speech -Lawrence-H.-Summers1.pdf.

4. Erik Brynjolfsson and Andrew McAfee, *The Second Machine Age: Work, Progress, and Prosperity in a Time of Brilliant Technologies* (New York: W. W. Norton, 2014), 202.

5. Alan Krueger, "Rise and Consequences of Inequality in the United States,"

remarks at the Center for American Progress, January 12, 2012, https://www
.whitehouse.gov/sites/default/files/krueger_cap_speech_final_remarks.pdf.

6. Diamond and Saez, "The Case for a Progressive Tax: From Basic Research to Policy Recommendations."

7. James Fallows, "Why the Conard Interview Matters—or, Why the Democrats Need Karl Rove," *Atlantic,* June 8, 2012, http://www.theatlantic.com/politics/ archive/2012/06/why-the-conard-interview-matters-or-why-the-democrats -need-karl-rove/258303.

8. Gerald A. Carlino, "Knowledge Spillovers: Cities' Role in the New Economy," *Business Review, Federal Reserve Bank of Philadelphia,* 2001, https://webcache .googleusercontent.com/search?q=cache:3tfK2DlpWPUJ:https://www.phila delphiafed.org/research-and-data/publications/business-review/2001/q4 /brq401gc.pdf+&cd=1&hl=en&ct=clnk&gl=us.

9. Stefano Scarpetta and Ignazio Visco, "The Sources of Economic Growth in OECD Countries," OECD, 2003, http://www.oecd-ilibrary.org/economics/ the-sources-of-economic-growth-in-oecd-countries_9789264199460-en.

10. Leo Sveikauskas, "R&D and Productivity Growth: A Review of the Literature," Bureau of Labor Statistics, September 2007, http://www.bls.gov/ore/pdf/ ec070070.pdf.

11. Peter Kuhn and Fernando Lozano, "The Expanding Workweek? Understanding Trends in Long Work Hours among U.S. Men, 1979–2006," *Journal of Labor Economics* 26, no. 2 (2007): 311–43, http://www.econ.ucsb .edu/~pjkuhn/Research%20Papers/LongHours.pdf.
    Samuel Bowles and Yongjin Park, "Emulation, Inequality, and Work Hours: Was Thorsten Veblen Right?" *Economic Journal* 115, no. 507 (2005): 397–412, http://tuvalu.santafe.edu/~bowles/veblen.

12. Diamond and Saez, "The Case for a Progressive Tax."

13. Ibid.

14. Ibid.

15. David Leonhardt and Kevin Quealy, "The American Middle Class Is No Longer the World's Richest," *New York Times,* April 22, 2014, http://www.nytimes .com/2014/04/23/upshot/the-american-middle-class-is-no-longer-the -worlds-richest.html?_r=0.

16. "The United States of Entrepreneurs," *Economist,* May 12, 2009, http://www .economist.com/node/13216037.

17. Stijn Broecke, Glenda Quintini, and Marieke Vandeweyer, "Wage Inequality and Cognitive Skills: Re-Opening the Debate," National Bureau of Economic Research, February 2016, http://www.nber.org/papers/w21965.

18. Paul Krugman, "The Conscience of a Liberal: Reagan! Reagan! Reagan!" *New York Times,* November 7, 2009, http://krugman.blogs.nytimes.com/2009/11/07 /reagan-reagan-reagan.

19. Edward Conard, "Ed Conard Debates Austan Goolsbee at the Center for American Progress," August 1, 2012, http://www.edwardconard.com/cap.

20. Christopher Chantrill, "Total Spending in Percent of GDP," *U.S. Government Spending,* accessed May 11, 2016, http://www.usgovernmentspending.com/ spending_chart_1990_2020USp_16s1li111mcn_F0t_Total_Spending_In _Percent_GDP.

21. Paul Krugman, "Left Coast Rising," *New York Times,* July 24, 2014, http://www .nytimes.com/2014/07/25/opinion/paul-krugman-california-tax-left-coast -rising.html.

22. Tino Sanandaji, "The American Left's Two Europes Problem," *American,* February 29, 2012, https://www.aei.org/publication/the-american-lefts-two -europes-problem.

23. "Snapshot of Performance in Mathematics, Reading and Science," *PISA 2012 Results in Focus,* Organisation of Economic Co-operation and Development, http://www.oecd.org/pisa/keyfindings/PISA-2012-results-snapshot-Volume -I-ENG.pdf.

24. "Quarterly Growth Rates of Real GDP, Change over Previous Quarter," Quarterly National Accounts, Organisation of Economic Co-operation and Development, accessed September 30, 2015, https://stats.oecd.org/index .aspx?queryid=350.

"Income Inequality Gini Coefficient," Organisation of Economic Co-operation and Development, accessed May 11, 2016, https://data.oecd.org/ inequality/income-inequality.htm.

25. William D. Nordhaus, "Schumpeterian Profits and the Alchemist Fallacy," Yale Economic Applications and Policy Discussion Paper No. 6, April 2, 2005, http://papers.ssrn.com/sol3/papers.cfm?abstract_id=820309.

26. Ibid.

27. Edward Conard, *Unintended Consequences: Why Everything You've Been Told About the Economy Is Wrong* (New York: Portfolio, 2012), 255.

28. Adam Davidson, "The Purpose of Spectacular Wealth, According to a Spectacularly Wealthy Guy," *New York Times Magazine,* May 1, 2012, http://www .nytimes.com/2012/05/06/magazine/romneys-former-bain-partner-makes -a-case-for-inequality.html?pagewanted=1&ref=magazine&_r=0.

29. Ibid.

30. Ibid.

31. Ibid.

32. Karen E. Dynan, Jonathan Skinner, and Stephen P. Zeldes, "Do the Rich Save More?" *Journal of Political Economy* 112, no. 2 (2004): 397–444. Also available at https://www.dartmouth.edu/~jskinner/documents/DynanKEDothe Rich.pdf.

33. Carmen DeNavas-Walt and Bernadette D. Proctor, "Income and Poverty in the United States: 2013," *U.S. Census Bureau's Current Population Reports,* September 2014, http://www.census.gov/content/dam/Census/library/publica tions/2014/demo/p60-249.pdf.

34. "Growth in Means-Tested Programs and Tax Credits for Low-Income Households," *CBO Report,* Congressional Budget Office, February 11, 2013, https:// www.cbo.gov/publication/43934#title0.

35. Carmen DeNavas-Walt and Bernadette D. Proctor, "Income and Poverty in the United States: 2014," United States Census Bureau, September 2015, http://www.census.gov/content/dam/Census/library/publications/2015/ demo/p60-252.pdf.

36. "Civilian Labor Force Participation Rate," *Labor Force Statistics from the Current Population Survey,* Bureau of Labor Statistics, accessed September 16, 2015, http://data.bls.gov/timeseries/LNS11300000.

37. Robert Frank, "Darwin, the Market Whiz," *New York Times,* September 17, 2011, http://www.nytimes.com/2011/09/18/business/darwin-the-market-whiz.html.

Robert Frank, "The Invisible Hand Trumped by Darwin?" *New York Times,* July 12, 2009, http://www.nytimes.com/2009/07/12/business/economy/12view .html?_r=0.

38. "Poverty Overview," World Bank, updated April 6, 2015, http://www.world bank.org/en/topic/poverty/overview.

39. Peter Kuhn and Fernando Lozano, "The Expanding Workweek? Understanding Trends in Long Work Hours Among U.S. Men, 1979–2004," NBER Working Paper no. 11895 (December 2005).
    Bowles and Park, "Emulation, Inequality, and Work Hours."

40. Kristin J. Forbes, "A Reassessment of the Relationship Between Inequality and Growth," *American Economic Review* 90, no. 4 (2000): 869–87, http://web.mit.edu/~kjforbes/www/Papers/Inequality-Growth-AER.pdf.

41. Robert J. Barro, "Inequality and Growth in a Panel of Countries," *Journal of Economic Growth* 5 (March 2000): 5–32, http://scholar.harvard.edu/files/barro/files/inequality_growth_1999.pdf.

42. Jens Arnold, "Do Tax Structures Affect Aggregate Economic Growth? Empirical Evidence from a Panel of OECD Countries," Organisation of Economic Co-operation and Development, Economics Department Working Paper No. 643, October 14, 2008, http://dx.doi.org/10.1787/2360 01777843.
    Asa Johansson, Christopher Heady, Jens Arnold, Bert Brys, and Laura Vartia, "Tax and Economic Growth," OECD Economics Department Working Paper No. 620, July 11, 2008, https://www.oecd.org/tax/tax-policy/41000592.pdf.

43. Ibid.

44. Jonathan D. Ostry, Andrew Berg, and Charalambos G. Tsangarides, "Redistribution, Inequality, and Growth," *IMF Staff Discussion Note*, February 2014, http://www.imf.org/external/pubs/ft/sdn/2014/sdn1402.pdf.

45. Dan Andrews, Christopher Jencks, and Andrew Leigh, "Do Rising Top Incomes Lift All Boats?" IZA Discussion Paper No. 4920, April 2010, http://ftp.iza.org/dp4920.pdf.

46. Ibid.

47. Sutirtha Bagchi and Jan Svejnar, "Does Wealth Inequality Matter for Growth? The Effect of Billionaire Wealth, Income Distribution, and Poverty," IZA Discussion Paper No. 7733, November 2013, http://ftp.iza.org/dp7733.pdf.

48. Ana Swanson, "Why Some Billionaires Are Bad for Growth, and Others Aren't," *Washington Post*, August 20, 2015, http://www.washingtonpost.com/news/wonkblog/wp/2015/08/20/why-some-billionaires-are-bad-for-growth-and-others-arent.

49. Aart Kraay and David Dollar, "Growth Is Good for the Poor," *Policy Research Working Papers*, April 2001, http://elibrary.worldbank.org/doi/abs/10.1596/1813-9450-2587.
    David Dollar, Tatjana Kleineberg, and Aart Kraay, "Growth, Inequality and Social Welfare: Cross-Country Evidence," *Economic Policy* 81, issue C (2014): 68–85, http://www.worldbank.org/en/news/feature/2014/07/03/growth-inequality-and-social-welfare-cross-country-evidence.
    David Dollar, Tatjana Kleineberg, and Aart Kraay, "Growth Still Is Good for the Poor," *European Economic Review* 81, issue C (2016): 68–85, http://econpapers.repec.org/article/eeeeecrev/v_3a81_3ay_3a2016_3ai_3ac_3ap_3a68-85.htm.

50. Rakesh Kochhar, "How Americans Compare with the Global Middle Class," *Pew Research Center's Fact Tank*, July 9, 2015, http://www.pewresearch.org/fact-tank/2015/07/09/how-americans-compare-with-the-global-middle-class.

Chapter 4: The Myth That Success Is Largely Unearned

1. Thomas Piketty, *Capital in the Twenty-First Century* (Cambridge, MA: Harvard University Press, 2013).
2. Ibid.
3. Arvid Malm and Tino Sanandaji, "The Role of Entrepreneurship in Rising Wealth and Income Inequality," Royal Institute of Technology, Paper No. 398, CESIS: (2015), https://static.sys.kth.se/itm/wp/cesis/cesiswp 398.pdf.

   Jon Bakija, Adam Cole, and Bradley T. Heim, "Jobs and Income Growth of Top Earners and the Causes of Changing Income Inequality: Evidence from U.S. Tax Return Data," November 2010, http://piketty.pse.ens.fr/files/ Bakijaetal2010.pdf.
4. Bakija, Cole, and Heim, "Jobs and Income Growth of Top Earners and the Causes of Changing Income Inequality."
5. Seth H. Giertz and Jacob A. Mortenson, "Recent Income Trends for Top Executives: Evidence from Tax Return Data," *National Tax Journal* 66, no. 4 (2013): 913–38, http://digitalcommons.unl.edu/cgi/viewcontent.cgi?article =1089&context=econfacpub.
6. Jae Song, David J. Price, Fatih Guvenen, and Nicholas Bloom, Till von Wachter, "Firming Up Inequality," National Bureau of Economic Research Working Paper No. 21199 (May 2015), http://www.nber.org/papers/ w21199?utm_campaign=ntw&utm_medium=email&utm_source=ntw.
7. Lawrence Mishel and Natalie Sabadish, "CEO Pay and the Top 1%: How Executive Compensation and Financial Sector Pay Have Fueled Income Inequality," *Economic Policy Institute Brief 331* (May 2, 2012).
8. Piketty, *Capital in the Twenty-First Century.*
9. Ibid.
10. Song et al., "Firming Up Inequality."
11. Mishel and Sabadish, "CEO Pay and the Top 1%."
12. Piketty, *Capital in the Twenty-First Century.*
13. Song et al., "Firming Up Inequality."
14. Malm and Sanandaji, "The Role of Entrepreneurship in Rising Wealth and Income Inequality."

    Steven N. Kaplan and Joshua D. Rauh, "Family, Education, and Sources of Wealth among the Richest Americans, 1982–2012," *American Economic Review* 103, no. 3 (2013), https://ideas.repec.org/a/aea/aecrev/v103y2013i3p158-62 .html.
15. Malm and Sanandaji, "The Role of Entrepreneurship in Rising Wealth and Income Inequality."
16. Brian Raub, Barry Johnson, and Joseph Newcomb, "A Comparison of Wealth Estimates for America's Wealthiest Decedents Using Tax Data and Data from the Forbes 400," *Compilation of Federal Estate Tax and Personal Wealth Studies: Chapter 7—Studies Linking Income and Wealth* (n.d.): 811–25, 2010, http://www .irs.gov/pub/irs-soi/11pwcompench7ewealth.pdf.

    Malm and Sanandaji, "The Role of Entrepreneurship in Rising Wealth and Income Inequality."
17. Ibid.
18. Lawrence H. Summers, "The Inequality Puzzle," *Democracy,* 2014, http://www .democracyjournal.org/33/the-inequality-puzzle.php?page=all.

19. Jason Schloetzer, Melissa Aguilar, and Matteo Tonello, "Departing CEO Age and Tenure," *The Conference Board, CEO Succession Practices: 2013 Edition*, 2013, https://www.conference-board.org/retrievefile.cfm?filename=TCB -CW-019.pdf&type=subsite.

20. Raj Chetty, Nathaniel Hendren, Patrick Kline, Emmanuel Saez, and Nicholos Turner, "Where Is the Land of Opportunity? The Geography of Intergenerational Mobility in the United States," NBER Working Paper 19844, January 2014, http://www.equality-of-opportunity.org/files/mobility_trends.pdf.

21. Paul Krugman, "Why We're in a New Gilded Age," *New York Review of Books*, May 8, 2014, http://www.nybooks.com/articles/archives/2014/may/08/ thomas-piketty-new-gilded-age.

22. Joseph E. Stiglitz, "In No One We Trust," *New York Times*, December 21, 2013, http://opinionator.blogs.nytimes.com/2013/12/21/in-no-one-we-trust.

23. Ibid.

24. Piketty, *Capital in the Twenty-First Century*.

25. Ronald A. Heifetz and Marty Linsky, *Leadership on the Line: Staying Alive Through the Dangers of Leading* (Cambridge, MA: Harvard Business School Press, 2002).

26. M. H. Lopez, Jeffrey Passel, and Molly Rohal, "Modern Immigration Wave Brings 59 Million to U.S., Driving Population Growth and Change Through 2065: Views of Immigration's Impact on U.S. Society Mixed," Pew Research Center, September 28, 2015, http://www.pewhispanic.org/files/ 2015/09/2015-09-28_modern-immigration-wave_REPORT.pdf.

27. Steven N. Kaplan, "Executive Compensation and Corporate Governance in the U.S.: Perceptions, Facts and Challenges," National Bureau of Economic Research, 2012, http://papers.ssrn.com/sol3/papers.cfm?abstract_id=2134208

28. Ibid.
    Schloetzer et al., "Departing CEO Age and Tenure."

29. Lawrence Summers, "The Future of Work in the Age of the Machine: A Hamilton Project Policy Forum," National Press Club, February 19, 2015, http:// www.hamiltonproject.org/events/the_future_of_work_in_the_age_of_the _machine.
    Joseph E. Stiglitz, "The Origins of Inequality, and Policies to Contain It," *National Tax Journal* 68 (2015): 425–48, https://www0.gsb.columbia.edu/ faculty/jstiglitz/download/papers/2015%20Origins%20of%20Inequality.pdf.
    Robert Reich, *Saving Capitalism: For the Many, Not the Few* (New York: Knopf, 2015).
    Paul Krugman, "Challenging the Oligarchy," *New York Review of Books*, December 17, 2015.

30. Lawrence Summers, "The Future of Work in the Age of the Machine."

31. "ExxonMobil," Wikipedia, retrieved September 30, 2015, https://en.wikipedia .org/wiki/ExxonMobil.

32. Brianna Cardiff-Hicks, Francine Lafontaine, and Kathryn Shaw, "Do Large Modern Retailers Pay Premium Wages?" National Bureau of Economic Research, Working Paper No. 20313, July 2014, http://www.nber.org/papers/ w20313.

33. Theo Francis and Ryan Knutson, "Wave of Megadeals Tests Antitrust Limits in U.S.," *Wall Street Journal*, October 18, 2015, http://www.wsj.com/articles/ wave-of-megadeals-tests-antitrust-limits-in-u-s-1445213306.
    Gustavo Grullon, Yelena Larkin, and Roni Michaely, "The Disappearance of Public Firms and the Changing Nature of U.S. Industries," SSRN, May 2015, http://papers.ssrn.com/sol3/papers.cfm?abstract_id=2612047.

34. Richard Dobbs et al., "The New Global Competition for Corporate Profits," *McKinsey Global Institute Report,* September 2015, http://www.mckinsey.com/ insights/corporate_finance/the_new_global_competition_for_corporate _profits.

35. Ibid.

36. Ibid.

37. Michael Moritz, "The Fall and Rise of Technology Juggernauts," *Financial Times,* December 4, 2015, https://next.ft.com/content/6b859714-99ba-11e5 -9228-87e603d47bdc.

38. Diane Mulcahy, Bill Weeks, and Harold Bradley, "We Have Met the Enemy . . . and He Is Us," Kauffman Foundation, May 2012, http://www.kauffman .org/~/media/kauffman_org/research%20reports%20and%20cov ers/2012/05/we_have_met_the_enemy_and_he_is_us.pdf.

39. "Too Much of a Good Thing." *Economist,* March 23, 2016, http://www.econo mist.com/news/briefing/21695385-profits-are-too-high-america-needs -giant-dose-competition-too-much-good-thing.

40. Ibid.

41. Michael Feroli, "Is Monopoly Power Restraining Capital Spending?" JP Morgan Chase, April 2016, https://markets.jpmorgan.com/research/email/ -8oud8i0/-oXS8c3RAh cAi1iSCozY8g/GPS-1999083-0.

42. Stephen Dubner, "How Much Does Campaign Spending Influence the Election? A Freakonomics Quorum," *Freakonomics Blog,* January 17, 2012, http:// freakonomics.com/2012/01/17/how-much-does-campaign-spending- influence-the-election-a-freakonomics-quorum.

　　Steven Levitt, "Policy Watch: Congressional Campaign Finance Reform," *Journal of Economic Perspectives,* Winter 1995, http://pricetheory.uchicago .edu/levitt/Papers/LevittPolicyWatchCongressional1995.pdf.

　　Stephen Ansolabehere, John de Figueiredo, and James Snyder Jr., "Are Campaign Contributions Investment in the Political Marketplace or Individual Consumption? Or 'Why Is There So Little Money in Politics?'" *MIT Sloan Working Paper,* October 2002, http://web.mit.edu/jdefig/www/papers/ invest_or_consumpt.pdf.

43. Kenneth P. Vogel, Dave Levinthal, and Tarini Parti, "Obama, Romney Both Topped $1B," *Politico,* December 7, 2012, http://www.politico.com/story/2012/12/ barack-obama-mitt-romney-both-topped-1-billion-in-2012-084737.

44. Lawrence Summers, "Worker Voice Critical in US Growth Agenda," *Financial Times, Larry Summer's Blog,* September 10, 2015, http://blogs.ft.com/larry -summers/2015/09/10/worker-voice-critical-in-us-growth-agenda.

45. "Earnings and Unemployment Rate by Educational Attainment," United States Department of Labor, Bureau of Labor Statistics, accessed February 12, 2016, http://www.bls.gov/emp/ep_chart_001.htm.

46. David Card and Alan Krueger, "Minimum Wages and Employment: A Case Study of the Fast Food Industry in New Jersey and Pennsylvania," National Bureau of Economic Research, October 1993, http://www.nber.org/papers/ w4509.

47. David Neumark, J. M. Ian Salas, and William Wascher, "Revisiting the Minimum Wage-Employment Debate: Throwing Out the Baby with the Bathwater?" National Bureau of Economic Research, January 2013, http://journalistsre source.org//uploads/2013/02/2013-paper.pdf.

　　David Fairris and Leon Fernandez Bujanda, "The Dissipation of Minimum Wage Gains for Workers Through Labor-Labor Substitution: Evidence

from the Los Angeles Living Wage Ordinance," *Southern Economic Journal,* 2008, http://econpapers.repec.org/article/sejancoec/v_3a75_3a2_3ay_3a2008_3ap_3a473-496.htm#.UqeJP5lfD-I.emai.
48. Neumark, Salas, and Wascher, "Revisiting the Minimum Wage-Employment Debate."
49. Jeffrey Clemens and Michael Wither, "The Minimum Wage and the Great Recession: Evidence of Effects on the Employment and Income Trajectories of Low-Skilled Workers," National Bureau of Economic Research, November 24, 2014, http://econweb.ucsd.edu/~mwither/pdfs/Effects%20of%20Min%20Wage%20on%20Wages%20Employment%20and%20Earnings.pdf.
50. "The Effects of a Minimum-Wage Increase on Employment and Family Income," Congressional Budget Office, February 2014, http://www.cbo.gov/sites/default/files/cbofiles/attachments/44995-MinimumWage.pdf.
51. "Response to a Request by Senator Grassley About the Effects of Increasing the Federal Minimum Wage Versus Expanding the Earned Income Tax Credit," Congressional Budget Office, January 9, 2007, https://www.cbo.gov/sites/default/files/cbofiles/ftpdocs/77xx/doc7721/01-09-minimumwageeitc.pdf.
52. "The Effects of a Minimum-Wage Increase on Employment and Family Income."
53. European Commission, "Unemployment Rate by Sex and Age," *Eurostat,* accessed April 8, 2016, http://appsso.eurostat.ec.europa.eu/nui/show.do.

*Chapter 5:* The Myth That Investment Opportunities Are in Short Supply

1. Carol A. Corrado, Charles R. Hulten, and Daniel E. Sichel, "Intangible Capital and Economic Growth," *Finance and Economics Discussion Series,* April 2006, http://www.federalreserve.gov/pubs/feds/2006/200624/200624pap.pdf.
2. Lawrence Summers, "U.S. Economic Prospects: Secular Stagnation, Hysteresis, and the Zero Lower Bound," 2014, http://larrysummers.com/wp-content/uploads/2014/06/NABE-speech-Lawrence-H.-Summers1.pdf.
3. Ibid.
4. Ibid.
5. Robert B. Reich, *Aftershock: The Next Economy and America's Future* (New York: Alfred A. Knopf, 2010).
6. Federico Cingano, "Trends in Income Inequality and Its Impact on Economic Growth," *OECD Social, Employment and Migration Working Papers 163,* 65, December 9, 2014, http://www.oecd-ilibrary.org/docserver/download/5jxrjncwxv6j.pdf?expires=1436996856&id=id&accname=guest&checksum=955AFBFEDF59ABFE3EF706272D0B3459.
7. Ben Bernanke, "Why Are Interest Rates So Low, Part 2: Secular Stagnation," *Ben Bernanke's Blog,* March 31, 2015, http://www.brookings.edu/blogs/ben-bernanke/posts/2015/03/31-why-interest-rates-low-secular-stagnation.
8. Ibid.
9. David M. Weil, *Economic Growth* (Boston: Pearson, 2005), figure 3.1, *GDP and Capital per Worker, 2000,* 49.
10. N. Gregory Mankiw, *Macroeconomics,* 6th Edition (Worth Publishers, 2007).
11. Bernanke, "Why Are Interest Rates So Low, Part 2: Secular Stagnation."
12. "Gross Savings (% of GDP) 1980–2014," World Bank National Accounts Data, accessed May 11, 2016, http://data.worldbank.org/indicator/NY.GNS.ICTR

.ZS?order=wbapi_data_value_2013%20wbapi_data_value%20wbapi_data
_value-last&sort=desc.

13. "Global Wealth Report 2015," Credit Suisse Research, October 2015, https://
publications.credit-suisse.com/tasks/render/file/?fileID=F2425415
-DCA7-80B8-EAD989AF9341D47E.

14. Chris Gaither and Dawn Chmielewski, "Fears of Dot-Com Crash, Version 2.0,"
*Los Angeles Times*, July 16, 2006, http://articles.latimes.com/2006/jul/16/
business/fi-overheat16.

15. Carmen Reinhart and Kenneth Rogoff, *This Time Is Different: Eight Centuries
of Financial Folly* (Princeton, NJ: Princeton University Press, 2009).

16. Lawrence Summers, "The Future of Work in the Age of the Machine: A Hamilton Project Policy Forum," National Press Club, February 19, 2015, http://
www.hamiltonproject.org/events/the_future_of_work_in_the_age_of_the
_machine.

17. Robert McIntyre, Richard Phillips, and Phineas Baxandall, "Offshore Shell
Games 2015: The Use of Offshore Tax Havens by Fortune 500 Companies,"
Citizens for Tax Justice, 2015, http://ctj.org/pdf/offshoreshell2015.pdf.

18. Richard Foster and Sarah Kaplan, *Creative Destruction: Why Companies That Are
Built to Last Underperform the Market—and How to Successfully Transform Them*
(New York: Crown, 2001), 13. First chapter available at: http://itech.fgcu.edu/fac
ulty/bhobbs/Creative%20destruction%20McKinsey%20Report%20CDch1.pdf.

19. Michael Moritz, "The Fall and Rise of Technology Juggernauts," *Financial
Times*, December 4, 2015, https://next.ft.com/content/6b859714-99ba-11e5
-9228-87e603d47bdc#axzz3tJPF7UAb.

20. "Is the U.S. Trade Deficit a Problem? What Is the Link Between the Trade
Deficit and Exchange Rates?" *Dr. Econ*, Federal Reserve Bank of San Francisco, June 2007, http://www.frbsf.org/education/publications/doctor
-econ/2007/june/trade-deficit-exchange-rate.

21. "Saving, Spending and Living Paycheck to Paycheck in America," Nielsen,
July 28, 2015, http://www.nielsen.com/us/en/insights/news/2015/saving
-spending-and-living-paycheck-to-paycheck-in-america.html.

22. Atif Mian and Amir Sufi, "The Consequences of the Mortgage Credit Expansion: Evidence from the 2007 Mortgage Default Crisis," National Bureau of
Economic Research, December 12, 2008, http://www.nber.org/papers/
w13936.

23. Sun Young Park, "The Size of the Subprime Shock," Unpublished Paper, Korea Advanced Institute of Science and Technology, 2011, https://83f7afa3-a
-62cb3a1a-s-sites.googlegroups.com/site/sanovs/home/subprime_shock
.pdf?attachauth=ANoY7cqkVpPSablq3egaIQpB3paaS4jtBGFDqt5dmoWXFf
0nxvmpaKBX4FbO_jikuAjqkFOhpDnt1fnGRoBjoT9xzQZkR097dflGE219ht
ENVMAYAcCDdjsV5tjKL9KfErymlL5qe4ZbG3NpP63cPmsT_84ZeFmui8qC
CeLSc6m5KHlNR3CcwkkTRxllyxqJ-IiqsILHxpd9licRJ6ITynr7bWK
CR8xymw%3D%3D&attredirects=0.

    Financial Crisis Inquiry Commission, "The Financial Crisis Inquiry Re-
port: Final Report of the National Commission on the Causes of the Financial and Economic Crisis in the United States" (Public Affairs, 2011), 228–29.

24. Bethany McClean and Joe Nocera, *All the Devils Are Here: The Hidden History of
the Financial Crisis* (New York: Portfolio, 2010).

25. "The Role of Government Affordable Housing Policy in Creating the Global
Financial Crisis of 2008," Staff Report to the Committee on Oversight and
Government Reform, US House of Representatives, 111th Congress, July 1,

2009, https://oversight.house.gov/report/the-role-of-government-affordable
-housing-policy-in-creating-the-global-financial-crisis-of-2008/.

26. Reinhart and Rogoff, *This Time Is Different: Eight Centuries of Financial Folly.*

27. *St. Louis Adjusted Monetary Base* [BASE], retrieved from FRED, Federal Reserve Bank of St. Louis, accessed January 3, 2016, https://research.stlouis fed.org/fred2/series/BASE.

28. Edward Conard, *Unintended Consequences: Why Everything You've Been Told About the Economy Is Wrong* (New York: Portfolio, 2012), Chapter 6, Footnote 2.

29. Anat Admati and Martin Hellwig, "The Bankers' New Clothes: What's Wrong with Banking and What to Do About It," (Princeton, NJ: Princeton University Press, 2012).

Laurence Kotlikoff, *Jimmy Stewart Is Dead: Ending the World's Ongoing Financial Plague with Limited Purpose Banking* (Hoboken, NJ: Wiley, 2011).

John Cochrane, "Toward a Run-Free Financial System," National Bureau of Economic Research, 2014, https://faculty.chicagobooth.edu/john.co chrane/research/papers/run_free.pdf.

Edward Lazear, "How Not to Prevent the Next Financial Meltdown," *Wall Street Journal,* October 2, 2015, http://www.wsj.com/articles/how-not-to-pre vent-the-next-financial-meltdown-1443827426.

30. Conard, *Unintended Consequences.*

31. Robert Gordon, *The Rise and Fall of American Growth* (Princeton, NJ: Princeton University Press, 2016).

Tyler Cowen, *The Great Stagnation: How America Ate All the Low-Hanging Fruit of Modern History, Got Sick, and Will (Eventually) Feel Better* (New York: Dutton, 2011).

32. John Maynard Keynes, *The Economic Consequences of Peace* (New York: Harcourt, Brace and Howe, 1920).

33. Paul Krugman, "The Conscience of a Liberal: Stimulus Arithmetic (Wonkish but Important)," *New York Times,* January 6, 2009, http://krugman.blogs.ny times.com/2009/01/06/stimulus-arithmetic-wonkish-but-important.

34. Paul Krugman, "The Conscience of a Liberal: "Why Am I a Keynesian," *New York Times,* June 6, 2015, http://krugman.blogs.nytimes.com/2015/06/06/ why-am-i-a-keynesian.

35. Christopher Chantrill, "U.S. Federal Government Spending," *U.S. Government Spending,* accessed May 11, 2016, http://www.usgovernmentspending.com/ spending_chart_1900_2020USp_XXs1li111mcn_F0f_US_Federal_Govern ment_Spending.

36. "Time Series Chart of Federal Revenue by Type," *U.S. Government Revenue,* accessed May 11, 2016, http://www.usgovernmentrevenue.com/revenue _chart_1985_2020USp_XXs1li011mcn_30f40f11f12f60f_Federal_Revenue _by_Type.

37. "Federal Debt Held by the Public as Percent of Gross Domestic Product," FRED Economic Data, Federal Reserve Bank of St. Louis (2015), https:// research.stlouisfed.org/fred2/series/FYGFGDQ188S.

38. Valerie Ramey, "Identifying Government Spending Shocks: It's All in the Timing," *Quarterly Journal of Economic Affairs,* 2011, http://qje.oxfordjournals .org/content/early/2011/03/21/qje.qjq008.full.

39. Paul Krugman, "The Conscience of a Liberal: Nobody Understand the Liquidity Trap (Wonkish)," *New York Times,* July 14, 2010, http://krugman.blogs .nytimes.com/2010/07/14/nobody-understands-the-liquidity-trap-wonkish.

40. Paul Krugman, "Failure to Rise," *New York Times*, February 12, 2009, http://www.nytimes.com/2009/02/13/opinion/13krugman.html?ref=paulkrugman.

41. Lawrence Summers, "Why Public Investment Really Is a Free Lunch," *Financial Times*, October 6, 2014, http://www.ft.com/intl/cms/s/2/9b591f98-4997-11e4-8d68-00144feab7de.html#axzz3mNLQzKa6.

42. Ramey, "Identifying Government Spending Shocks."

43. Teresa Ter-Minassian, Mark Allen et al., International Monetary Fund, "Public Investment and Fiscal Policy," March 12, 2004, figure 1, "Investment Trends in Advanced OECD and Selected Latin American Countries, 1970–2000 (In Percent of GDP)," https://www.imf.org/external/np/fad/2004/pifp/eng/pifp.pdf.

44. Martin Fackler, "Japan's Big-Works Stimulus Is Lesson," *New York Times*, February 5, 2009, http://www.nytimes.com/2009/02/06/world/asia/06japan.html?pagewanted=all&_r=1&.

45. Pascale Harter, "The White Elephants That Dragged Spain into the Red," BBC News, July 26, 2012, http://www.bbc.com/news/magazine-18855961.

46. Andrew M. Warner, "Public Investment as an Engine Growth," *IMF Working Paper 14/148*, August 2014, http://www.imf.org/external/pubs/ft/wp/2014/wp14148.pdf.

47. Congressional Budget Office, "The Budget and Economic Outlook: 2015 to 2025," *CBO Report* (January 26, 2015): p. 49, https://www.cbo.gov/publication/49892.

48. Paul Krugman, "The Conscience of a Liberal: The Four Percent Solution," *New York Times*, May 24, 2013, http://krugman.blogs.nytimes.com/2013/05/24/the-four-percent-solution.

49. "St. Louis Adjusted Monetary Base," FRED Economic Data, Federal Reserve Bank of St. Louis, accessed September 24, 2015, https://research.stlouisfed.org/fred2/series/BASE.

50. "Excess Reserves of Depository Institutions," FRED Economic Data, Federal Reserve Bank of St. Louis, accessed December 17, 2015, https://research.stlouisfed.org/fred2/series/EXCSRESNS.

51. J. Bradford DeLong, "The Tragedy of Ben Bernanke," *Project Syndicate*, October 29, 2015, https://www.project-syndicate.org/commentary/bernanke-memoir-monetary-policy-lessons-by-j—bradford-delong-2015-10.

52. Angus Deaton, "Measuring and Understanding Behavior, Welfare and Poverty," Nobel Prize Lecture, December 8, 2015, http://www.nobelprize.org/nobel_prizes/economic-sciences/laureates/2015/deaton-lecture.html.

53. Paul Krugman, "The Conscience of a Liberal: Monetary Policy in a Liquidity Trap," *New York Times*, April 11, 2013, http://krugman.blogs.nytimes.com/2013/04/11/monetary-policy-in-a-liquidity-trap.

54. Martin Wolf, "Lunch with the FT: Ben Bernanke," *Financial Times*, October 23, 2015, http://www.ft.com/intl/cms/s/0/0c07ba88-7822-11e5-a95a-27d368e1ddf7.html.

55. "Pushing on a String," Wikipedia, accessed December 18, 2015, https://en.wikipedia.org/wiki/Pushing_on_a_string.

56. Paul Krugman, "The Conscience of a Liberal: Rethinking Japan," *New York Times*, October 20, 2015, http://krugman.blogs.nytimes.com/2015/10/20/rethinking-japan.

57. John Cochrane, "The Fed Needn't Rush to 'Normalize,'" *Wall Street Journal*, September 16, 2015, http://www.wsj.com/articles/the-fed-neednt-rush-to-normalize-1442441737.

*Chapter 6:* The Myth That Progress Hollows Out the Middle Class

1. Erik Brynjolfsson and Andrew McAfee, *The Second Machine Age: Work, Progress, and Prosperity in a Time of Brilliant Technologies* (New York: W. W. Norton, 2014), 202.
2. Christopher Matthews, "How Silicon Valley Is Hollowing Out the Economy (and Stealing from You to Boot)," *Time,* May 7, 2013, http://business.time.com/2013/05/07/how-silicon-valley-is-hollowing-out-the-economy-and-stealing-from-you-while-theyre-at-it.
3. Erik Brynjolfsson, "The Future of Work in the Age of the Machine: A Hamilton Project Policy Forum," National Press Club, Washington, DC, February 19, 2015, http://www.hamiltonproject.org/assets/legacy/files/download_and_links/2015_02_24_THP_Future_of_Work_in_Machine_Age_transcript_unedited.pdf.
4. Thomas Piketty, *Capital in the Twenty-First Century* (Cambridge, MA: Harvard University Press, 2013).
5. Bradford Delong, "Over at the Washington Center for Equitable Growth: Piketty Day Here at Berkeley: The Honest Broker for the Week of April 26 2014," Grasping Reality with the Invisible Hand, April 23, 2014, http://delong.typepad.com/sdj/2014/04/piketty-day-here-at-berkeley-the-honest-broker-for-the-week-of-april-26-2014.html.
6. Lawrence Summers, "The Inequality Puzzle," *Democracy,* 2014, http://democracyjournal.org/magazine/33/the-inequality-puzzle/?page=all.
7. Robert Putnam, *Our Kids: The American Dream in Crisis* (New York: Simon & Schuster, 2015), 73.
8. Sara McLanahan and Christopher Jencks, "Was Moynihan Right?" *Education Next,* Spring 2015, http://educationnext.org/was-moynihan-right.
9. Sabrina Tavernise, "Education Gap Grows Between Rich and Poor, Studies Say," *New York Times,* February 9, 2012, http://www.nytimes.com/2012/02/10/education/education-gap-grows-between-rich-and-poor-studies-show.html.
10. Charles Murray, *Coming Apart: The State of White America, 1960–2010* (New York: Crown Forum, 2012).
11. Ibid and Raghuram Rajan, *Fault Lines: How Hidden Fractures Still Threaten the World Economy* (Princeton, NJ: Princeton University Press, 2010).
12. Brynjolfsson and McAfee, *The Second Machine Age.*
13. David Autor, "The Polarization of Job Opportunities in the U.S. Labor Market: Implications for Employment and Earnings," The Center for American Progress and The Hamilton Project, 2010, http://www.brookings.edu/research/papers/2010/04/jobs-autor.
14. "The American Middle Class Is Losing Ground," Pew Research Center, December 9, 2015, http://www.pewsocialtrends.org/files/2015/12/2015-12-09_middle-class_FINAL-report.pdf.
15. Ibid.
16. "Percentage of Persons 25 to 29 Years Old with Selected Levels of Educational Attainment, by Race/Ethnicity and Sex: Selected Years, 1920 Through 2014," National Center for Education Statistics, U.S. Department of Education, accessed December 17, 2015, https://nces.ed.gov/programs/digest/d14/tables/dt14_104.20.asp.
17. "Historical Income Tables: Households," U.S. Census Bureau, accessed January 4, 2016, http://www.census.gov/hhes/www/income/data/historical/household.

18. Mark Perry, "Some Demographic Trends That Might Explain the Stagnation and Decline in US Household Income," *Carpe Diem*, American Enterprise Institute, December 19, 2015, http://www.aei.org/publication/some-demographic-trends-that-might-explain-the-stagnation-and-decline-in-us-household-income/?utm_source=paramount&utm_medium=email&utm_content=AEITODAY&utm_campaign=122215.

19. Ibid.

20. "Current Population Survey," U.S. Census Bureau, tabulation of data by Sentier Research, accessed November 2015.

21. Ibid.

22. Ibid.

23. Ibid.

24. Ibid.

25. Thomas Piketty and Emmanuel Saez, "Income Inequality in the United States, 1913–1998," *Quarterly Journal of Economics* 118, no. 1 February 2003. https://eml.berkeley.edu/~saez/pikettyqje.pdf.

26. Philip Armour, Richard V. Burkhauser, and Jeff Larrimore, "Deconstructing Income and Income Inequality Measures: A Crosswalk from Market Income to Comprehensive Income," *American Economic Review* 103, no. 3 (May 2013): 173–77, https://www.aeaweb.org/articles.php?doi=10.1257/aer.103.3.173.

27. Eduardo Porter, "Sizing Up Hillary Clinton's Plans to Help the Middle Class," *New York Times*, July 14, 2015, http://www.nytimes.com/2015/07/15/business/sizing-up-hillary-clintons-plans-to-help-the-middle-class.html?_r=0.

28. Robert Z. Lawrence, "The Growing Gap Between Real Wages and Labor Productivity," *Peterson Institute for International Economics*, July 21, 2015, http://www.capx.co/external/why-are-wages-lagging-productivity-in-the-us.

    James Sherk, "Productivity and Compensation: Growing Together," *Heritage Foundation Backgrounder*, 2825, July 17, 2013, http://www.heritage.org/research/reports/2013/07/productivity-and-compensation-growing-together.

29. Karen E. Dynan, Jonathan Skinner, and Stephen P. Zeldes, "Do the Rich Save More?" *Journal of Political Economy* 112, no. 2 (2004): 397–444, https://www.dartmouth.edu/~jskinner/documents/DynanKEDotheRich.pdf.

30. Bruce D. Meyer and James X. Sullivan, "The Material Well-Being of the Poor and the Middle Class Since 1980," *American Enterprise Institute Working Paper 44* (2011), http://www3.nd.edu/~jsulliv4/well_being_middle_class_poor4.3.pdf.

31. Putnam, *Our Kids*.

32. Murray, *Coming Apart*.

33. Putnam, *Our Kids*.

34. Ray Chetty and Nathaniel Hendren, "The Impacts of Neighborhoods on Intergenerational Mobility: Childhood Exposure Effects and County-Level Estimates," Unpublished Manuscript, April 2015, http://scholar.harvard.edu/hendren/publications/impacts-Neighborhoods-Intergenerational-Mobility-Childhood-Exposure-Effects-And.

35. Joyce A. Martin, Brady E. Hamilton, Michelle J. K. Osterman, Sally C. Curtin, and T. J. Matthews, "Births: Final Data for 2013," *National Vital Statistics Reports* 64, no. 1 (2015), http://www.cdc.gov/nchs/data/nvsr/nvsr64/nvsr64_01.pdf.

    Stephanie J. Ventura and Christine A. Bachrach, "Nonmarital Childbearing in the United States, 1940–99," Centers for Disease Control

and Prevention, *National Vital Statistics Reports* 48, no. 16 (2000), http://www
.cdc.gov/nchs/data/nvsr/nvsr48/nvs48_16. pdf.

36. Robert Putnam, "E Pluribus Unum: Diversity and Community in the Twenty-
    First Century, the 2006 Johan Skytte Prize Lecture," *Scandinavian Political
    Studies* 30, no. 2 (2007): 137–91, http://onlinelibrary.wiley.com/doi/10.1111/
    j.1467-9477.2007.00176.x/epdf.

37. Michael Jonas, "The Downside of Diversity," *Boston Globe*, August 5, 2007,
    http://www.boston.com/news/globe/ideas/articles/2007/08/05/the_down
    side_of_diversity/?page=full.

38. Rajan, *Fault Lines*.

39. Michael D. Bordo and Christopher M. Meissner, "Does Inequality Lead to a
    Financial Crisis?" *Journal of International Money and Finance* (2012), http://
    www.economics.hawaii.edu/research/abstracts/mar16_12Bordo.pdf.

40. Sandra E. Black, Paul Devereux, Petter Lundborg, and Kaveh Majlesi, "Poor
    Little Rich Kids? The Determinants of Intergenerational Transmission of
    Wealth," National Bureau of Economic Research, Working Paper 21409 (July
    2015), http://www.nber.org/papers/w21409.

41. Ron Unz, "The Myth of American Meritocracy," *American Conservative*, No-
    vember 28, 2012, http://www.theamericanconservative.com/articles/the
    -myth-of-american-meritocracy.

42. Derek Thompson, "How America's Top Colleges Reflect (and Massively Dis-
    tort) the Country's Racial Evolution," *Atlantic*, January 23, 2013, http://www
    .theatlantic.com/national/archive/2013/01/how-americas-top-colleges-re
    flect-and-massively-distort-the-countrys-racial-evolution/267415.

43. Stacy Dale and Alan Krueger, "Estimating the Return to College Selec-
    tivity over the Career Using Administrative Earnings Data," National Bu-
    reau of Economic Research, June 2011, http://www.nber.org/papers
    /w17159.

44. Ana Ferrer and W. Craig Riddell, "The Role of Credentials in the Canadian
    Labour Market," *Canadian Journal of Economics*, 2002, http://papers.econom
    ics.ubc.ca/legacypapers/dp0116.pdf.
        W. Craig Riddell, "Understanding 'Sheepskin Effects' in the Returns to
    Education: The Role of Cognitive Skills," Canada Department of Economics,
    University of Toronto, November, 2008, http://www.clsrn.econ.ubc.ca/hrsdc/
    papers/Paper%20no.%202%20-%20Craig%20Riddell%20-%20Sheep
    skin%20Effects.pdf.

45. Seth Zimmerman, "The Returns to College Admission for Academically Mar-
    ginal Students," *Journal of Labor Economics*, 2014, http://pantheon.yale
    .edu/~sdz3/Zimmerman_JoLE_5_2013.pdf.

46. Jaison R. Abel and Richard Deitz, "College May Not Pay Off for Everyone,"
    *Liberty Street Economics*, Federal Reserve Bank of New York, September 4,
    2014, http://libertystreeteconomics.newyorkfed.org/2014/09/college-may
    - not-pay-off-for-everyone.html#.VgrSQMJ0yY.
        Kartik Athreya and Janice Eberly, "The Education Risk Premium," Pre-
    liminary Draft, July 2010, revised December 22, 2010, http://citeseerx.ist.psu
    .edu/viewdoc/summary?doi=10.1.1.364.5315.

47. Jaison R. Abel, Richard Deitz, and Yaqin Su, "Are Recent College Graduates
    Finding Good Jobs?" *Current Issues in Economics and Finance*, Federal Reserve
    Bank of New York, 2014, https://www.newyorkfed.org/medialibrary/media/
    research/current_issues/ci20-1.pdf.

"Voice of the Graduate," McKinsey and Company, May 2013, http://mckin seyonsociety.com/downloads/reports/Education/UXC001%20Voice %20of%20the%20Graduate%20v7.pdf.

48. Lawrence Summers, "The Future of Work in the Age of the Machine: A Hamilton Project Policy Forum," National Press Club, Washington, DC, February 19, 2015, http://www.hamiltonproject.org/assets/legacy/files/downloads _and_links/2015_02_24_THP_Future_of_Work_in_Machine_Age_transcript _unedited.pdf.

49. "Promising Models and a Call to Action," Executive Office of the President, The White House, January 2014, https://www.whitehouse.gov/sites/default/ files/docs/white_house_report_on_increasing_college_opportunity_for _low-income_students.pdf.

50. "Net Prices by Income over Time: Public Sector," College Board, 2015, http:// trends.collegeboard.org/college-pricing/figures-tables/net-prices-income -over-time-public-sector.

51. "Trends in Student Aid 2014," *Trends in Higher Education Series,* College Board, 2014, https://secure-media.collegeboard.org/digitalServices/misc/ trends/2014-trends-student-aid-report-final.pdf.

52. Lamar Alexander, "College Too Expensive? That's a Myth," *Wall Street Journal,* July 6, 2015, http://www.wsj.com/articles/college-too-expensive-thats-a-myth college-too-expensive-thats-a-myth-1436212158?tesla=y.

53. Ibid.

54. Ibid.

55. "Educational Indicators in Focus," Organisation for Economic Co-operation and Development, June 2012, https://www.oecd.org/edu/skills-beyond -school/Education%20Indicators%20in%20Focus%206%20June% 202012.pdf.

56. David Lucca, Taylor Nadauld, and Karen Shen, "Credit Supply and the Rise in College Tuition: Evidence from the Expansion in Federal Student Aid Programs," Federal Reserve Bank of New York, July 2015, https://www.newyork fed.org/research/staff_reports/sr733.html.

*Chapter 7:* The Myth That Mobility Has Declined

1. Alan Krueger, "Transcript: The Rise and Consequences of Inequality in the United States," remarks at the Center for American Progress, January 12, 2012, https://www.whitehouse.gov/sites/default/files/krueger_cap_speech _final_remarks.pdf.

2. Raj Chetty, Nathaniel Hendren, Patrick Kline, Emmanuel Saez, and Nicholas Turner, "Is the United States Still a Land of Opportunity? Recent Trends in Intergenerational Mobility," National Bureau of Economic Research, Working Paper 19844 (2014): 8–9, http://www.equality-of-opportunity.org/files/ mobility_trends.pdf.

3. Ibid.

4. Thomas Hertz, "Trends in the Intergenerational Elasticity of Family Income in the United States," *Industrial Relations: A Journal of Economy and Society* 46, no. 1 (2007): 22–50.

5. Chul-In Lee and Gary Solon, "Trends in Intergenerational Income Mobility," *Review of Economics and Statistics* 91, no. 4 (2009): 766–72.

6. Chetty et al., "Is the United States Still a Land of Opportunity?"

7. Markus Jäntti et al., "American Exceptionalism in a New Light: A Comparison of Intergenerational Earnings Mobility in the Nordic Countries, the United Kingdom and the United States," *Institute for the Study of Labor (IZA) DP no. 1938* (2006), http://ftp.iza.org/dp1938.pdf.

Jason DeParle, "Harder for Americans to Rise from Lower Rungs," *New York Times,* January 4, 2012, http://www.nytimes.com/2012/01/05/us/harder-for-americans-to-rise-from-lower-rungs.html.

8. "The Ins and the Outs," *Economist,* January 31, 2013, http://www.economist.com/news/special-report/21570836-immigration-and-growing-inequality-are-making-nordics-less-homogeneous-ins-and.

9. Silje Vatne Pettersen and Lars Ostby, "Immigrants in Norway, Sweden and Denmark," *Samfunnsspeilet,* May 2013, https://www.ssb.no/en/befolkning/artikler-og-publikasjoner/immigrants-in-norway-sweden-and-denmark.

10. Richard V. Reeves, "Saving Horatio Alger, Equality, Opportunity, and the American Dream," Brookings Essay, August 20, 2014, http://www.brookings.edu/research/essays/2014/saving-horatio-alger.

11. Ibid.

12. Ibid.

DeParle, "Harder for Americans to Rise from Lower Rungs."

13. Reeves, "Saving Horatio Alger, Equality, Opportunity, and the American Dream."

14. Robert Doar, "What Malcolm Gladwell Gets Wrong About Poverty," *Federalist,* August 27, 2015, http://www.aei.org/publication/what-malcolm-gladwell-gets-wrong-about-poverty/?utm_source=paramount&utm_medium=email&utm_content=AEITODAY&utm_campaign=083115.

15. Chetty et al., "Is the United States Still a Land of Opportunity?"

16. Sara McLanahan and Christopher Jencks, "Was Moynihan Right?" *Education Next,* Spring 2015. http://educationnext.org/was-moynihan-right.

17. Jennifer DePaoli, Jonanna Fox, Erin Ingram, Mary Maushard, John Bridgeland, and Robert Balfanz, "2015 Building a Grad Nation Report," Alliance for Excellent Education, America's Promise Alliance, Civic Enterprises, Everyone Graduates Center at Johns Hopkins University, May 12, 2015, http://www.gradnation.org/report/2015-building-grad-nation-report.

18. Reeves, "Saving Horatio Alger, Equality, Opportunity, and the American Dream."

19. Joyce A. Martin, Brady E. Hamilton, Michelle J. K. Osterman, Sally C. Curtin, and T. J. Matthews, "Births: Final Data for 2013," Centers for Disease Control and Prevention, *National Vital Statistics Reports* 64, no. 1 (2015), http://www.cdc.gov/nchs/data/nvsr/nvsr64/nvsr64_01.pdf.

Stephanie J. Ventura and Christine A. Bachrach, "Nonmarital Childbearing in the United States, 1940–99," Centers for Disease Control and Prevention, *National Vital Statistics Reports* 48, no. 16 (2000), http://www.cdc.gov/nchs/data/nvsr/nvsr48/nvs48_16.pdf.

"Number and Percentage Distribution of Spring 2002 High School Sophomores, Table 104.91," National Center for Education Statistics, U.S. Department of Education, http://nces.ed.gov/programs/digest/d14/tables/dt14_104.91.asp.

20. Reeves, "Saving Horatio Alger, Equality, Opportunity, and the American Dream."

21. Chetty et al., "Is the United States Still a Land of Opportunity?"
    N. Greg Mankiw, "How Much Income Inequality Is Explained by Varying Parental Resources?" *Greg Mankiw's Blog*, January 24, 2014, http://greg mankiw.blogspot.com/2014/01/how-much-inequality-does-parental.html.

22. Miles Corak, Matthew J. Lindquist, and Bhashkar Mazumder, "A Comparison of Upward and Downward Intergenerational Mobility in Canada, Sweden and the United States," *Labour Economics* 30 (October 2014): 185–200, http://su.diva-portal.org/smash/get/diva2:708146/FULLTEXT01.pdf.

23. Peter Diamond and Emmanuel Saez, "The Case for Progressive Tax: From Basic Research to Policy Recommendations," *Journal of Economic Perspectives*, Fall 2011, http://pubs.aeaweb.org/doi/pdfplus/10.1257/jep.25.4.165.

24. Lawrence Summers, "The Future of Work in the Age of the Machine: A Hamilton Project Policy Forum," National Press Club, February 19, 2015, http://www.hamiltonproject.org/events/the_future_of_work_in_the_age_of_the_machine.

25. Jonathan D. Ostry, Andrew Berg, and Charalambos G. Tsangarides, "Redistribution, Inequality, and Growth," International Monetary Fund, Discussion Note, February 2014, http://www.imf.org/external/pubs/ft/sdn/2014/sdn1402.pdf.

26. Often attributed to Winston Churchill. BrainyQuote.com, Xplore Inc., 2015, http://www.brainyquote.com/quotes/quotes/w/winstonchu103564.html.

*Chapter 8:* Our Moral Obligation to Help Those Less Fortunate

1. Charlie Spiering, "Full Text: Bobby Jindal's Dynamite Speech to the Republican National Committee in Charlotte," *Washington Examiner*, January 25, 2013, http://www.washingtonexaminer.com/full-text-bobby-jindals-dyna mite-speech-to-the-republican-national-committee-in-charlotte/article/2519682.

2. Rakesh Kochhar, "How Americans Compare with the Global Middle Class," Pew Research Center, July 9, 2015, http://www.pewresearch.org/fact -tank/2015/07/09/how-americans-compare-with-the-global-middle-class.

3. Ibid.

4. Panel Study of Income Dynamics, "Household Total Hours Worked by Income Quintile," Survey Research Center, Institute for Social Research, University of Michigan, Ann Arbor, MI, 2015, https://www.dropbox.com/s/a7711 k65nahsqmn/Basic%20results.xlsx?dl=0.

5. "Modern Immigration Wave Brings 59 Million to U.S. Driving Population Growth and Change Through 2065," Pew Research Center, September 28, 2015, http://www.pewhispanic.org/files/2015/09/2015-09-28_modern-immi gration-wave_REPORT.pdf.

6. "Poverty Overview," World Bank, April 6, 2015, http://www.worldbank.org/ en/topic/poverty/overview.
    "International Comparison Program," World Bank, 2011, http://sitere sources.worldbank.org/ICPEXT/Resources/ICP_2011.html.

7. Axel Dreher, "Does Foreign Aid Boost Growth?" World Economic Forum, October 22, 2015, https://agenda.weforum.org/2015/10/does-foreign-aid -boost-growth.

8. Leigh Ann Henion, "A Job That Nourishes the Soul, If Not the Wallet," *New York Times*, January 2, 2016, http://www.nytimes.com/2016/01/03/jobs/a-job -that-nourishes-the-soul-if-not-the-wallet.html?_r=0.

9. Scott Sumner, "There's Only One Sensible Way to Measure Economic Inequality," *EconLog*, Library of Economics and Liberty, April 24, 2014, http://econlog.econlib.org/archives/2014/04/theres_only_one.html.

10. Christopher Chantrill, "Federal, State, and Local Spending in 20th Century," U.S. Government Spending, accessed May 11, 2016, http://www.usgovern mentspending.com/spending_chart_1900_2020USp_XXs1li111mcn _F0xF0sF0lF0f_Federal_State_and_Local_Spending_in_20th_Century.

11. "Federal Debt Held by the Public as Percent of Gross Domestic Product," FRED Economic Data, Federal Reserve Bank of St. Louis (2015), https://research.stlouisfed.org/fred2/series/FYGFGDQ188S.

12. Anna Merritt, Daniel Effron, and Benoit Monin, "Moral Self-Licensing: When Being Good Frees Us to Be Bad," *Social and Personality Psychological Compass*, 2010, http://www-psych.stanford.edu/~monin/papers/Merritt, %20Effron%20%26%20Monin%202010%20Compass%20on%20Moral%20 Licensing.pdf.

13. Dalton Conley, "Poverty and Life Chances: The Conceptualization and Study of the Poor," *The Handbook of Sociology* (U.K.: Sage Limited, 2005), 329, edited by Craig Calhoun, Chris Rojek, and Bryan Turner. https://wagner.nyu.edu/files/faculty/publications/poverty_chapter.pdf.

14. Rajendra Pachauri et al., "Climate Change 2014: Synthesis Report," Contribution of Working Groups I, II and III to the Fifth Assessment Report of the Intergovernmental Panel on Climate Change, IPCC, Geneva, Switzerland, 2014, 151 pp., http://ipcc.ch/pdf/assessment-report/ar5/syr/SYR _AR5_FINAL_full_wcover.pdf.

15. "The Distribution of Federal Spending and Taxes in 2006," Congressional Budget Office, November 7, 2013, http://www.cbo.gov/sites/default/files/44698-Distribution_11-2013.pdf.

16. Cheryl H. Lee, Tereese Dyson, Matthew Park, Calvin Handy, and Marquita Buchanan Reynolds, "State Government Finances Summary: 2013," U.S. Census Bureau, February 2015, http://www2.census.gov/govs/state/g13-asfin.pdf.

17. "Growth in Means-Tested Programs and Tax Credits for Low-Income Households," Congressional Budget Office, February 11, 2013, https://www.cbo.gov/publication/43934#title0.

18. "Current Population Survey," U.S. Census Bureau, tabulation of data by Sentier Research, accessed November 2015.

   Gene Falk, Alison Mitchell, Karen Lynch, Maggie McCarty, William Morton, and Margot Crandall-Hollick, "Need-Tested Benefits: Estimated Eligibility and Benefit Receipt by Families and Individuals," Congressional Research Service, December 30, 2015, https://www.fas.org/sgp/crs/misc/R44327.pdf.

19. Falk et al., "Need-Tested Benefits: Estimated Eligibility and Benefit Receipt by Families and Individuals."

   Michael Tanner and Charles Hughes, "The Work Versus Welfare Trade-Off: 2013," Cato Institute (2013), http://object.cato.org/sites/cato.org/files/pubs/pdf/the_work_versus_welfare_trade-off_2013_wp.pdf.

   Robert Rector and Rachel Sheffield, "The War on Poverty After 50 Years," Heritage Foundation (2014), http://www.heritage.org/research/reports/2014/09/the-war-on-poverty-after-50-years.

20. "Current Population Survey," U.S. Census Bureau, tabulation of data by Sentier Research, accessed November 2015.

21. "Social Spending During the Crisis: Social Expenditure (SOCX) Data Update 2012," Organisation for Economic Co-operation and Development,

2012, http://www.oecd.org/els/soc/OECD2012SocialSpendingDuring
TheCrisis8pages.pdf.

Price V. Fishback, "Social Welfare Expenditures in the United States and
the Nordic Countries: 1900–2003," National Bureau of Economic Research,
Working Paper 15982, May 2010, http://www.nber.org/papers/w15982.pdf.

22. Neil Irwin, "A Big Safety Net and Strong Job Markets Can Coexist. Just Ask
Scandinavia," *New York Times*, December 17, 2014, http://www.nytimes
.com/2014/12/18/upshot/nordic-nations-show-that-big-safety-net-can-allow
-for-leap-in-employment-rate-.html.

23. P. J. O'Rourke, *Eat the Rich* (New York: Atlantic Monthly Press, 1998).

24. Nima Sanandaji, "Scandinavian Unexceptionalism: Culture, Markets, and
the Failure of Third-Way Socialism," Institute of Economic Affairs (2015),
http://www.iea.org.uk/sites/default/files/publications/files/Sanandajinima
-interactive.pdf.

25. Ibid.

26. "Labor Force Characteristics by Race and Ethnicity, 2013," U.S. Bureau of
Labor Statistics, *BLS Reports*, August 2014, http://www.bls.gov/opub/reports/
race-and-ethnicity/archive/race_ethnicity_2013.pdf.

27. "Employment Status of the Civilian Population 25 Years and Over by Educational Attainment, Table A-4," Bureau of Labor Statistics (2015), http://www
.bls.gov/news.release/empsit.t04.htm.

28. Sanandaji, "Scandinavian Unexceptionalism."

29. Samuel Bowles and Yonglin Park, "Emulation, Inequality, and Work Hours:
Was Thorsten Veblen Right? *Economic Journal* (2005), http://tuvalu.santafe
.edu/~bowles/veblen.

30. Peter Kuhn and Fernando Lozano, "The Expanding Workweek? Understanding Trends in Long Work Hours Among U.S. Men, 1979–2006," University of
California–Santa Barbara, November 2007, http://www.econ.ucsb
.edu/~pjkuhn/Research%20Papers/LongHours.pdf.

31. Chuck Marr, Chye-Ching Huang, Arloc Sherman, and Brandon Debot,
"EITC and Child Tax Credit Promote Work, Reduce Poverty, and Support
Children's Development," Center on Budget and Policy Priorities (2015),
http://www.cbpp.org/research/federal-tax/eitc-and-child-tax-credit
-promote-work-reduce-poverty-and-support-childrens.

32. Bowles and Park, "Emulation, Inequality, and Work Hours: Was Thorsten
Veblen Right?"

Kuhn and Lozano, "The Expanding Workweek? Understanding Trends
in Long Work Hours Among U.S. Men, 1979–2006."

33. "Household Total Hours Worked by Income Quintile," Panel Study of Income
Dynamics, Survey Research Center, Institute for Social Research, University
of Michigan, 2015, https://www.dropbox.com/s/a7711k65nahsqmn/
Basic%20results.xlsx?dl=0.

34. Ibid.

35. "Employer Costs For Employee Compensation," U.S. Bureau of Labor Statistics, March 10, 2016, http://www.bls.gov/news.release/pdf/ecec.pdf.

36. "What Are Poverty Rates Among Working Adults?" University of California–
Davis Center for Poverty Research, http://poverty.ucdavis.edu/faq/what-are
-poverty-rates-among-working-adults.

Carmen DeNavas-Walt and Bernadette D. Proctor, "Income and Poverty in the
United States: 2014," U.S. Census Bureau, September 2015, http://www
.census.gov/content/dam/Census/library/publications/2015/demo/p60-252.pdf.

37. Lawrence M. Mead, "Overselling the Earned Income Tax Credit," *National Affairs* 21, Fall 2014, http://www.nationalaffairs.com/publications/detail/overselling-the-earned-income-tax-credit.

38. Lawrence M. Mead, *The New Politics of Poverty: The Nonworking Poor in America* (New York: Basic Books, 1993).

39. "Growth in Means-Tested Programs and Tax Credits for Low-Income Households," Congressional Budget Office, February 11, 2013, https://www.cbo.gov/sites/default/files/113th-con gress-2013-2014/reports/43934-Means-TestedPrograms.pdf.

40. Christopher Wimer, Liana Fox, Irv Garfinkel, Neeraj Kaushal, and Jane Waldfogel, "Trends in Poverty with an Anchored Supplemental Poverty Measure," Institute for Research on Poverty, University of Wisconsin–Madison, 2013, http://www.gc.cuny.edu/CUNY_GC/media/LISCenter/Readings%20for%20workshop/Madrick2.pdf.

41. W. Gregory Guedel, "Sovereignty, Economic Development, and Human Security in Native American Nations," *American Indian Law Journal* 3 no. 1, Fall 2014, http://www.law.seattleu.edu/Documents/ailj/Fall%202014/Guedel.pdf.

42. "Of Slots and Sloth: How Cash from Casinos Makes Native Americans Poorer," *Economist,* January 17, 2015, http://www.economist.com/news/united-states/21639547-how-cash-casinos-makes-native-americans-poorer-slots-and-sloth.

43. Charles M. Blow, "Jeb Bush, 'Free Stuff,' and Black Folks," *New York Times,* http://www.nytimes.com/2015/09/28/opinion/charles-m-blow-jeb-bush-free-stuff-and-black-folks.html.

44. "Poverty 2014 Highlights," U.S. Census Bureau, *Current Population Survey: 2015 Annual Social and Economic Supplement,* accessed September 29, 2015, https://www.census.gov/hhes/www/poverty/about/overview.

45. "POV24, Reason for Not Working or Reason for Spending Time Out of the Labor Force-Poverty Status of People Who Did Not Work or Who Spent Time Out of the Labor Force," U.S. Census Bureau, *Current Population Survey 2015 Annual Social and Economic Supplement,* accessed May 10, 2016, https://www.census.gov/hhes/www/cpstables/032015/pov/pov24_100.htm.

46. Sarah Jane Glynn, "Families Need More Help to Care for Their Children," Center for American Progress, August 16, 2012, https://www.americanprogress.org/issues/labor/news/2012/08/16/11978/fact-sheet-child-care/.

47. Sarah Minton and Christin Durham, "Low-Income Families and the Cost of Child Care: State Child Care Subsidies, Out-of-Pocket Expenses, and the Cliff Effect," Urban Institute, December 2013, http://www.urban.org/sites/default/files/alfresco/publication-pdfs/412982-Low-Income-Families-and-the-Cost-of-Child-Care.PDF.

48. Gene Falk, et al., "Need-Tested Benefits: Estimated Eligibility and Benefit Receipt by Families and Individuals."

49. Child Care Information Services, "CCIS Frequently Asked Questions," accessed March 2, 2016, http://www.ccisinc.org/categories/child-care-subsidy/frequently-asked-questions.html.

50. Anne Fisher, "U.S. Retail Workers Are No. 1 . . . in Employee Theft," *Forbes,* January 26, 2015, http://fortune.com/2015/01/26/us-retail-worker-theft.

51. Barack Obama, "Remarks by the President in Conversation on Poverty at Georgetown University," The White House, May 12, 2015, http://www.georgetown.edu/news/poverty-summit-2015-with-obama.html.

52. Thomas Sowell, "Why Racists Love the Minimum Wage Laws," *New York Post,* September 17, 2013, http://nypost.com/2013/09/17/why-racists-love-the-minimum-wage-laws.

## *Chapter 9:* The Limitations of Education

1. Alan Borsuk, "Arne Duncan on Milwaukee's Chronic Woes: 'A national disgrace,'" *Milwaukee Journal Sentinel,* January 23, 2016, http://www.jsonline.com/news/education/arne-duncan-on-milwaukees-chronic-woes-a-national-disgrace-b99656481z1-366329791.html.
   Lauren Camera, "Low-Income Students Shortchanged on Math Curriculum," *U.S. News & World Report,* September 30, 2015, http://www.usnews.com/news/articles/2015/09/30/low-income-students-shortchanged-on-math-curriculum.
   Joseph Stiglitz, "Inequality and the American Child," Project Syndicate, December 11, 2014, http://www.project-syndicate.org/commentary/american-children-lack-equal-opportunity-by-joseph-e—stiglitz-2014-12.
2. Anatoly Karlin, "Berlin Gets Bad News from PISA," *The AK Blog,* May 12, 2012, http://akarlin.com/2012/05/berlin-gets-bad-news-from-pisa.
3. Ran Abramitzky, Leah Platt Boustan, and Katherine Eriksson, "Europe's Tired, Poor, Huddled Masses: Self-Selection and Economic Outcomes in the Age of Mass Migration," *American Economic Review* (2012): 1832–56, http://www.econ.ucla.edu/lboustan/research_pdfs/research11_massmigration.pdf.
4. Martin Carnoy and Richard Rothstein, "What Do International Tests Really Show About US Student Performance," *Economic Policy Institute* (2013), http://www.epi.org/files/2013/EPI-What-do-international-tests-really-show-about-US-student-performance.pdf.
5. "PISA 2009 Results: Overcoming Social Background—Equity in Learning Opportunities and Outcomes (Volume II)," Organisation for Economic Cooperation and Development (2010), http://www.oecd.org/pisa/pisaproducts/48852584.pdf.
6. "Untapped Skills: Realising the Potential of Immigrant Students," Organisation for Economic Co-operation and Development (2012): 27, http://www.oecd.org/edu/Untapped%20Skills.pdf.
7. Martin Carnoy, Emma Garcia, and Tatiana Khavenson, "Bringing It Back Home," Economic Policy Institute, October 30, 2015, http://www.epi.org/publication/bringing-it-back-home-why-state-comparisons-are-more-useful-than-international-comparisons-for-improving-u-s-education-policy.
8. Ibid.
9. "2013 National Assessment of Educational Progress Reading and Mathematics: Summary of State Results," Massachusetts Department of Elementary and Secondary Education, November 2013, http://www.doe.mass.edu/mcas/naep/results/2013ReadingMath.pdf.
   Amanda Ripley, "Your Child Left Behind," *Atlantic,* December 2010, http://www.theatlantic.com/magazine/archive/2010/12/your-child-left-behind/308310.
   Carnoy et al., "Bringing It Back Home."
10. "2013 National Assessment of Educational Progress Reading and Mathematics: Summary of State Results."

11. Ibid.
12. "QuickFacts Massachusetts," U.S. Census Bureau, accessed December 17, 2015, http://www.census.gov/quickfacts/table/PST045214/25,00.
13. Ibid.
14. Ibid.
15. Caroline M. Hoxby, Sonali Murarka, and Jenny Kang, "How New York City's Charter Schools Affect Achievement, August 2009 Report," Second report in series. Cambridge, MA: New York City Charter Schools Evaluation Project September 2009, http://users.nber.org/~schools/charterschoolseval/how _NYC_charter_schools_affect_achievement_sept2009.pdf.
16. Joshua Angrist, Parag Pathak, and Christopher Walters, "Explaining Charter School Effectiveness," Institute for the Study of Labor, April 2012, http://ftp .iza.org/dp6525.pdf.
17. Ron Oxburgh et al., "Report of the International Panel Set up by the University of East Anglia to Examine the Research of the Climatic Research Unit," University of East Anglia, April 14, 2010, http://www.uea.ac.uk/docu ments/3154295/7847337/SAP.pdf/a6f591fc-fc6e-4a70-9648-8b943d 84782b.
18. Joshua Angrist, Susan Dynarski, Thomas Kane, Parag Pathak, and Christopher Walters, "Who Benefits from KIPP?" IZA Discussion Paper No. 5690 (May 2011), http://economics.mit.edu/files/6965.
19. Mike Klonsky, "NAACP Resolution on Charter Schools," National Education Policy Center, January 3, 2012, http://nepc.colorado.edu/blog/naacp-resolu tion-charter-schools.
20. Joshua S. Wyner, John M. Bridgeland, and John J. DiIulio Jr., "Achievement Trap: How America Is Failing Millions of High-Achieving Students from Lower-Income Families," Civic Enterprises (2007), http://www.jkcf.org/as sets/1/7/Achievement_Trap.pdf.
21. Joshua Angrist et al., "Explaining Charter School Effectiveness."
    Richard Rothstein, "Class and Schools: Using Social, Economic, and Educational Reform to Close the Black-White Achievement Gap" (2004), Economic Policy Institute, Washington, DC, http://www.epi.org/publication/ books_class_and_schools.
22. Raj Chetty, John N. Friedman, and Jonah E. Rockoff, "The Long-Term Impacts of Teachers: Teacher Value-Added and Student Outcomes in Adulthood," Working Paper 17699, National Bureau of Economic Research (2011), http://www.rajchetty.com/chettyfiles/value_added.pdf.
    Raj Chetty, John N. Friedman, and Jonah E. Rockoff, "Measuring the Impacts of Teachers II: Teacher Value-Added and Student Outcomes in Adulthood," *American Economic Review* 104, no. 9 (2014): 2633–79, http://www .rajchetty.com/chettyfiles/w19424.pdf.
23. Chetty et al., "Measuring the Impacts of Teachers II."
24. Ibid.
25. Ibid.
26. Betty Hart and Todd R. Risley, "The Early Catastrophe: The 30 Million Word Gap by Age 3," *American Educator* 27, no. 1 (2003): 4–9, American Federation of Teachers, http://www.aft.org//sites/default/files/periodicals/TheEarly Catastrophe.pdf.
27. "Building the Future for Our Kids, Our Community and Our Country: 2012–2013 Biennial Report," Harlem Children's Zone (2013), http://wac.adef.edge

castcdn.net/80ADEF/hcz.org/wp-content/uploads/2014/04/biennial
-2012-13LO-resSingles.pdf.

28. Grover J. Whitehurst and Michelle Croft, "The Harlem Children's Zone,
Promise Neighborhoods, and the Broader, Bolder Approach to Education,"
Brown Center on Education Policy at the Brookings Institution, July 20, 2010,
http://www.brookings.edu/~/media/research/files/reports/2010
/7/20-hcz-whitehurst/0720_hcz_whitehurst.pdf.

29. Ibid.

30. Lawrence Schweinhart, Jeanne Montie, Zongping Xiang, W. Steven Barnett,
et al., "Lifetime Effects: The High/Scope Perry Preschool Study Through Age
40," High/Scope Press (2006), http://www.highscope.org/file/Research/Per
ryProject/specialsummary_rev2011_02_2.pdf.

31. Ibid.

32. "Hawthorne Effect," Wikipedia, retrieved September 2015, https://en.wikipedia
.org/wiki/Hawthorne_effect.

33. Mark Lipsey, Dale Farran, and Kerry Hofer, "A Randomized Control Trial of
a Statewide Voluntary Prekindergarten Program on Children's Skills and Behaviors through Third Grade," Peabody Research Institute, Vanderbilt University, September 2015, http://peabody.vanderbilt.edu/research/pri/
VPKthrough3rd_final_withcover.pdf.

34. Ibid.

35. Katharine Stevens and Elizabeth English, "Studies Used to Promote Pre-K
Actually Make the Case for a Different Approach," American Enterprise Institute, April 2016, http://www.aei.org/multimedia/studies-used-to-promote
-pre-k- actually-make-the-case-for-a-different-approach/?utm_source
=paramount&utm_medium=email&utm_content=AEITODAY&utm_cam
paign=041316.

36. Katharine Stevens and Elizabeth English, "Does Pre-K Work? The Research
on Ten Early Childhood Programs—and What It Tells Us," American Enterprise Institute, April 2016, http://www.aei.org/wp-content/uploads/2016/04/
Does-Pre-K-Work.pdf.

37. Peter Diamond and Emmanuel Saez, "The Case for a Progressive Tax: From
Basic Research to Policy Recommendations," *Journal of Economic Perspectives*
25 (Fall 2011): 165–90, http://pubs.aeaweb.org/doi/pdfplus/10.1257/
jep.25.4.165.

38. "Chapter B: Financial and Human Resources Invested in Education," *Education at a Glance,* Organisation for Economic Co-operation and Development
(2011): 203–23, http://www.oecd.org/education/skills-beyond-school/
48630868.pdf.

Sheila Murray and Kim Reuben, "Racial Disparities in Education Finance: Going Beyond Equal Revenues," Urban Institute, November 3, 2008,
http://www.urban.org/research/publication/racial-disparities-education
-finance-going-beyond-equal-revenues.

Jason Richwine, "The Myth of Racial Disparities in Public School Funding," *Heritage Foundation Backgrounder 2548,* April 20, 2011, http://www.heri
tage.org/research/reports/2011/04/the-myth-of-racial-disparities-in
-public-school-funding.

"The Nation's Report Card: Trends in Academic Progress 2012," National Center for Education Statistics, U.S. Department of Education, http://nces
.ed.gov/nation sreportcard/subject/publications/main2012/pdf/2013456.pdf.

39. Barbara Kantrowitz, "Scientists Bring New Rigor to Education Research," *Scientific American,* July 15, 2014, http://www.scientificamerican.com/article/ scientists-bring-new-rigor-to-education-research.

40. Eric Schulzke, "Bill Gates Says Education Reform Is Tougher Than Eradicating Polio, Malaria or Tuberculosis," *Deseret News,* July 2, 2014, http://national .deseret news.com/article/1800/bill-gates-says-education-reform-is-tougher -than-eradicating-polio-malaria-or-tuberculosis.html.

41. Paul Krugman, "The Conscience of a Liberal: "Rip Van Skillsgap," *New York Times,* February 22, 2015, http://krugman.blogs.nytimes.com/2015/02/22/ rip-van-skillsgap.

42. Ibid.

43. Lawrence Summers, "The Future of Work in the Age of the Machine: A Hamilton Project Policy Forum," National Press Club, February 19, 2015, http:// www.hamilton project.org/events/the_future_of_work_in_the_age_of_the _machine.

44. Schulzke, "Bill Gates Says Education Reform Is Tougher Than Eradicating Polio, Malaria or Tuberculosis."

45. Tinca J. C. Polderman, Beben Benyamin, Christiaan A. de Leeuw, Patrick Sullivan, et al., "Meta-Analysis of the Heritability of Human Traits Based on Fifty Years of Twin Studies," *Nature Genetics* 47 (2015): 702–9, http://www.nature .com/ng/journal/v47/n7/full/ng.3285.html.

   Kaili Rimfeld, Yulia Kovas, Philip S. Dale, and Robert Plomin, "Pleiotropy Across Academic Subjects at the End of Compulsory Education," *Scientific Reports,* 2015, http://www.nature.com/articles/srep11713.

46. Raj Chetty, Nathaniel Hendren, Patrick Kline, Emmanuel Saez, and Nicholas Turner, "Is the United States Still a Land of Opportunity? Recent Trends in Intergenerational Mobility," National Bureau of Economic Research, Working Paper 19844 (2014): 8–9, http://www.equality-of-opportunity.org/files/ mobility_trends.pdf.

47. N. Greg Mankiw, "How Much Income Inequality Is Explained by Varying Parental Resources?" *Greg Mankiw's Blog,* January 24, 2014, http://greg mankiw.blogspot.com/2014/01/how-much-inequality-does-parental.html.

48. Joseph Stiglitz and Bruce Greenwald, *Creating a Learning Society: A New Approach to Growth, Development, and Social Progress* (New York: Columbia University Press, 2014).

49. "A-16. Employment Status of the Civilian Non-Institutional Population 16 to 24 Years of Age by School Enrollment, Age, Sex, Race, Hispanic or Latino Ethnicity, and Educational Attainment," U.S. Bureau of Labor Statistics, accessed March 9, 2016, http://www.bls.gov/web/empsit/cpseea16.htm#cps_eande_m16.f.1.

50. Robert J. Barro and Jong-Wha Lee, "A New Data Set of Educational Attainment in the World, 1950–2010," *Journal of Development Economics* 104 (2013): 184–98, http://barrolee.com/papers/Barro_Lee_Human_Capital_Update _2012April.pdf.

51. Ibid.

52. Jorge Guzman and Scott Stern, "The State of American Entrepreneurship: New Estimates of the Quantity and Quality of Entrepreneurship for 15 US States, 1988–2014," National Bureau of Economic Research, March 2016, http://static1.squarespace.com/static/53d52829e4b0d9e21c9a6940 /t/56d9a05545bf217588498535/1457102936611/Guzman+Stern+—+State+o f+American+Entrepreneurship+FINAL.pdf.

53. Vivek Wadhwa, Richard Freeman, and Ben Rissing, "Education and Tech Entrepreneurship," Ewing Marion Kaufmann Foundation (2008), http://www.kauffman.org/what-we-do/research/2009/04/education-and-tech-entrepreneurship.

54. Charles I. Jones, "Sources of U.S. Economic Growth in a World of Ideas," *American Economic Review* 92, no. 1 (2002), http://web.stanford.edu/~chadj/SourcesAER2002.pdf.

55. Giovanni Peri, "The Economic Windfall of Immigration Reform," *Wall Street Journal,* February 12, 2013, http://www.wsj.com/articles/SB10001424127887324196204578297850464590498.

56. Scott Anderson, "Immigrants and Billion Dollar Startups," National Foundation for American Policy, March 2016, http://nfap.com/wp-content/uploads/2016/03/Immigrants-and-Billion-Dollar-Startups.NFAP-Policy-Brief.March-2016.pdf.

57. "Digest of Education Statistics: 2012, Table 316," National Center for Education Statistics, U.S. Department of Education (2012), http://nces.ed.gov/programs/digest/d12/tables/dt12_316.asp.

58. "A National Talent Strategy: Ideas for Securing U.S. Competitiveness and Economic Growth," *Microsoft: On the Issues,* September 27, 2012, http://news.microsoft.com/download/presskits/citizenship/MSNTS.pdf.

59. Daniel Costa, "STEM Labor Shortages? Microsoft Report Distorts Reality About Computing Occupations," Economic Policy Institute, November 19, 2012, http://www.epi.org/publication/pm195-stem-labor-shortages-microsoft-report-distorts/#_ref1.

60. Lindsay B. Lowell, Hal Salzman, Hamutal Bernstein, and Everett Henderson, "Steady as She Goes? Three Generations of Students Through the Science and Engineering Pipeline," Annual Meetings of the Association for Public Policy Analysis and Management, Washington, DC, November 7, 2009, http://www.ewa.org/sites/main/files/steadyasshegoes.pdf.

61. Enrico Moretti, "Local Multipliers," *American Economic Review, Papers and Proceedings* 100 (2010), http://eml.berkeley.edu//~moretti/multipliers.pdf.

62. "Digest of Education Statistics: Table 104.91, 2014" National Center for Education Statistics, U.S. Department of Education, 2014, http://nces.ed.gov/programs/digest/d14/tables/dt14_104.91.asp.

## *Chapter 10:* Real Solutions

1. "Current Population Survey," U.S. Census Bureau, tabulation of data by Sentier Research, accessed November 2015.

2. B. Lindsay Lowell, Hal Salzman, Hamutal Bernstein, and Everett Henderson, "Steady as She Goes? Three Generations of Students Through the Science and Engineering Pipeline," Annual Meetings of the Association for Public Policy Analysis and Management, Washington, DC, November 7, 2009, http://www.ewa.org/sites/main/files/steadyasshegoes.pdf.

3. "The Distribution of Household Income and Federal Taxes, 2011," Congressional Budget Office, November 12, 2014, https://www.cbo.gov/publication/49440.

4. Steven Rattner, "We're Making Life Too Hard for Millennials," *New York Times,* July 31, 2015, http://www.nytimes.com/2015/08/02/opinion/sunday/were-making-life-too-hard-for-millennials.html?ref=topics&_r=2.

Jordan Weissmann, "Millennials Aren't Quite as Poor as You Think," *Slate*, August 3, 2015, http://www.slate.com/blogs/moneybox/2015/08/03/millen nials_aren_t_as_poor_as_you_think.html.

5. Peter Zeihan, *The Accidental Superpower: The Next Generation of American Pre-eminence and the Coming Global Disorder* (New York: Twelve/Hachette, 2014).

6. Chris Isidore, "U.S. Corporate Tax Rate: No. 1 in the World," *CNN Money*, March 27, 2014, http://money.cnn.com/2012/03/27/pf/taxes/corporate -taxes.

7. Warren Buffett, "America's Growing Trade Deficit Is Selling the Nation Out from Under Us. Here's a Way to Fix the Problem—and We Need to Do It Now," *Fortune*, November 10, 2003, http://www.berkshirehathaway.com/let ters/grow ing.pdf.

8. Edward Conard, *Unintended Consequences: Why Everything You've Been Told About the Economy Is Wrong* (New York: Portfolio, 2012).

9. "The Distribution of Federal Spending and Taxes in 2006," Congressional Budget Office, November 7, 2013, https://www.cbo.gov/publication/44698.

10. Ibid.

11. Ibid.

12. Ibid.

13. "Federal Debt Held by the Public as Percent of Gross Domestic Product," FRED Economic Data, Federal Reserve Bank of St. Louis and U.S. Office of Management and Budget (2015), https://research.stlouisfed.org/fred2/se ries/FYGFGDQ188S.

14. Peter Kuhn and Fernando Lozano, "The Expanding Workweek? Understand-ing Trends in Long Work Hours Among U.S. Men, 1979–2006," *Journal of Labor Economics* 26, no. 2 (2007): 311–43, http://www.econ.ucsb.edu/~pjkuhn /Research%20Papers/LongHours.pdf.

# ILLUSTRATION SOURCES

**Figure 1-1: Growth in Incomes by Level of Income**

Daniel Hirschman, "Visualizing Inequality in the U.S., 1947–2011," A (Budding)
Sociologist's Commonplace Book, April 12, 2013, https://asociologist
.com/2013/04/12/visualizing-inequality-in-the-us-1947-2011.

Facundo Alvaredo, Tony Atkinson, Thomas Piketty, Emmanuel Saez, and Gabriel Zucman,
"The World Wealth and Income Database," http://www.wid.world/#Home.

**Figure 1-2: Effect of Productivity on Wages**

David Leonhardt and Kevin Quealy, "The American Middle Class Is No Longer the
World's Richest," *New York Times*, April 22, 2014, http://www.nytimes.com/2014/04/23
/upshot/the-american-middle-class-is-no-longer-the-worlds-richest.html.

Luxembourg Income Study Database, http://www.lisdatacenter.org/.

**Figure 1-3: 99 Percent's Share of GDP over Time**

Jan Behringer and Till van Treeck, "Income Distribution, Aggregate Demand and Current
Account: A Sectoral Perspective," IMK Working Paper, October 21, 2013, http://www
.boeckler.de/pdf/v_2013_10_24_behringer_van_treeck.pdf.

Alan Heston, Robert Summers, and Bettina Aten, Penn World Table Version 7.1. (2012),
Center for International Comparisons of Production, Income and Prices at the
University of Pennsylvania, http://pwt.econ.upenn.edu/.

**Figure 1-4: U.S. Investment in Intangibles as a Percentage of GDP**

Peter Coy, "The Rise of the Intangible Economy: U.S. GDP Counts R&D, Artistic Creation,"
Bloomberg, July 18, 2013, http://www.bloomberg.com/news/articles/2013-07-18/
the-rise-of-the-intangible-economy-u-dot-s-dot-gdp-counts-r-and-d-artistic-creation.

Carol Corrado, Jonathan Haskel, Cecilia Jona-Lasinio, and Massimiliano Lommi,
"Intangible Capital and Growth in Advanced Economies: Measurement Methods and
Comparative Results," Institute for the Study of Labor (IZA), July 2012, http://repec.iza
.org/dp6733.pdf.

**Figure 1-5: High-Potential U.S. Start-Ups**

Jorge Guzman and Scott Stern, "The State of American Entrepreneurship: New Estimates
of the Quantity and Quality of Entrepreneurship for 15 U.S. States, 1988–2014,"
National Bureau of Economic Research, March 2016, http://www.nber.org/papers/
w22095.

**Figure 4-1: Corporate Profits Relative to GDP**

U.S. Bureau of Economic Analysis, Corporate Profits After Tax (without IVA and CCAdj)
[CP], Federal Reserve Bank of St. Louis, May 19, 2016, https://research.stlouisfed.org/
fred2/series/CP.

**Figure 4-2: U.S. Private Business Investment (Net of Depreciation)**

U.S. Bureau of Economic Analysis, Net Domestic Investment: Private: Domestic Business [W790RC1Q027SBEA], Federal Reserve Bank of St. Louis, May 19, 2016, https://research.stlouisfed.org/fred2/series/W790RC1Q027SBEA.

**Figure 4-3: U.S. Productivity Growth**

Eric Morath, "Sputtering Worker Productivity Vexes Economy," *Wall Street Journal*, August 11, 2015, http://www.wsj.com/articles/u-s-productivity-increases-at-1-3-pace-in-second-quarter-1439296327.

U.S. Labor Department.

Federal Reserve Bank of St. Louis.

**Figure 4-4: Growth in Federal Spending on Means-Tested Programs and Tax Credits for Low-Income Households**

Congressional Budget Office Staff, "Growth in Means-Tested Programs and Tax Credits for Low-Income Households," Congressional Budget Office, February 2013, http://www.cbo.gov/sites/default/files/cbofiles/attachments/43934-Means-TestedPrograms.pdf.

**Figure 5-1: Value of Technology vs. Manufacturing Companies**

"Does Deutschland Do Digital," *Economist*, November 21, 2015, http://www.economist.com/news/business/21678774-europes-biggest-economy-rightly-worried-digitisation-threat-its-industrial.

**Figure 5-2: Personal Saving Rate as a Percentage of Disposable Income**

U.S. Bureau of Economic Analysis, Personal Saving Rate, Federal Reserve Bank of St. Louis, May 19, 2016, https://research.stlouisfed.org/fred2/series/PSAVERT.

**Figure 5-3: Mortgage Lending by Credit Score**

"Quarterly Report on Household Debt and Credit," Federal Reserve Bank of New York, February 2016, https://www.newyorkfed.org/medialibrary/interactives/householdcredit/data/pdf/HHDC_2015Q3.pdf.

**Figure 5-4: Government Investment as a Percentage of GDP (U.S. vs. Japan)**

Martin Fackler, "Japan's Big-Works Stimulus Is Lesson," *New York Times*, February 5, 2009, http://www.nytimes.com/2009/02/06/world/asia/06japan.html.

**Figure 6-1: Income Distribution, Full-Time White Workers, 25 to 64 Years Old**

U.S. Census Bureau, 2013, via Sentier Research, 2015, "Current Population Survey," http://www.census.gov/.

**Figure 6-2: Income Distribution, Full-Time African American Workers, 25 to 64 Years Old**

U.S. Census Bureau, 2013, via Sentier Research, 2015, "Current Population Survey," http://www.census.gov/.

**Figure 6-3: Income Distribution, All Full-Time Workers, 25 to 64 Years Old**

U.S. Census Bureau, 2013, via Sentier Research, 2015, "Current Population Survey," http://www.census.gov/.

**Figure 6-4: U.S. Income Growth by Income Quintile over Time**

Philip Armour, Richard V. Burkhauser, and Jeff Larrimore, "Deconstructing Income and Income Inequality Measures: A Crosswalk from Market Income to Comprehensive Income," *American Economic Review* 103, no. 3 (May 2013): 173–77, https://www.aeaweb.org/articles.php?doi=10.1257/aer.103.3.173.

**Figure 6-5: Productivity vs. Wage Growth**

Robert Lawrence, "The Growing Gap Between Real Wages and Labor Productivity," Peterson Institute for International Economics, July 21, 2015, https://piie.com/blogs/realtime-economic-issues-watch/growing-gap-between-real-wages-and-labor-productivity.

Bureau of Economic Analysis and Bureau of Labor Statistics.

**Figure 6-6: Share of White Students at Select Universities**

Derek Thompson, "How America's Top Colleges Reflect (and Massively Distort) the Country's Racial Evolution," *Atlantic,* January 23, 3013, http://www.theatlantic .com/national/archive/2013/01/how-americas-top-colleges-reflect-and-massively -distort-the-countrys-racial-evolution/267415/.

National Center for Education Statistics.

**Figure 6-7: Value of Education to Marginal Students**

Jaison Abel and Richard Deitz, "Do the Benefits of College Still Outweigh the Costs?" *Current Issues in Economics and Finance,* 2014, https://www.newyorkfed.org/medialibrary/ media/research/current_issues/ci20-3.pdf.

**Figure 7-1: U.S. Income Mobility over Time**

Raj Chetty, Nathaniel Hendren, Patrick Kline, Emmanuel Saez, and Nicholas Turner, "Integrational Mobility Estimates for the 1971–1993 Birth Cohorts (Figure 2)," in "Is the United States Still a Land of Opportunity? Recent Trends in Intergenerational Mobility," National Bureau of Economic Research, Working Paper 19844 (2014): 8–9, http://www .equality-of-opportunity.org/files/mobility_trends.pdf.

**Figure 7-2: Income Mobility: U.S. vs. Denmark**

"Comparing Economic Mobility," *New York Times,* http://www.nytimes.com/ interactive/2012/01/04/us/comparing-economic-mobility.html.

Markus Jäntti et al., "American Exceptionalism in a New Light: A Comparison of Intergenerational Earnings Mobility in the Nordic Countries, the United Kingdom and the United States," Institute for the Study of Labor (IZA) DP No. 1938 (2006), http:// ftp.iza.org/dp1938.pdf.

**Figure 7-3: Effect of Race on Income Mobility**

Richard Reeves, "Saving Horatio Alger, Equality, Opportunity, and the American Dream," Brookings Essay, August 20, 2014, http://www.brookings.edu/research /essays/2014/saving-horatio-alger; Tax Policy Center, Urban Institute, and Brookings Institution.

**Figure 7-4: Mobility of Poor White Americans Compared to Denmark's Population**

Richard Reeves, "Saving Horatio Alger, Equality, Opportunity, and the American Dream," Brookings Essay, August 20, 2014, http://www.brookings.edu/research/essays/2014/ saving-horatio-alger.

Tax Policy Center, Urban Institute, and Brookings Institution.

"Comparing Economic Mobility," *New York Times,* http://www.nytimes.com/interactive/ 2012/01/04/us/comparing-economic-mobility.html.

**Figure 7-5: Effect of Marriage on Income Mobility**

Richard Reeves, "Saving Horatio Alger, Equality, Opportunity, and the American Dream," Brookings Essay, August 20, 2014, http://www.brookings.edu/research/essays/2014/ saving-horatio-alger.

Tax Policy Center, Urban Institute, and Brookings Institution.

**Figure 7-6: Effect of Dropping Out of High School on Income Mobility**

Richard Reeves, "Saving Horatio Alger, Equality, Opportunity, and the American Dream," Brookings Essay, August 20, 2014, http://www.brookings.edu/research/essays/2014/ saving-horatio-alger

Tax Policy Center, Urban Institute, and Brookings Institution.

**Figure 7-7: Comparisons of Causes of Poverty**

Richard Reeves, "Saving Horatio Alger, Equality, Opportunity, and the American Dream," Brookings Essay, August 20, 2014, http://www.brookings.edu/research/essays/2014/ saving-horatio-alger

Tax Policy Center, Urban Institute, and Brookings Institution.

Figure 7-8: Effect of a College Degree on Income Mobility

Richard Reeves, "Saving Horatio Alger, Equality, Opportunity, and the American Dream," Brookings Essay, August 20, 2014, http://www.brookings.edu/research/essays/2014/saving-horatio-alger

Tax Policy Center, Urban Institute, and Brookings Institution.

Figure 8-1: U.S. Spending on Income Support

Office of Management and Budget, "Historical Tables, Table 8.5—Outlays for Mandatory and Related Programs: 1962–2021," April 28, 2016. https://www.whitehouse.gov/omb/budget/Historicals.

Figure 8-2: Change in Poverty by Source of Income

Christopher Wimer et al., "Official vs Supplemental Overall Poverty Rates, 1967–2012, (Figure 2)," in "Trends in Poverty with an Anchored Supplemental Poverty Measure," Institute for Research on Poverty, University of Wisconsin–Madison, 2013, https://courseworks.columbia.edu/access/content/group/c5a1ef92-c03c-4d88-0018-ea43dd3cc5db/Working%20Papers%20for%20website/Anchored%20SPM.December7.pdf.

Figure 10-1: Federal Government Expenditures and Taxes by Household Type

Congressional Budget Office, "Distribution of Federal Spending and Taxes in 2006," November 7, 2013; "Exhibit 7 Average Transfers and Taxes per Household, by Type of Household, 2006," and "Exhibit 18 Average Transfers and Taxes per Nonelderly Household, by Income Group 2006," Author's Calculations, https://www.cbo.gov/publication/44698.

# INDEX

Also by EDWARD CONARD

NEW YORK TIMES BESTSELLER

# UNINTENDED CONSEQUENCES

## WHY EVERYTHING YOU'VE BEEN TOLD ABOUT THE ECONOMY IS WRONG

"There are an amazing number of good ideas and interesting points made in this book. The thinking underlying it, and the obvious depth of understanding of the author, are very impressive."
— STEVEN LEVITT, Coauthor of *Freakonomics*; 2004 John Bates Clark Medal Winner

## EDWARD CONARD

FORMER MANAGING DIRECTOR OF BAIN CAPITAL, LLC